Series Editors:

Jan Broekhoff, PhD
Michael J. Ellis, PhD
Dan G. Tripps, PhD

University of Oregon
Eugene, Oregon

The 1984
Olympic Scientific
Congress
Proceedings
Volume 7

Sport and Politics

Edited by Gerald Redmond, PhD
University of Alberta

Human Kinetics Publishers, Inc.
Champaign, Illinois

Library of Congress Cataloging-in-Publication Data

Olympic Scientific Congress (1984 : Eugene, Or.)
    Sport and politics.

    (1984 Olympic Scientific Congress proceedings ; v. 7)
    Bibliography: p.
    1. Sports and state—Congresses.   2. Olympic games—
Congresses.   I. Redmond, Gerald, 1934-   .   II. Title.
III. Series: Olympic Scientific Congress (1984 : Eugene,
Or.).   1984 Olympic Scientific Congress proceedings ;
v. 7.
GV565.O46   1984 vol. 7   796 s   85-18114
[GV706.8]   [796] $L \, S \, S \, L \, 9$
ISBN 0-87322-007-2

Managing Editor: Susan Wilmoth, PhD
Developmental Editor: Susan Wilmoth, PhD
Production Director: Sara Chilton
Copyeditor: Olga Murphy
Typesetter: Yvonne Winsor
Text Layout: Gail Irwin
Cover Design and Layout: Jack Davis
Printed By: Braun-Brumfield, Inc.

ISBN: 0-87322-006-4   (10 Volume Set)
ISBN: 0-87322-007-2

Printed in the United States of America

10 9 8 7 6 5 4 3 2 1

Human Kinetics Publishers, Inc.
Box 5076, Champaign, IL 61820

Contents

Series Acknowledgments

The Congress organizers realize that an event as large and complex as the 1984 Olympic Scientific Congress could not have come to fruition without the help of literally hundreds of organizations and individuals. Under the patronage of UNESCO, the Congress united in sponsorship and cooperation no fewer than 64 national and international associations and organizations. Some 50 representatives of associations helped with the organization of the scientific and associative programs by coordinating individual sessions. The cities of Eugene and Springfield yielded more than 400 volunteers who donated their time to make certain that the multitude of Congress functions would progress without major mishaps. To all these organizations and individuals, the organizers express their gratitude.

A special word of thanks must also be directed to the major sponsors of the Congress: the International Council of Sport Science and Physical Education (ICSSPE), the United States Olympic Committee (USOC), the International Council on Health, Physical Education and Recreation (ICHPER), and the American Alliance for Health, Physical Education, Recreation and Dance (AAHPERD). Last but not least, the organizers wish to acknowledge the invaluable assistance of the International Olympic Committee (IOC) and its president, Honorable Juan Antonio Samaranch. President Samaranch made Congress history by his official opening address in Eugene on July 19, 1984. The IOC further helped the Congress with a generous donation toward the publication of the Congress papers. Without this donation it would have been impossible to make the proceedings available in this form.

Finally, the series editors wish to express their thanks to the volume editors who selcted and edited the papers from each program of the Congress. Special thanks go to Gerald Redmond of the University of Alberta for his work on this volume.

Jan Broekhoff,
Michael J. Ellis, and
Dan G. Tripps

Series Editors

Series Preface

Sport and Politics contains selected proceedings from this interdisciplinary program of the 1984 Olympic Scientific Congress, which was held at the University of Oregon in Eugene, Oregon, preceding the Olympic Games in Los Angeles. The Congress was organized by the College of Human Development and Performance of the University of Oregon in collaboration with the cities of Eugene and Springfield. This was the first time in the history of the Congress that the event was organized by a group of private individuals, unaided by a federal government. The fact that the Congress was attended by more than 2,200 participants from more than 100 different nations is but one indication of its success.

The Congress program focused on the theme of Sport Health and Well-Being and was organized in three parts. The mornings of the eight-day event were devoted to disciplinary sessions, which brought together specialists in various subdisciplines of sport science such as sport medicine, biomechanics, sport psychology, sport sociology, and sport philosophy. For the first time in the Congress' history, these disciplinary sessions were sponsored by the national and international organizations representing the various subdisciplines. In the afternoons, the emphasis shifted toward interdisciplinary themes in which scholars and researchers from the subdisciplines attempted to contribute to crossdisciplinary understanding. In addition, three evenings were devoted to keynote addresses and presentations, broadly related to the theme of Sport, Health, and Well-Being.

In addition to the scientific programs, the Congress also featured a number of associative programs with topics determined by their sponsoring organizations. Well over 1,200 papers were presented in the various sessions of the Congress at large. It stands to reason, therefore, that publishing the proceedings of the event presented a major problem to the organizers. It was decided to limit proceedings initially to interdisciplinary sessions which drew substantial interest from Congress participants and attracted a critical number of high-quality presentations. Human Kinetics Publishers, Inc. of Champaign, Illinois, was selected to produce these proceedings. After considerable deliberation, the following interdisciplinary themes were selected for publication: Competitive Sport for Children and Youths; Human Genetics and Sport; Sport and Aging; Sport and Disabled Individuals; Sport and Elite Performers; Sport, Health, and Nutrition; and Sport and Politics. The 10-volume set published by Human Kinetics Publishers is rounded out by the disciplinary proceedings of Kinanthropometry, Sport Pedagogy, and the associative program on the Scientific Aspects of Dance.

Jan Broekhoff,
Michael J. Ellis, and
Dan G. Tripps

Series Editors

Preface

Sport has been traditionally viewed in many quarters as an apolitical institution to which the addition of political considerations was undesirable (the "sport and politics do not mix" syndrome). The historian, however, can easily document various, consistent affinities between sport and politics since the civilizations of the ancient world. Hardly ever, in fact, has sport been free of politics, a point born out by reference to the related literatue. As sport itself has become the focus of research on an unparalleled scale—giving rise to numerous and specific associations, conferences and congresses, referred journals and the like—the area of "sport and politics" is now an urgent and valid field of study in its own right in many countries, an academic genre of increasing contemporary significance, and of international social concern.

This relationship between sport and politics has indeed intensified in recent years at local, national, and international levels. This fact has been reflected in the quite dramatic increase in the related literature. The *Cultures* Journal (Vol. IV, No. 2, 1977), published by UNESCO, included a bibliography on sport and politics of selected works in English, French, and German, accompanied by brief essays, which was quite comprehensive in spite of the rigid selection. Yet in only the 7 years which have transpired it is already considerably out-of-date, overwhelmed, and made largely redundant by the large number of pertinent studies which have been completed since then. This "explosion," if we may term it that without too much exaggeration (see Part V: Suggestions for Further Reading, p. 215), confirms the urgency and validity of the relationship between sport and politics in our world society. It is both crucial and fragile, full of uncertain promise, and imbued with both positive and negative aspects. Above all, the relationship is inescapable, and poses problems for those involved in sport and/or politics which today really means a mass of people everywhere, in their insatiable roles as participants and spectators, and citizen consumers within their country.

As Peter McIntosh stated succinctly in 1963:

> The relationship may turn bad in at least two ways, by too much interaction and by the debasement of either one of the two agents. The injection of too much sport into politics might reduce the most serious of human activities to puerilism, while the seriousness of politics, if carried into sport in too great measure, could destroy its playfulness and so change its very nature.

Today it would be naive to ignore the increasing interaction and the obvious worry that "too much" had already been reached or exceeded; or to deny that in terms of "debasement," the most worrisome trend is of too much politics getting into sport. Because of the peculiar interdependent economic, political, religious, social, and technological factors affecting our modern world, perhaps this is unavoidable. In any case, the relationship between sport and politics, and its disturbing as well as optimistic trends, can be readily identified within many dimensions: Sport competitions representing conflicting ideologies; patronage and use of sport by political authorities; financial control and/or support of sport by different levels of government; legislation affecting sport; radical protests (even terrorism) within sport; and so on.

It is difficult for anyone interested in this relationship to keep abreast of important and rapid developments. The sheer volume of pertinent literature, products of our computerbased "paperback revolution" allied to modern mass-marketing methods, can discourage even the most conscientious student. An encyclopedia or a similar exceedingly large work would be needed to do full justice to sport and politics within a single volume. This book is *not* such a comprehensive volume, but its selection of well-researched topics is a valuable contribution for all who are interested in the area. Not surprisingly, as many academic meetings in recent years have done likewise, the successful 1984 Olympic Scientific Congress held at Eugene, Oregon, from July 19-26, had an interdisciplinary session entitled "Sport and Politics" in its program. There, more than 30 scholars from 10 countries presented papers within a variety of themes, and the selection presented here represents a variety of factors which vitally affects the relationship between sport and politics in a number of ways. The information and insights provided into such international aspects as historical and contemporary government involvement in sport, perspectives on elite and mass sport, and of course the political problems associated with the Olympic Games, should assist the reader to better understand the complexity of the problems involved.

Gerald Redmond,
Editor

The 1984
Olympic Scientific
Congress
Proceedings
Volume 7

Sport and Politics

PART I

The Role of Government

SECTION A
Government Involvement in Australia, Canada, and the United States

1

Pragmatic Coercion: The Role of Government in Sport in the United States

Roy A. Clumpner
WESTERN WASHINGTON UNIVERSITY
BELLINGHAM, WASHINGTON, USA

This paper attempts to update an earlier work on American government involvement in sport to 1984 (Clumpner, 1976). The study concerned itself with various branches, agencies, and bureaus of the federal govenment, including the executive branch (but not the personal exercise/sport habits and interests of the president). Not included in the study were the armed forces and organizations which seemingly would have had little connection with sport such as the Department of Agriculture, and so forth. In addition, the National Rifle Association, school military programs, conservation efforts related to recreation, and other semirelated aspects were not included. In instances where military material and personnel were used in a supportive role for a sport competition, the information was included. The study was further delineated to include aspects of gambling in as far as it was connected with sport. An overview of the research previously dealing with American government involvement will not be presented here due to the length of this paper. The reader can refer to the author's original work along with works by the following authors: Zingale, 1973; Lindop and Sares, 1964; Metcalfe, 1966; Drew, 1944; Applin, 1968; DeKoff, 1962; Chase, 1973; Corran, 1981; and Semotiuk, 1970.

Federal Involvement

Today, the powers entrusted to the American federal government have greatly expanded from those outlined in the original Constitution. Greater and greater involvement by the federal sector in the lives of all Americans has occurred. Sport (organized sport, physical fitness, and physical education) is not far removed from this increase in federal involvement. By the end of 1983, the American government had involved itself in the following 11 areas relating to sport:

- Antitrust
- Criminal activities
- Restructuring Sport
- Discrimination
- Capital support
- Tax/Duty exemption
- Social/work projects
- Sponsored publicity
- Health/Fitness promotion
- Boycott
- International athletic tours/exchanges

Antitrust

Application of the antitrust laws to sport has continually involved the federal government since the latter part of the 19th century. Much of the antitrust involvement surrounded the 1922 Supreme Court's decision to exempt baseball from the antitrust laws (*Federal Baseball Club of Baltimore*, 1922). Other professional sports attempted but were refused inclusion in this exemption in 1955 (*U.S.* v. *International Boxing Club of New York*, 1955) and 1957 (*Rodovich* v. *National League*, 1957). Partial exemptions to the antitrust laws have been granted, most notably the merger of the American Football League with the National Football League in 1966, and in the area of telecommunications. Although Congress had passed a racially biased law in 1920 prohibiting the transport of prize fight films across state lines (repealed in 1940), interest in sport telecommunications did not surface until post-World War II with the advent of television sport. In 1961, Congress authorized professional football, baseball, basketball, and hockey to package and sell league games to television networks while at the same time protecting college football games in a 75-mile radius from professional telecasts when college games were to be played on Friday evenings, Saturday afternoon, or evenings in-season Public Law (PL) 331.

Congress once again intervened in 1973 with PL107 which outlawed the practice by professional teams of blacking out games which were sold out 72 hours in advance. More recently, the Supreme Court ruled, in 1984, that the NCAA's practice of selling television packages of college football games to the television networks was in violation of the antitrust laws. Other areas of increasing interest to Congress pertaining to sport and antitrust have been the impact of cable television programming on sport and the movement of professional sport franchises from city-owned stadiums.

Criminal Activities

With the outcome of most sporting events largely unknown, it comes as no surprise that sport has had numerous problems with regard to gambling and racketeering. Congress has passed legislation twice during the period under study. The first involved the fixing of sporting events and resulted in PL316 in 1963 which amended the law making it a crime to use any instrumentality of commerce, the mails, or travel in commerce in order to regulate or fix any amateur or professional athletic contest or event. The second instance was related to organized crime in horseracing, betting, and the management of race tracks. Recently, Congress has held hearings on violence in sport. While no legislation has been passed, Congressional interest encouraged the professional leagues to take stricter measures in dealing with the problem.

Restructuring Sport

Federal efforts to restructure sport met with both failure and success during the period under study. Attempts to institute reforms in professional boxing have all met with failure since the first efforts began in 1951. The cycle of attempted legislation usually corresponds with media exposure of underworld connections to the sport, questionable outcomes of fights (fixing), or the deaths of fighters. Attempts to restructure the sport have continued with hearings held in Congress in 1965, 1970, 1979, and 1983. All efforts failed primarily due to the general nervousness of Congress about involving itself directly in the regulation and control of a private, professional sport business.

Inactivity on the federal part was not the case, however, when American success in international amateur athletic competition was threatened; the result was passage of the Amateur Sports Act of 1978 which forced the restructuring of amateur sport in America. Efforts to solve amateur sport's problems, arising primarily from disputes between the NCAA and the AAU, began in 1962 and included numerous hearings by Congress, investigations by presidentially appointed committees, and an arbitration board, before final passage. The result was the most comprehensive piece of amateur sport legislation in the history of the country and resulted in a more streamlined, amateur-sport system.

Discrimination

In addition to the Amateur Sports Act of 1978, another significant piece of legislation pertaining to sport in this study was passage of the Education Amendment of 1972 (Title IX) which withheld federal funds to any educational program which denied participants on the basis of sex. The application of the law, specifically to physical education and to athletes, did not occur until 1975. Since then, it has proven to be the greatest boost to the development of women's sports in American schools in the 20th century. Hand in hand with Title IX has been the federal government's interest in the handicapped. In 1966, PL749 provided money to colleges for programs to train physical educators for the mentally retarded and handicapped. This was followed in 1967 by PL170, the training of physical education and recreational personnel for mentally retarded and handicapped children. Probably the greatest boost came, however, in 1975 when the Education for All Handicapped Children Act of 1975 was passed (PL142) which granted physical education to all children with provision for the handicapped to be included in regular physical education programs. With passage of this legislation, the United States became a model nation internationally for the handicapped.

Capital Funding

Direct federal funding of sport is a relatively recent phenomenon in the United States. Instances of assistance were related to the staging of international amateur athletic events on American soil. Financial assistance of $500,000 for the transporting of Latin American athletes to the 1959 Pan American Games in Chicago was provided that year by PL15. The Arctic Winter Games also received Congressional support of $150,000 in 1973 when they were hosted by Alaska. By far, the largest appropriations by Congress have been for the Olympic Games when hosted by the United States. While the federal government first involved itself in support of the American Olympic Committee in 1920, by supplying a sailing vessel for the athletes to compete in Belgium, actual direct funding for the Games from the federal government did not take place until recently. Generally speaking, the United States government has assisted various organizing committees with direct funding, most recently in the area of security. Basically, federal monies have been appropriated for three Olympics: The Squaw Valley Winter Olympics received 4½ million dollars; Lake Placid, over $70 million; and, most recently, Los Angeles, $50 million. While there have been numerous attempts to get the federal government involved financially in sport, by and large, it has proven to be an extremely difficult task, probably because of the attitude in Congress that sport is not an area in which the government should be involved. When American prestige is on the line, however, government assistance seems much more possible.

Tax/Duty Exemptions

Somewhat related to capital funding were exemptions from taxes or duties granted by Congress to sport organizations. One of the first occurred in 1935 when PL528 allowed excess monies from the Los Angeles Olympic Games to be free of federal taxes. In 1950, the first American government recognition of an amateur athletic organization took place with PL805, incorporating the United States Olympic Association. The incorporation granted the committee tax-exempt status. Two years later, Congress exempted all sport programs conducted for the benefit of the Red Cross from tax (PL465), and in 1959, admissions tax exemptions (PL319) were granted for any athletic games conducted for the benefit of crippled or retarded children. More recently, Congress granted a federal charter to the Volunteer National Ski Patrol in 1980 (PL489). One other area of exemption from taxes involved the importation of sport equipment; in 1952 and 1956, racing shells were granted tax-exempt status and in 1977, bobsleds.

Social/Work Projects

The concept of federally sponsored, sport-related projects for social or work purposes began during the Depression. A creation of Franklin Roosevelt, the Works Progress Administration (WPA) in 1935 built or improved 8,000 parks, 12,800 playgrounds, and erected 5,900 schools (*Newsweek*, 1975). In the 1960s, besides the WPA, two additional projects which used sport in a work or social setting were created. The Peace Corps, created in 1961 by executive order, incorporated sport, particularly coaches, into its program. By 1972,

283 American coaches were serving in 25 countries (Quinn, 1972). A second social/work project, developed in 1968, known as the National Summer Youth Sports Program, was implemented which involved the President's Council on Physical Fitness and Sports. The program was to aid urban youth during the summer by opening college sporting facilities to them. The program has since been funded very sporadically on a temporary status. In 1972, the program's name was officially changed to Youth Recreation and Sports Program.

Sponsored Publicity

Sponsored publicity of sport by the federal government has been an easy method for the federal government to demonstrate approval of sport without outlaying capital funds for implementation. One form has been a formal invitation by Congress and the President to hold a sporting event in the United States. Invitations were made by Congress in 1949 and 1951 to hold the Pan American Games, and, in 1960, an invitation was extended to foreign countries to an international parachuting contest. By far, the greatest number of invitations have been for the Olympic Games. A total of 6 invitations have been extended by Congress. In addition, the naming of a specific day, week, month, or months in honor of sport or physical fitness has occurred.

Finally, the minting of commemorative Olympic coins has been another example of government-sponsored publicity. Recently, this type of legislation was passed for the 1984 Los Angles Games (PL220, 1980).

Health/Fitness Promotion

There have been numerous attempts in the 20th century to pass physical education legislation and numerous examples of federal departments in charge of fitness during World War II. Very little legislation occurred with respect to health-fitness promotion until President Eisenhower created, by executive order, the President's Council on Youth Fitness to combat low fitness scores. Throughout its existence, the Council has undergone numerous changes and reorganization. It currently operates out of the Health and Human Services Department with an operating budget in 1982 of approximately $1 million (Budget of the U.S. Government 1984).

With governments picking up a greater share of health costs in the early 1970s, the federal government turned its attention to the concept of health promotion. In 1978, PL626 was enacted which amended the Public Health Service Act and established the Office of Health Information, Health Promotion, and Physical Fitness, and Sports Medicine. Its duties were to be a coordinator for all activities related to health information, health promotion, preventive health services, and education in the appropriate use of health care in the department. Its 1984 estimated budget is over $3 million (Ibid).

Boycott

There was no greater direct interference in the affairs of American sport than the decision by President Carter in 1980 to pressure the United States Olympic Committee into boycotting the Moscow Summer Olympic Games of 1980 in retaliation for the Soviet invasion of Afghanistan. Direct federal pressure was applied, both within the country on the United States Olympic Committee and outside the country, on American allies, to boycott. The pressure succeeded; the boycott took place, and shortly after, the Carter administration announced that $10 million would be appropriated to the U.S.O.C. from Congress (*New York Times*, May 26, 1980). In July, PL306 was signed authorizing the minting of gold-plated medals to the athletes of the summer Olympic team.

International Athletic Tours/Exchanges

The final area where the federal government was involved in sport was federally sponsored, sport-related tours or exchanges which were done to enhance the American image abroad. Although there is evidence of government-sponsored sports tours during and after World War II, the major instances occurred with passage of the Fulbright Act in 1946 and the Smith-Mundt Act of 1948. Both of these programs sent scholars overseas, and, in several cases, physical educators were among the chosen. In the 1960s, Americans began to systematically send athletes and coaches overseas as a direct counter to Soviet sport-cultural exchanges. Although several studies have been undertaken by the federal government which indicated sport was an appropriate tool for foreign policy objectives, very little has been done in this area by the Department of State, except for periodical forays such as the Chinese tour of American swimmers in 1973, and, more recently, the defection of a Chinese tennis star. The Department of State has sponsored several conferences dealing with sport; however, it has chosen to maintain a low profile in this area.

Conclusion

In summarizing American government involvement in sport, government intervention is assured when the laws of the country are abridged, as in the application of antitrust legislation, criminal activities, and sex discrimination. At the same time, however, Congress has altered or exempted sport from the law when public opinion and pressure was evident, such as in the merging of the two professional football leagues in 1966.

In spite of these exceptions, it can be said that the American government adheres to a "less-government-the-better" rule when it comes to sport. There have been numerous instances in the past which indicate that government has been slow in acting (the NCAA-AAU controversy) and, in some cases, has never acted, even though the evidence suggested repeated need for action such as attempts to clean up professional boxing.

Often, the applications of existing laws and public sentiment clash as in recent attempts to restrict professional sports' franchise movement, and contribute to Congressional inaction. On the other hand, Congress has indicated that it will act, especially if international prestige is on the line (The Amateur Sports Act of 1980). When international prestige is coupled with political survival, as was the case in 1980, then government action is immediate as demonstrated by the government's actions in the 1980 boycott.

Sports, as an international goodwill ambassador for the United States, has never seriously been accepted and it is very likely to continue to remain as such. Working against all involvement is cost which always enters into any decision regarding American involvement in sport. Recently, with an increasing amount of money being spent by the federal government on health care, there has been interest in the area of health promotion, especially physical fitness; it seems evident that more attention will be paid to this aspect by the government.

In almost all cases of involvement, the American government has demonstrated a very practical, pragmatic approach, often coupled with coercion. At the same time, it has repeatedly emphasized that sport should attempt to handle its own problems outside government. In spite of its so-called laissez-faire approach to sport, the American government has changed and altered the direction and emphasis of sport in the modern era. Three instances of intervention which stand out as having the greatest possible influence have been the implementation of Title IX, the Amateur Sports Act of 1978, and the numerous pieces of legislation for the handicapped. While it might dislike the concept of involvement, government's actions in these three instances resulted in strengthened sports and expanded athletic opportunities.

References

Applin, A. (1968). *National legislation for health, physical education and recreation: The Schwert Bills, H.R. 10606 and H.R. 1074, a study of why they failed.* Unpublished master's thesis, The Pennsylvania State University, University Park.

Budget of U.S. Government, fiscal 1984, p. I K25.

Chase, J. (1973). *Politics and nationalism in sports: Soviet and American government involvement in amateur sports as an aspect of the Cold War.* Master's thesis, San Jose State University, San Jose.

Clumpner, Roy A. (1976). *American government involvement in sport*, 1848-1973. Unpublished doctoral dissertation. University of Alberta, Edmonton.

Corran, R. (1981). Federal government involvement in sport and physical education. *The Physical Educator*, pp. 193-198.

DeKoff, I. (1962). *The rule of government in the Olympics.* Unpublished doctoral dissertation, Teacher's College, New York, NY.

Department of State Cultural Presentations Program Tours (1954-1958). FY-1955 through FY-1958. Mimeo paper.

Drew, G. (1944). *A historical study of the concern of the federal government for the physical fitness of non-age youth with reference to the schools.* Unpublished doctoral dissertation, University of Pittsburgh, Pittsburgh.

Federal baseball club of Baltimore, Inc. v *National League of professional baseball clubs, et al.* (1922). 269 Fed. 681; 50 App. D.C. 165, (pp. 208-209).

History of the office of the coordinator of inter-American affairs. (1947). Washington, D.C., U.S. Government Printing Office.

Interagency committee on international athletics (draft of a report). (1965, January). p. 7.

Interagency committee on international athletics. (1965, November). A study on the achievement of U.S. foreign policy objectives, pp. 1-5.

Metcalfe, A. (1966). *The contributions of John F. Kennedy to physical education and recreation.* Unpublished master's thesis, University of Wisconsin.

Newsweek. (1975, January 20). p. 57.

New York Times. (1964, February 14). Humphrey urges White House to help raise U.S. sport level.

New York Times. (1980, January 12) 1:3; (1980, January 24) 6:5; (1980, February 21) 1:4; (1980, May 26) 1:5; and (1983, March 4).

Press release, United States Information Agency, 1956.

Quinn, T. (1972, March). Sports corps builds teams. . .and nations. *Washington News.*

Radovich v National League (1957). 352 U.S. 445.

Report to the President of the United States. (1965). Amateur sport in America: An appraisal and proposal. Arthur D. Little & Co.

Semotiuk, D. (1970). *The development of a theoretical framework for analyzing the role of national government involvement in sport and physical education and its application to Canada.* Unpublished doctoral dissertation, The Ohio State University, Columbus.

United States Department of State, Office of International and Cultural Affairs. (1945-1946). List of professors in the Western Hemisphere.

United States v International Boxing Club of New York (1955). 348 U.S. 236.

Zingale, D. (1973). *A history of the involvement of the American presidency in school and college physical education and sports during the Twentieth Century.* Unpublished doctoral dissertation, The Ohio State University, Columbus.

2

Deuce or Double Fault? The Defection of Tennis Player Hu Na[1]: A Study of China-United States Sport Diplomacy

Brian B. Pendleton
VANCOUVER COMMUNITY COLLEGE
BRITISH COLUMBIA, CANADA

During the night of Tuesday, July 20, 1982, 19-year-old Chinese tennis player Hu Na disappeared from her room at the Marriott Hotel in Santa Clara, California. Later that week, lawyer Edward C.Y. Lau contacted the U.S. State Department, and on Monday, July 26, the San Francisco attorney filed papers with the Immigration and Naturalization Service requesting political asylum for the young athlete on the grounds that she was being pressured and persecuted by Communist Party officials in China. Subsequent events, in what was to become known in Chinese circles as the *Hu Na Shijian* (the "Hu Na Incident") suggest that there is a two-way interaction between sport and diplomacy often resulting in decisions being made at the highest political levels; this paper presents the results of research into the case of tennis player Hu Na. In particular, the essay examines initial and subsequent reactions in both China and the United States, identifies the involvement of key figures in the dispute, and discusses the broader issues underlying already strained Sino-American relations during this period.

[1]Romanization of Chinese characters to English follows the *hanyu pinyin* system adopted for use in the People's Republic of China in 1979. Furthermore, the Chinese practice of placing the surname first (e.g. *Hu* has been followed throughout this paper; thus Hu Na—*never* Na Hu—is the accepted form of address for Miss Hu.

Initial Response and Reaction

As the drama unfolded, public reaction was mixed. Tennis officials expressed concern and dismay on hearing of the defection ("Chinese promise," 1982). U.S. Tennis Association Vice-President Hunter L. Delatour Jr. remarked, "We feel terrible about what happened. We're the host nation and we want to keep our very good relations with the Chinese. But we certainly couldn't put guards on the doors of all the players." (p. 28). Commenting on Hu's disappearance, another USTA official said, "It's not unusual for coaches and agents to be at events like this looking for young talent, but this smacks of the slave trade, snatching bodies from other countries" (p. 28).

Meanwhile, Immigration District Director David Ilchert was quoted as saying that he would make the final decision after receiving an advisory opinion from the State Department in Washington. Noting that the process could take several weeks, Ilchert remarked, "We have 8,500 applications pending here [fewer than 1,000 were Chinese], but in this case, because of all the publicity, it will probably be expedited" ("*Request*," 1982). In Washington, a concurrent resolution (Congressional Record [CR], 1982, p. E3733) urging the State Department to grant the asylum request was introduced in Congress on August 5 by Representatives Tom Lantos (Dem-CA) and Jack Kemp (Rep-NY). The issue was again raised on Capital Hill when Representative Edward J. Derwinski (Rep-IL) quoted from an editorial in a suburban Chicago Publication, the *Southern Economist*:

> One of the prices communist governments pay for oppressing their citizenry is the embarrassment caused whenever some of them defect to free countries. The price is double [*sic*] high when the defector is an especially talented or prominent person enjoying the best that life has to offer in your standard workers' paradise. . . .Shouldn't young Hu Na, said to be a potential world class player, have the right to be compensated in full for her talent and achievement? No one considered packing Martina Navratilova back to Czechoslovakia when she defected in 1975. (*CR*, 1982, p. E4055)

Similar expressions of support came from various organizations in Taiwan. The Taipei Tennis Association extended a welcome to Hu, offering living expenses and the services of a coach, while the Free China Relief Association sent cables to the International Red Cross and other groups urging support for Hu's asylum application.

While the official media in China remained silent, an editorial in the pro-China *Wen Wei Po* (Foreign Broadcast Information Service [FBIS], 1982, August 16, p. W1) in Hong Kong argued that because Hu Na's visit to the United States had been arranged in accordance with the Sino-American agreement on cultural exchanges, the United States government had the duty of ensuring her safety, regardless whether the invitation had come from a governmental or nongovernmental organization. Foreshadowing future developments, a spokesman for the Chinese Foreign Ministry in Beijing (Peking) stated that China held the United States responsible for Hu's safe return and noted that "such an incident is sure to adversely affect the cultural exchanges between the two countries" ("Return tennis star," 1982). As summer turned to autumn, and autumn limped into winter, behind the scenes discussions continued in Beijing and Washington. In January 1983, Hu's lawyer publicly expressed concern at the lengthy delay in reaching a decision. In response, Immigration Director Ilchert remarked,

> It's been going back and forth. We are reviewing the State Department's comments in the matter and will probably seek some further elaboration . . . .We will go upon what she has said and what the State Department has advised and make the determination of whether she has a well-founded fear of persecution ("Defector worries," 1983)

One indication of the sensitivity surrounding the issue was that, as late as March 25—8 months after the controversy arose—queries directed to officials in Washington received a terse, "No comment!" (Gerol, 1983). Considering the contentious nature of the problem, we might now ask, Who is Hu Na?

Rising Tennis Star Hu Na

Hu Na was born in 1963 to a sporting family in central China's Sichuan province. Her mother, Wen Ruying, is a staff member at the provincial Physical Culture and Sport Commission, while her father, Hu Yunpu, is a coach with the Chengdu Army unit basketball team. She has an older sister, Hu Shan, and a younger brother, Hu Bo, who is also a promising tennis player. Hu took up tennis at age 8 under the guidance of her grandfather, Wen Ling, a former provincial team coach, and her aunt, Wen Ruyu, a spare time sport school coach who was a nationally ranked player in the 1960s. Three years after entering a sport school, Hu Na won the singles title at the 1975 National Sparetime Schools tournament. In 1978, she captured the national junior singles crown at age 15. In March, 1980, she upset number one ranked Yu Liqiao in tournament play and went on to win the national singles title in 1981. Hu first traveled to the United States in August 1979, competing at tournaments in New York and Boston. Between 1979 and 1982, she competed abroad on 10 occasions, visiting the United State three times and touring Hong Kong, Rumania, Spain, Italy, France, and Mexico. Her international success included partnering Li Xinyi to the doubles title at the 3rd Casablanca Cup tournament in 1981 and winning the singles crown at the same tournament a year later in January 1982.

As a rising sport star, she was featured in several press articles, was the subject of a cover story (Li, 1982) in China's *Xin Tiyu* (*New Sports*) magazine, and appeared in a Canadian television documentary on China. Her sporting achievements also led to recognition as a member of the Sichuan provincial Women's Federation, a model worker in Chengdu city, and a member of the municipal Youth Federation. At the time of her defection, she was reported to have applied for membership in the Communist Party.

Response to the Asylum Decision

On Monday, April 4, 1983, U.S. Justice Department spokesman, Arthur P. Brill, released the following statement:

> Hu Na has been granted asylum under the Refugee Act of 1980, which provides asylum in cases where the applicant establishes a well-founded fear of persecu-

tion, due to their race, religion, nationality, political opinion or membership in a special social group. (*New York Times*, 1983, April 5)

In a short statement issued to the press, Hu expressed thanks to the American people and government and noted that no one in China knew in advance of her planned defection or of the personal agony she faced in choosing to leave her homeland ("Chinese defector," 1983). In Washington, reports circulated that President Reagan had "decided to pay any price" to assure Hu remained in the U.S. Republican Party official, Richard Vigurie, quoted Reagan as saying, "I would rather adopt her myself than send her back" (*FBIS*, 1983, April 11, p. B1).

Support for the government's decision came from several quarters, while its most prominent critic was the Speaker of the House of Representatives, Thomas P. O'Neill, Jr. (Dem-MA). Press reports (*FBIS*, 1983, April 14, p. B1) attribute the following remarks to O'Neill: "I honestly believe this government would be better off if we took the advice of the highly paid and educated people the State Department sends to that part of the world. They know the country and understand it." Clearly, O'Neill was suggesting that the decision taken was far from unanimous. The Speaker's comments drew an immediate response in Washington, with one Congressman saying,

> In choosing to side with totalitarianism against Hu Na, the Speaker has made the Statue of Liberty blush; but perhaps what he has said tells us in an unvarnished way how far liberals have gone toward abandoning the goals of freedom to the immoral challenge of Communists [*sic*] dictatorship. (CR, 1983, p. H2003)

Capital Hill's most damning comments, however, came from Representative Newt Gingrich (Rep-GA) who spoke for 30 minutes assailing what he characterized as a liberal, proslavery policy, evidenced by recent opposition to the United States' involvement in Central America, support for a nuclear freeze resolution, and O'Neill's criticism of the Hu Na decision (CR, 1983, pp. H2090-2092).

In Beijing, the Director of the Information Department of the Ministry of Foreign Affairs, Qi Huaiyuan, called the asylum decision, "a grave political incident long premeditated and deliberately created by the United States" (*Tiyu Bao*, 1983). Media response was similarly vitriolic. Radio Beijing, *Xinhua* (the New China News Agency), *Renmin Ribao* (The People's Daily) and *Tiyu Bao* (*Sports News*) published interviews with Hu's family, teachers, and coaches which cited the care and assistance she had received over the years and denied that she had been persecuted in any way, noting that, like many young people, Hu had applied for Party membership, but that her application had not yet been considered. In addition, editorial writers questioned how a quiet girl with average schooling could have written a request for asylum using such sophisticated wording as, "I would like to drop my pen here, and wish you golden peace"—a traditional, classical Chinese expression commonly used in Taiwan (*FBIS*, 1983, April 8, p. B2). On April 7, the Director of the Bureau for Cultural Relations with Foreign Countries of the Ministry of Culture, Ding Gu, met with Charles Freeman of the United States' embassy staff and announced the cancellation of nine bilateral exchanges scheduled for the remainder of 1983. Among the cancelled programs were art exhibitions, performing arts group tours, a film festival, journalist and publisher visits, and an exchange between Radio Beijing and Voice of America personnel (*FBIS*, 1983, April 7). On the same day, a spokesman for the All-China Sports Federation announced China's withdrawal from 10 international events slated to be held in the United States. Included in the announcement were a waterpolo tournament in May; softball and track and field competitions in June; cycling, equestrian and windsurfing events in July; the America's Cup swimming meet in August; rowing and canoeing programs in September; and a pre-Olympic volleyball tournament in October (*FBIS*, 1983, April 7). In announcing China's withdrawal, the ACSF official stated that, instead of guaranteeing the safety of participants in international events, the host country had in this case "connived at the enticement and coercion of Hu Na by a handful of Americans working in collusion with special agents from Taiwan" (FBIS, 1983, April 7, p. B4).

Reaction to the Chinese cancellations and withdrawals in the United States was low key. The State Department expressed regret at China's "overreaction," and White House spokesman Larry Speakes remarked that "good relations between the United States and China are a benefit to both sides and it's important that we view our differences in the perspective of the broader bilateral relationship" ("U.S. calls," 1983). Meanwhile, representatives of several sporting organizations expressed surprise at China's announced withdrawal, as many groups had known for months that Chinese athletes would not attend. A spokesman for the Coors International Cycling Classic, scheduled for Boulder, Colorado, remarked, "We invited them as a favor because they are an emerging cycling team. . .[they] wouldn't last very long if they did come" (*New York Times*, 1983, April 8, p. A8). To most government and sporting organizations, then, China's cancellations and withdrawals were viewed as being of little significance.

Analysis and Comment

Any discussion of the "Hu Na Incident" must place the controversy in the context of broader Sino-American relations. Since the normalization of diplomatic ties in January 1979, a pattern has emerged in dealings between the two nations characterized by Chinese bluster and warnings, responded to by calm, often indifferent, American reassurances. During 1982-83, disagreements arose in three areas: trade, technology, and Taiwan. With regard to trade, the two nations negotiated at length on textile quotas until the United States unilaterally imposed restrictions in January 1983, a move which led to a Chinese embargo on American imports including wheat. Technology transfer from the United States to China proved similarly contentious as officials in Washington moved cautiously on the export of dual-use computer systems and military hardware although relations improved somewhat when the People's Republic was granted "friendly and non-allied" status in June 1983. The principal, longstanding obstacle to improved relations, however, remained Taiwan. Beijing viewed Washington's continued arms sales to Taipei as a symbol of the Administration's failure to honor the terms of the 1979 and 1982 U.S.-China accords; moreover, American opposition to Taiwan's ouster from the

Asian Development Bank was seen as further, unwarranted support for the Republic of China. In sporting circles, the "two Chinas" debate was rekindl-ed in July 1982 when China refused to send a team to the Women's World Softball Championships in Taiwan which had the support of the American Presi-dent of the International Softball Federation, Donald Porter. Thus, notwith-standing the overall expansion of Sino-American ties over the past decade several irritants fueled the defection controversy in the weeks and months following Hu Na's disappearance.

Attempts to solve the dispute were hindered as excessive publicity heightened Chinese sensitivities. As one official in Beijing noted, "China will never, for the sake of its relations with the United States, abandon its principled stand of safeguarding its state sovereignty and national dignity" (*FBIS*, 1983, April 7, p. B1). By June 1983, however, Chinese press accounts acknowledged that the issue was not Hu Na herself but the broader question of political support for Taiwan and a perceived miscarriage of the American tradition of granting asylum to genuine victims of persecution ("Hu Na Case," 1983). In the end, the decision to grant Hu's request was made in the White House and, as one editorial writer wryly noted, "It was a case of weighing the offense to China against the alienation of President Reagan's conservative supporters. China lost" ("She wins," 1983, p. 4).

It would, perhaps, be easy to conclude this essay with the observation that the "Hu Na Incident" was resolved, in tennis terms: "Game, Set and Match—Miss Hu." Such an approach, however, ignores the substantive issues involved: Hu Na's future, subsequent U.S.—China exchange programs, and American response to requests for asylum.

As for Hu Na, she moved to the Nick Bollettiere Tennis Academy in Braden-ton, Florida, and resumed training with such players as Carling Bassett and Jimmy Arias prior to entering her first tournament in June 1983 in Erie, Penn-sylvania, where she lost her first round match to Mexico's number-two-ranked Claudia Hernandez. Hu's future, however, is uncertain as her mastery of English and adaptation to Western society remain immediate concerns.

As for the cancelled exchanges, little long-term damage was done, and Sino-American ties have not been dramatically impaired. Although the cancella-tions were possibly significant at the time, they were limited to those exchanges covered by formal, bilateral agreements, and the majority of programs handled through private channels continued as planned. By December 1983, discus-sions were underway on resumption of the state-to-state exchange program.

As for the United States' response to defectors, present procedures must be questioned. Hu Na should indeed feel privileged as she is among but a small number of Chinese who have been granted asylum in recent years. Bureaucratic indecision may have needlessly magnified the "Hu Na Incident" although, given the publicity the case received, there should have been little doubt as to the outcome. While some officials saw the appeal as a test case, possibly resulting in a deluge of asylum requests from the thousands of Chinese students and scholars in the United States, American immigration authorities have accepted only some 20-odd applicants in the past three years. In the case of Hu Na, were there winners or losers?

References

Chinese defector happy in U.S. (1983, April 5). *Vancouver Sun*, p. A14.

Chinese promise no recriminations (1982, July 26). *Santa Barbara Tribune*, p. 28.

Congressional Record. (1982, August 5). Political asylum for Hu Na. *Proceedings and Debates*, p. E3733.

Congressional Record. (1982, September 8). Chinese tennis star deserves asylum in United States. *Proceedings and Debates*, p. E4055.

Congressional Record. (1983, April 13). Liberals criticize granting of asylum for young Chinese girl. *Proceedings and Debates*, p. H2003.

Congressional Record. (1983, April 14). Liberal foreign policy is proslavery. *Proceedings and Debates*, pp. H2090-2092.

Daily Report: China. Foreign Braodcast Information Service. (1982, August 16), (1983, April 7, pp. B1, B3, B4, B4-5), (1983, April 8), (1983, April 11), and (1983, April 14).

Gerol, I. (1983, March 27). China tennis star trapped in limbo of human rights politics. *Vancouver Province*, p. B3.

Hu Na case—An unfortunate incident in China-U.S. relations. (1983, June). *China Reconstructs*, pp. 25-26.

Li, Gaozhong. (1982, April). Baigongbei wangqiu guanjun Hu Na [Casablanca cup tennis champion Hu Na]. *Xin Tiyu*, pp. 2-5.

New York Times. (1983, April 5), pp. A1, 10.

New York Times. (1983, April 8), p. A8.

Request for asylum expected to get OK. (1982, July 28). *Vancouver Sun*, p. C2.

Return tennis star: China. (1982, August 3). *Toronto Star*, p. F7.

She wins point, set, match. (1983, April 6). *Vancouver Province*, p. 4.

Tiyu Bao. (1983, April 6), p. 1.

U.S. calls Chinese move overreaction. (1983, April 8). *Vancouver Sun*, p. A14.

3

Canadian Government Involvement in Sport: Some Consequences and Issues

Donald Macintosh and C.E.S. Franks
QUEEN'S UNIVERSITY
KINGSTON, CANADA

Tom Bedecki
CAHPER NATIONAL OFFICE
OTTAWA, ONTARIO, CANADA

This paper discusses some of the consequences and issues raised by federal government involvement in sport in Canada, namely, national unity and a Canadian sport identity; the sport bureaucracy; the federal government's role in sport; and sport autonomy. The material in this paper is drawn from a larger study of government policy-making in sport in Canada since 1961.[1] It is the objective of this study to examine the processes and forces which were instrumental in bringing about sport legislation in 1961, and to examine subsequent events and forces which caused program emphasis to change from one of an indirect, passive role to one of direct, forceful involvement in the development of elite athletes.

National Unity and A Canadian Sport Identity

Perhaps the most significant characteristic of recent federal government involvement has been the role assigned to sport in contributing to national unity.

[1]This research project was funded by the Social Sciences and Humanities Research Council of Canada. The authors wish to acknowledge the contributions of associate investigator, Rick Gruneau, and research assistants, Donna Greenhorn, Robert Hollands, and Aniko Varpalotai.

The Grey Cup and Canada's international hockey teams had always been causes for national celebration or concern, depending upon the outcome. But the overt political use of sport as a unity symbol had its origin in a 1968 campaign speech when Prime Minister Trudeau linked sport with culture in promoting national unity, a major issue of the day. The breakdown of federal-provincial relations during the 1960s, the demands from Quebec for a special place in the confederation, and a rising economic nationalism in western Canada were all issues which begged for resolution. Sport, because of its affinity for television, became a household commodity in the 1960s; its greatly increased popularity made it attractive as an instrument to promote national unity.

Mr. Trudeau's election promise to establish a Task Force on Sport was fulfilled in 1969; on the basis of many of its recommendations, the federal government embarked in the 1970s on a course of direct, aggressive promotion of the development of high-performance athletes. The Canadian government's attempts to promote mass sports and fitness programs in the 1960s had been frustrated by federal-provincial jurisdictional disputes and by the magnitude of this task relative to the available resources. Success in elite sport, on the other hand, could be attained with a substantially smaller amount of money and could be easily verified in quantitative terms. Because of its high visibility, elite sport also had the potential for a much more attractive political payoff than did mass sport and fitness programs.

The Canadian government's efforts to improve performance levels of their amateur athletes in international sports competitions bore fruit in the late 1970s and early 1980s. Canada's athletes performed in a credible fashion at the 1976 Olympics in Montreal and improved substantially in the unofficial points' standings compared to the Munich Games 4 years earlier. The extensive television coverage of these Olympics fanned greater interest and higher expectations. These expectations were realized in the 1978 Commonwealth Games in Edmonton when Canada staged a spectacular sport triumph by finishing first ahead of the traditional winners, England and Australia. The Games were skillfully covered by the CBC, and Canadian successes were watched with satisfaction and pride by millions of Canadians. More recent Canadian successes in international skiing events, particularly the sensational downhill ski season in 1982 by Steve Podborski and the triple medal performance by Gaetan Boucher at the 1984 Winter Olympics, also served to illustrate that sport could transcend language and regional differences in Canada to promote a sense of national unity and pride.

Sport also appeals, although this is seldom mentioned, to intensely nationalistic and jingoistic emotions. The Canada Games, initiated in 1968 in Quebec City, significantly carried the symbol of "Unity Through Sport." Some observers feel, however, that these competitions, which subsequently have been held every 2 years, have had a divisive effect, perpetuating current regional and cultural differences in Canada.

The federal government's efforts to promote high-performance sport have also served to maintain and develop a Canadian sport identity. The attractiveness of sport on television and the use of sport to sell commodities and services have resulted in a North American professional sport image dominated by American telecasts, businesses, and sports enterprises. The expansion of professional hockey across the United States and the introduction of major league baseball in Montreal and Toronto gave additional impetus to this trend. The improved performance by "made in Canada" amateur athletes in international competitions provided Canadians with sport heroes who were not part of the North American sports package; this has played a role in countering the threat to Canadian identity of the pervasive mass culture of the United States.

The Sport Bureaucracy

Another important legacy of the federal government's involvement in sport in Canada is a burgeoning sport bureaucracy. The Task Force criticized amateur sports organizations for their "kitchen table" style of operation. National sports-governing bodies were characterized by part-time volunteer officers and officials, national executives who were typically drawn from only one or two regions of the country, and a high degree of inefficiency and disorganization. Few of the nation's sports-governing bodies had full-time, paid officials. But not even the most zealous sports afficionado would have anticipated the size and scope of today's sport bureaucracy. The Fitness and Amateur Sport Branch staff quadrupled in size from 30 in 1970 to 121 in 1984 (Canada, DNHW, 1971-72, 1984-85). In that same time, the professional, technical, and clerical staff which supports the national sports associations housed in Ottawa grew from 65 to 532 (Glynn, H., Personal Communication, April 4, 1984).

Increased federal government involvement in the 1970s, in promoting elite sport and the success of the Canada Games stimulated a parallel growth of sport bureaucracies in most provinces, which before had concentrated most of their efforts on mass recreation and fitness programs. For example, the Ontario Sports Center, established in 1970, today has a full-time staff of 90; in addition, currently there are about 130 full-time administrative and technical personnel attached directly to provincial sports associations (Furlani, A., Personal Communication, May 9, 1984). This expansion mirrored the general provincial bureaucratic growth of the 1970s and was, in part, a response to growing demands by Canadians and a counter-balance to the federal government's activities.

This formidable sport bureaucracy, along with the Coaching Association of Canada and its provincial delivery systems, has provided an administrative and technical competency for Canadian amateur sport to a degree unthought of in the 1960s. This support system is the envy of many western democratic nations and certainly is a major factor behind Canada's increased stature on the international sport scene. But this sport bureaucracy is not without problems. Because the salaries of these bureaucrats are largely paid by governmental funds, the loyalties of these executive, technical, and program directors are divided between representing the views of their respective organizations and respecting the wishes and views of the governmental agency which supports them. This has contributed substantially to their acquiescence to the federal government's penchant for promoting high performance sport and to the disappearance of an independent voice for amateur sport, an issue which will be discussed later in this paper.

The Federal Government's Role in Sport

The government's role in western capitalistic countries has two aspects. On one hand, it should support and nurture private enterprise, the major part of the economy. On the other, it should provide for the disadvantaged and promote equal opportunity for all. The role of sports programs here is contentious. The monies governments have allocated to build sport facilities, however, quite clearly support the private sector. These expenditures have been very substantial in comparison to program spending. For instance, the federal government spent $100 million on sport programs in the decade 1970-79 (FAS Annual Reports). But over $800 million was spent to build the sport facilities for the Montreal Olympics (Quebec, 1980), and $36 million at the 1978 Commonwealth Games in Edmonton (Commonwealth Games Foundation Report, 1978). Many such sports facilities, constructed with public tax monies, have been of most direct benefit to professional sports organizations. The most conspicuous of these are the Olympic Stadium in Montreal, which serves as the home site for both the Montreal Expos and the Montreal Concordes; the Commonwealth Stadium in Edmonton, which houses the Edmonton Eskimo football team; the Saddledome in Calgary, which provides home ice for the Calgary Flames; and BC Place in Vancouver, the site for the British Columbia Lions' home football games. The operational expenses of such facilities usually prohibit their use by elite amateur sports groups and more recreationally oriented community-based organizations. Despite attempts by political activists to point out the anomaly of huge public expenditures on a domed stadium in Toronto when social service and welfare budgets are being reduced, this proposal is receiving wide support from civic and provincial governments. Funding massive spectator sports facilities is attractive because such projects appeal to both the private and public sectors.

A recent hosting policy by Sport Canada calls for a closer scrutiny of the "benefits" of hosting international sports events in the future (Canada, FAS, 1983). This policy recognizes that federal funds spent on major facility construction might better be used to develop high-performance sport. Ironically, the federal cabinet shortly thereafter approved expenditures of up to $50 million on a Canadian bid for the World Football Cup (Kidd, B., Personal Communication, March 2, 1984).

Sport Autonomy

Autonomy has been one of the most contentious issues surrounding federal government involvement in sport. When the Fitness and Amateur Sport Act was passed in 1961, care was taken to allay fears that control would pass from sports organizing and governing bodies to the federal government. Through most of the 1960s, the federal government's involvement in sport was limited largely to cost-sharing arrangements with the provinces and awarding grants to national sports governing bodies. These grants had few strings attached, and there was little in the way of accountability on the part of the recipients. In addition, the National Advisory Council, which under the terms of the new

Act was to advise government on fitness and amateur sport policy, actually assumed responsibilities for directing the program. Thus a good measure of independence from government was maintained.

But the failure of these early efforts to improve Canada's performances in international amateur sports events, coupled with other broader political and social events outlined earlier in this paper, caused the federal government to become more directly involved in the development of high-performance athletes. First, the role of the Advisory Council was reduced, and program direction and policy advice to the Minister was placed firmly in the hands of the public servants in the Fitness and Amateur Sport Directorate. Second, the federal government established a number of "arms length" agencies designed to provide more effective administrative and technical assistance to sport. The national sports-governing bodies found themselves in a position where their rent, services, and most of the salaries of their full-time administrative and technical staff were being paid by the government. In addition, the direct grants which they received became increasingly tied to meeting specific conditions regarding elite development and performance. By the late 1970s, it was estimated that 75% of these grants were awarded under such specific conditions (Kidd, 1981).

Besides assuming a larger role in determining sport policy, the federal government started using sport as a political instrument. In 1976, Prime Minister Trudeau would not issue visas to the Olympic team from Taiwan unless they agreed neither to display their flag nor play their national anthem, despite the fact that they had been granted permission to participate by the International Olympic Committee. When the federal government, following the United States' example, imposed an economic and cultural boycott on the United Socialist Soviet Republic because of its military intervention in Afghanistan, the Canadian Olympic Association followed suit, despite the fact that its executive committee, a month earlier, had voted overwhelmingly in favor of going to Moscow for the Games. Overt pressure which the federal government has put on athletes and sport events organizers to support its boycott of South Africa is another example of federal government control over sport.

The creation of a Minister of State for Fitness and Amateur Sport in 1976 also contributed to greater government control of sport. Previously, this responsibility was part of the portfolio of health and welfare, and sport was only a small part of a large and important ministry. Mrs. Iona Campagnolo, the first minister of sport, was able to use this position to maintain a high profile in the news media. Her most triumphant moment was the victory parade at the conclusion of the 1978 Commonwealth Games in Edmonton. Mrs. Campagnolo was an effective, hardworking, and knowledgeable advocate of high-performance sport in Canada, but her stint of office was terminated by the election of the short-lived Conservative government in 1979. The Liberal government, returning to power in 1980, has since used the sport and fitness portfolio in the same manner as other junior posts—to test new cabinet ministers. There have been no fewer than five such appointments in the most recent Liberal government term of office, and these ministers have tended to seize on current sports issues and make popular pronouncements on sport policy with little thought of the implications and without the benefit of appropriate background information and knowledge. Some recent examples are Celine

Hervieux-Payette's warning late in 1983 that Canadian athletes and sports federations must stop using performance-enhancing drugs or lose government funds; Jacques Olivier's pronouncement early in 1984 that grants to the Canadian Olympic Association would be reviewed in the light of its selection criteria which excluded some athletes from competing in the Sarajevo Olympics; and pressure from both these ministers on sports federations to increase the use of French or risk losing government funding.

Certainly, few would advocate a return to the era prior to the Fitness and Amateur Sport Act when government eschewed any role in developing elite sports programs. The "autonomy" of sports organizations was tainted because they often represented vested class and social interests which were at odds with desirable sports programs for all Canadians. Those who advocate that sport become financially independent of government and depend, instead, on the private sector for support, ignore the problem that one master of sport simply would be replacing another. Instead of serving the interests of government, sport would be dominated by efforts to sell goods and services, and the commodification of sport, which already has dominated professional and much amateur sport, would be complete.

Government has a legitimate, essential role to play in sport. Providing opportunities to develop potential talent and maintaining a Canadian sport identity justifies government support to the same extent as these functions are widely accepted in culture. If sport is to keep any distance from the political whims of the day, escape from the narrow definition of outcomes which currently prevail, maintain its spontaneity, and have any transformative function in society, the government's role must be mediated by a strong, independent, widely representative, national Sports Council. This concept was a naive expectation of the sport community when the Fitness and Amateur Act came into being in 1961. An independent Sports Canada was proposed by the Task Force in 1969, and a quasiindependent Sports Council was advocated in the 1979 White Paper on Sport. It is a concept which is long overdue.

References

Canada. (1969). *Report of the Task Force on Sports for Canadians*.

Canada. (1971-1979). *Fitness and amateur sport*. Annual Reports.

Canada. (1971-72, 1984-85). Department of National Health and Welfare, Fitness and amateur sport estimates.

Canada. (1979). *Fitness and amateur sport. Partners in pursuit of excellence*: A national policy on amateur sport.

Canada. (1983). *Fitness and amateur sport*. Sport Canada: Hosting Policy.

Commonwealth Games Foundation. (1978, August 3). The friendly games: XI Commonwealth Games, Edmonton, Official Edition.

Kidd, B. (1981). The Canadian state and sport: The dilemma of intervention. *Annual Conference Proceedings of the National Association for Physical Education in Higher Education* (pp. 239-250). Champaign: Human Kinetics.

Quebec. (1980). *Report of the Commission of Inquiry into the cost of the 21st Olympiad* (Vol. 2).

4

Australian Government Involvement in Sport: A Delayed, Eclectic Approach

Richard S. Baka
FOOTSCRAY INSTITUTE OF TECHNOLOGY
FOOTSCRAY, VICTORIA, AUSTRALIA

In comparison to most nations, Australia definitely exhibited a late entry into the field of governmental involvement in sport. This might be considered strange when one assesses Australia's history of sporting success in such areas as the Olympic and Commonwealth Games, Wimbledon Tennis, and other world-caliber athletic contests. In fact, Australia's "year of glory" in 1983 earned it the distinction of being named "Country of the Year" by the French magazine *L'Express*.

From both past and recent sporting achievements, it might readily be concluded that sport plays an important part in the sociocultural context of Australia. Under such conditions, one might also expect a high degree of governmental involvement in sport, particularly at the federal or commonwealth level. For a variety of reasons, however, this has not been the case. Only within the last decade has there been any significant government public policy and forthcoming programs with respect to sport.

Background to the Contemporary Setting

Despite a paucity of research into various areas of government involvement in sport in Australia, a few studies have examined different aspects concerning this topic. Some of the more prominent efforts include work by Strang (1984), Baka (1982), Deane (1982), Semotiuk (1982), Hartung (1980), and Jacques and Pavia (1976). Deane (1982) concluded that there were three phases of federal government involvement: 1901 to 1972, 1972 to 1975, and post-1975. Because Deane's work was completed in 1982, this author contends that a fourth phase began in March 1983, following the Labor election victory.

From Federation to the Seventies 1901-1972: Little Money, Limited Programs, Little Interest

As with most western, democratic states when they were formed, Australia's federation in 1901 did not concern itself in the *Constitution Act* with any mention of sport or the broader field of recreation. It received no attention under exclusively federal powers, concurrent state and federal powers, or residual powers (which fell almost entirely to the states) (Hamilton-Smith & Robertson, 1976). For the next 70 years, public sector interest in this area was a low-key affair characterized by an ad hoc approach.

This limited involvement consisted of a *National Fitness Act* passed in 1941. While the objective of this legislation had a military-linked motive, the overall impact on sport was not large other than very limited funding for community centers, sport coaching, and some recreation and physical education programs. Another example of low regard for sport in government is that, before 1972, the federal government did not have a department concerned with sport.

Some federal involvement took place with financial assistance for team travel and accommodations to Olympic and Commonwealth Games, and for costs associated with hosting such events (e.g., Sydney, 1938; Melbourne, 1956; and Perth, 1962). Another recipient of regular federal financial subsidies since 1951 were the Royal and Surf Life-Saving Associations (Deane, 1982). Overall, such support was relatively minor; for example, the federal government's contribution to the National Fitness Program, run in conjunction with state national fitness councils, amounted to less than 3 million pounds from the late thirties to the late sixties (Baka, 1982).

Labor Reform, 1972-1975: The Seed is Sown

This very brief 3-year period proved to be a watershed with respect to public-sector involvement in sport. Under a Gough Whitlam Labor government, which broke a 23-year rule by the Liberals, there was widespread interest in broad social policy including the areas of sport, recreation, and leisure; this was exemplified by the creation of a Department of Tourism and Recreation in 1972 and a commitment by the Labor government to greatly increase its support to sport through new programs and services. Examples of these include a Capital Assistance Program to provide sporting facilities, a Sports' Assistance Program to support national sports associations, and a fitness awareness campaign known as Fitness Australia. The government also commissioned a number of landmark reports (e.g., *The Role, Scope and Development of Recreation in Australia* [1973] and the *Report of the Australian Sports Institute Study Group* [1975]) to help guide future policy.

Meanwhile, the early seventies witnessed major undertakings by most of the state governments as they passed new legislation and created primary departments or agencies to administer youth, sport, and recreation services; actually the states merely filled a void created by the federal government's lack of action before the Labor government's initiative in 1972.

However, the new-found Labor interest in sport at the federal level did not take place without some criticism. Hartung (1980, p. 202) reported that

> The government came in for a great deal of criticism for overspending on sport and, in retrospect, sporting associations were ill-prepared to handle the increased physical and financial involvement in central government.

While such criticism was warranted to some extent, the flurry of activity in Canberra came to a near halt. In an extremely complex, bitter political battle in Canberra, the issue of "double dissolution" saw the Labor government relinquish power to a Liberal-National Country Party Coalition in 1975.

Liberal Conservatism and Caution: 1975-1983

When the new coalition, dominated by the Liberals, came to power, it immediately adopted a far more cautious approach to sport. While the innovative Labor-inspired policy was not totally abandoned, funding and services were cut back dramatically, and the Department of Tourism and Recreation was abolished. The low status of the primary sport agency was shown as it was shifted a total of three times, and it was under four different ministers during this 8-year period.

Liberal government involvement was not characterized by a total lack of support to sport but by a more conservative approach as compared to the previous Labor government. Due to pressure applied from the opposition Labor Party and a growing sport lobby, spearheaded by the Confederation of Australian Sport which was established in 1976, the Liberals reacted by maintaining some sports programs and services. Furthermore, one of the Liberal ministers responsible for sport from 1978 to 1980, Bob Ellicott, was a major catalyst in giving the Liberal government a better track record than might have been expected otherwise (Hartung, 1980; Semotiuk, 1982). Thus, a revised Sports Assistance Scheme, a revamped sport facility program, large grants for the 1982 Brisbane Commonwealth Games, the Australian Sports Institute in Canberra, and other programs were largely due to the efforts of a minister who did not have the total support of his party.

Labor Momentum Restored: 1983

With the popular Bob Hawke and his Labor Party assuming power in the 1983 election, the fourth era began. The incoming government had gone to great lengths preparing itself for its return to rule evidenced by its drafting of a comprehensive 127-page document titled *The Australian Labor Party Sport and Recreation Policy.* One of Labor's first tasks was the creation of a new Department of Sport, Recreation, and Tourism. Amidst this aura of optimism, staff were hired, programs were planned, and appropriations to sport were increased to record levels (see Table 1).

Two recent undertakings were the efforts to draft a national sport policy in concert with representative bodies of sport and the government's decision to create a new National Sports Commission, a type of super advisory/monitory body. Such moves highlight the Labor government's vital interest in and commitment to sport development in Australia.

Reasons for the Delayed, Eclectic Approach

The late public sector interest, to some extent, can be attributed to association with the motherland. Because Australia developed British-style institutions, including political philosophy and style of nongovernment intervention, it is not difficult to understand the hesitation of the public sector to become involved in a domain traditionally administered by the private sector (Baka, 1982).

Table 1.1. Federal spending on sport and recreation from 1941-1984 in million $

Year	Agency/department	Federal spending
1941-72	National Fitness Council/Health Department	7.9
1972-73	Department of Tourism and Recreation	1.2
1973-74	Department of Tourism and Recreation	3.8
1974-75	Department of Tourism and Recreation	8.1
1975-76	Environment, Housing and Community Development	11.4
1976-77	Environment, Housing and Community Development	7.6
1977-78	Environment, Housing and Community Development	5.6
1978-79	Home Affairs	5.8
1979-80	Home Affairs	6.8
1980-81	Home Affairs and Environment	9.0
1981-82	Home Affairs and Environment	13.1
1982-83	Home Affairs and Environment	14.5
1983-84	Sport, Recreation and Tourism	22.5

Note. From Deane (1982); Baka (1982); Department of Sport, Recreation, and Tourism Annual Report, 1982-83; and Strang (1984). Some discrepancies existed among the various sources reporting expenditures due to inconsistently recorded government figures.

Another explanation for the belated government intrusion into sport had to do with international prestige attained through success in international sporting circles. During the post-World War II period of the fifties and sixties, Australia literally rode the crest of a wave of international sporting success. With such a record, there seemed no need for governmental intervention.

Sport, itself, placed few, if any, pressures on the Commonwealth government to take a more active role in the delivery system. In effect, there was no active lobby group campaigning for increased public sector for funding, programs, or administration.

Finally, the Commonwealth government, particularly during Liberal rule from 1949 to 1972, had no political orientation or widespread interest in sport. Sport, simply put, was not a major part of Liberal party politics.

Analysis of Motives Underlying Federal Government Involvement in Sport in Australia

Semotiuk (1981) developed a model characterizing nine motives underlying national government involvement in sport. When specifically applied to Australia, some interesting analysis is possible.

Unlike many nations, especially those allied with the Eastern bloc, the Australian Federal Government has not overtly rationalized its involvement for reasons associated with a military function or a political indoctrination function. These might be labelled tertiary motives with the least application to the Australian context.

A number of motives outlined by Semotiuk have had some application in Australia and could be considered secondary motives. Included in this category is the Labor productivity function (e.g., interest in promoting employee health/fitness programs). There has also been some evidence of an economic function witnessed by the gambling profits in horse racing and sport lottery pools being used to fund government sport programs. The legislative function has had application in Australia with the federal level passing laws affecting sport (e.g., restricting smoking advertising in sporting events). As with many countries around the world, the Australian government has exhibited an international goodwill function through sporting exchanges. Finally, a socializing or nationalizing function has become more evident in the Australian context as the federal government appears to have devised programs designed to elicit nationalistic feelings (e.g., the Australian Institute of Sport in Canberra and the Australia Games).

Above all, two primary motives appear to have dominated Canberra's decision to be involved in the area of public sector sport policy. One of these is the individualizing function or the contribution that sport or physical activity makes toward the total development of the individual. It is a widely supported view that a major reason behind the Australian government's interest in sport policy was directly related to a national prestige function or success in international competition.

Summary and Conclusions

For the most part, a domestic, public-sector sport policy did not exist until the Labor government came to power in 1972, and the next 12 years were characterized by erratic development due to governmental changes. Reasons for the delay were interrelated and varied: adherence to British "ideals"; geographical factors; longstanding international sports' success without government involvement; nonexistence of an effective sport lobby; and party politics. When the Australian government eventually developed sport policy, it often adopted an eclectic approach by borrowing ideas from nations such as Canada. The most obvious motives underlying the Australian government's involvement in sport can be traced to a national prestige function and to an individualizing function. In the years ahead, despite governmental changes, it appears that Australian government sport policy will develop to such an advanced stage that there will be a guaranteed, active federal role in sport.

References

Australia, Department of Sport, Recreation and Tourism, (1983). *Annual Report, 1982-83*. Canberra: Government Printer.

Australia, Department of Tourism and Recreation. (1975). *Report of the Australian Sports Institute Study Group*. Canberra: Government Printer.

Australian Labor Party (1982). *The A.L.P. Sport and Recreation Policy*. (No publishing details.)

Baka, R.S. (1982). Similarities between Australian and Canadian government involvement in sport. *Proceedings of the Fifth Candian Symposium on the History of Sport and Physical Education* (pp. 462-473). University of Toronto, Ontario, Canada.

Bloomfield, J. (1973). *The role, scope and development of recreation in Australia*. Canberra: Government Printer.

Deane, J. (1982). *The development of the Department of Youth, Sport and Recreation in the state of Victoria*. Unpublished master's thesis, University of Liverpool, England.

Hamilton-Smith, E., & Robertson, R. (1976). Recreation and government in Australia. In D. Mercer (Ed.), *Leisure and Recreation in Australia* (pp. 175-187). Sydney, N.S.W., Australia: Holt-Rinehart Ltd.

Hartung, G. (1980). Sport and the Canberra lobby. In R. Cashman & M. McKernan (Eds.), *Sport: Money, morality and the media* (pp. 194-215). Kensington, N.S.W., Australia: University Press Ltd.

Jacques, T.D., & Pavia, G.R. (1976). The Australian government and sport. In T.D. Jacques & G.R. Pavia (Eds.), *Sport in Australia* (pp. 148-156). Sydney, N.S.W., Australia: McGraw-Hill.

Semotiuk, D.M. (1981). Motives underlying national government involvement in sport. *Comparative Physical Education and Sport Journal, 7*, 17-23.

Semotiuk, D.M. (1982). *National government involvement in amateur sport in Australia, 1972-81*. Paper presented at the Third International Seminar on Comparative Physical Education and Sport, Minneapolis, Minnesota, U.S.A.

Strang, G. (1984). *Federal commitment to sports development*. Paper presented at the 15th ACHPER Biennial Conference, Sydney, N.S.W., Australia.

SECTION B
Perspectives on Elite and Mass Sport

5

Politics of Elite Sport in East and West

James W. Riordan
UNIVERSITY OF BRADFORD
BRADFORD, GREAT BRITAIN

Communist nations have displaced capitalist nations as sports leaders in the Olympics and many other world championships. This paper examines why and how the change has occurred and implications for the future of world sport.

When the communist nations made their debut at the 1952 Summer Olympics, they won 29% of the medals; in 1972 they won 47%; in 1976, 57%. Yet the USA and its NATO allies have twice the population and four times the GNP of the Warsaw Pact states (Clumpner, 1980).

The German Democratic Republic (GDR) advanced from 15th to 2nd medal place in the Summer Olympics between 1956 and 1976, overtaking the USA; and from 16th to 1st in the Winter Olympics between 1956 and 1980, and again in 1984, overtaking the USSR. The GDR has fewer than 17 million people.

Socialist Cuba has improved from 53rd in the unofficial points total on its Summer Olympic debut in 1960 to 23rd in 1972, 8th in 1976, and 4th in 1980. In 1976, it won more medals (13) than the rest of the other 30 Latin American states put together (10). And at the Ninth Pan-American Games in 1983, it also won more gold medals (79) than Canada and the rest of Latin America combined, placing second only to the USA (in track and field it won 34 medals, 12 gold, to the USA's 38, 14 gold). Cuba has a population of 9 million; the USA, 200 million.

The USSR (population 272 million) has "won" every Olympics, summer and winter, for which it has entered, with the sole exception of the summer of 1968, and the winters of 1980 and 1984. It is also by far the most versatile nation in Olympic history, winning medals in 19 of the 21 sports at the 1976 Montreal Olympics. In the traditional track and field encounter with the USA between 1958 and 1983, the score is currently 14-3 in the Soviet favor.

Western nations do have compensations in some "open" world sports such as tennis and soccer, although even in ice hockey the USSR has dominated competition against North American professionals and won the Canada Cup in 1981. Communist leaders have, nonetheless, insisted that their main target is the Olympic Games. As the Soviet sports monthly *Teoriya i praktika fizicheskoi kultury* (1968) has editorialized, "In evaluating the significance of international sport, we must remember that while world and European championships are of great importance, victory at the Olympics acquires a political resonance." The point being made is that the Olympics bring more publicity and national prestige; they are, it is thought, *the* measure of a nation's health and power, and as UNESCO (1956) put it 30 years ago, "an important testing ground for the two great political units."

Communist states have made other contributions to world sport. Cuba, for example, has exploded the myth of supposed black inferiority in aquatic and field sports, providing black champions in swimming and diving and, at the 1980 Olympics, the first-ever black woman to win an Olympic throwing event (Colon in the javelin). Between 1952 and 1980, female participation has increased from 10 to 24% of all Olympic competitors, a fact not unconnected with the communist Olympic debut and the Moscow Olympics. Finally, the assistance to developing countries and the boycott of South Africa owes much to the initiative and backing of the communist countries; today, only Western-controlled sports, such as golf, rugby, cricket, horse- and motor-racing, continue contacts with South Africa.

Why Interest in Excellence?

Communist Nations

Three major reasons for concern by communist nations for sporting excellence are as follows: The first is *inspiration* and *patriotism*. Athletes are held in high esteem for their skill, grace, and strength—attributes to inspire young and old alike to be active and join in at all levels of sport. Sport for all is free and is energetically promoted in all communist states for a number of salient reasons: hygiene and health, integration and patriotism, defense training, and labor discipline. Top performers also encourage a sense of pride in one's team, nationality, and country, even in the political system that can produce such world-beaters. The patriotic pride generated by sports success, especially against the strongest capitalist states, helps further to integrate ethnically diverse societies such as the USSR and China.

Second, there is a strong belief in communist states in the *parity of mental and physical culture* in human development, and a conviction that talent in sport should be treated no differently from talent in art, music, or science. In other words, budding gymnasts should be treated the same as promising ballet dancers; they must be given every chance to develop their gifts for the benefit of both the individual and the community. Unlike the early administrators of amateur sport in the West, communist leaders have never been constrained by the notion that sport is an unworthy profession. Indeed, if it had not been for the need to play the game acording to Western "amateur" rules when joining the Olympic movement, communist nations would surely now be continuing Soviet pre-1951 practice of having openly remunerated, full-time professionals. As it is, all proficient athletes pursue one of two occupations: as a student or a serviceman under the sponsorship of a trade union or other (such as security forces—Dinamo—or army) sports society.

Third, communist sport follows *foreign policy* and has paramount functions to discharge. These include the following:

Gaining Recognition and Prestige in the World

In the face of Western intransigence, boycott and subversion in economic, military, political, and other social areas, sport has served uniquely some communist nations as a medium of international expression. For example, where other channels have been closed, sport seems to have helped the German Democratic Republic attain a measure of international recognition and prestige. As Party Secretary, Erich Honecker (1976), has attested, "Our state is respected in the world because of the excellent performance of our athletes." In Cuba, success in international sport has helped nurture and satisfy patriotic pride in the face of a United States' boycott and subversion. Castro (1976) has described Cuban Olympic success as, "a sporting, psychological, patriotic and revolutionary victory."

This function has also been apparent in Chinese sports policy of recent years and in the entry of Soviet athletes into world sport after World War II. Soviet sports official Rodichenko (1970) has written that "The main purpose of our international sports ties is to consolidate the authority of the Soviet Union by ensuring that Soviet athletes do well internationally."

Maintaining and Reinforcing the Unity of the Communist Countries

The bulk of East European sports competition, as with foreign trade, is with socialist states. In this, they not only have the advantage of central planning in sport but considerable integration and division of labor within the communist community. This includes joint training camps, regular meetings to share research findings and to decide on joint policies towards the West (e.g., sports ministers met just prior to the 1981 Olympic Congress), and to divide up responsibilities. Cooperation, however, exists up to a point, of course. As a GDR official told me recently, "You can share experience but not a gold medal." Nonetheless, substantial sports cooperation does take place both to promote a common assault on the "bourgeois fortress," and, as Romanov (1973) says, "To help reinforce fraternal cooperation and friendship and to develop a sense of patriotism and internationalism among young people of the socialist states."

Demonstrating the Advantages of the Communist Way of Life and Promoting Communist Foreign Policy

Since the end of the last war, and particularly since the USSR launched its policy of "peaceful coexistence between states with different political systems," communist leaders have regarded sport as an important (indeed, perhaps the *only*) medium for "defeating" their ideological opponents. Victories over bourgeois states would attest to the vitality of the communist system. This objective was spelled out in the Soviet party resolution of 1949, instructing all organizations "To help Soviet athletes win world supremacy in the major sports in the immediate future'' (*Kultura i zhizn*, 1949). Furthermore, after this target had evidently been met in the 1972 Olympics, the Soviet monthly *Sport v SSSR* noted,

> The mounting impact of socialist sport on the world sports movement is one of the best and most comprehensible means of explaining to people throughout the world the advantages which the socialist system has over capitalism.

Castro (1962) looks forward to the day when Cuba can prove the superiority of its national sport—baseball—over that of United States' baseball,

> One day, when the Yankees accept peaceful coexistence with our country, we shall beat them at baseball too and then the advantages of revolutionary over capitalist sport will be demonstrated!

Despite some sporting setbacks, there is ample evidence to show that the economically advanced communist states have gone a considerable way toward achieving their aim of world supremacy, above all in the Olympic Games.

Capitalist Nations

Western motives for promoting sports excellence are far less easy to define, owing to the more fragmented organizational structure of Western sport, the competing (and sometimes contradictory) aims and ideologies of the various institutions involved in sport, and the lack of formal integration within the Western community. Nonetheless, against the background of the three principal reasons given above for communist interest in excellence, the following points may be made.

First, the *inspirational* value of sports success is generally recognized. As the British Sports Council (1984) records,

> The nation lifts its head high when our national teams succeed. It also takes to the court, pitch or swimming pool when would-be champions have witnessed their idols demonstrating a high level of sports skills.

There is, too, a more or less vague notion that sports success helps to generate patriotism. In the Scandinavian states, patriotism through sport is made explicit and produces considerable state support for proficient athletes. In others where state support is weak and commercialism and professionalism strong, patriotism may come second to self-interest and profit. Whereas communist athletes owe the development of their talents entirely to state support, capitalist athletes often owe it to their families and to themselves. Although this situation is slowly changing with the encouragement of trusts, athletic scholarships, and undercounter payments, it has long resulted in social barriers in many sports and extensive wastage of untapped talent among the less privileged (the poor, the black, and women). As the Council of Europe (1977) warns, ''Social obstacles to participation are significant: some sports in some countries have developed social 'images' that limit participation.''

In general, Western sports stars do not have social or political duties and do not regard themselves as being responsible to the state (in fact, many regard themselves as having succeeded *despite* the state). Moreover, few seem to regard themselves as ambassadors for their countries or standard-bearers for capitalism, although several Western governments pressed for such a role when endeavoring to boycott the 1980 Moscow Olympics.

Second, Western sport, with its long traditions, now seems in transition from a traditional *amateur-elitist* to a *commercial-professional* ethos. The dominant credo of the former has been that sport should be divorced from politics, government interference and commercialism, professional coaches, sports schools, and the like, and that there should be a firm commitment to the Olympic ideal. The clash between this philosophy and the commercial-professional has occurred in different forms in different states. At best, the evolution toward the latter has produced encouragement for the spotting, nurturing, and rewarding of sports talent, the development of sports schools, and the entry into sport of a far wider social community than ever before. At worst, it has resulted in sport that is looked upon as a source of profit for commercial agents and go-betweens, for hand-outs and retainers, and for governments who shift their responsibility for sport onto willing entrepreneurs whose interest is not sport but its exploitation in order to sell their product and line their pockets. One does not have to look far from Oregon for an example of that. What is apparent, as the American Pavek (1983) writes, is

> The communist nations give priority to preparing athletes for success in the Olympics, while the West generally gives priority to preparing an athlete for gaining a professional contract in a major sport with high financial rewards.

Third, the older Western nations do not seem to have such ambition to gain recognition and prestige in the world as do the younger states. It is the former who, having had their days of glory, alone claim that the Olympics have become too nationalistic, unwieldy, and political. As the British Sports Council (1982) claims for Britain,

> Some countries invest vast public funds in special facilities, training programmes and financial and status rewards for elite athletes, in order to win prestige and trade internationally. It is neither tradition nor policy to treat top level sport in this way in Britain.

In other words, Western nations do not seem *to need to win* as much as developing countries do, trying to establish themselves in the world.

On the other hand, there is a growing awareness that somehow the West is losing out in some well-publicized propaganda battle with communism in sports arenas; thus, efforts have been made, especially since the 1980 Olympic boycott fiasco (the reinforcing of the U.S. vanguard position within the Western bloc is amply demonstrated by the lack of a British boycott of the Los Angeles Games over the U.S. invasion of the British Commonwealth member Grenada!) to draw Western states together and to make a concerted attempt to beat the communist nations on American soil (or at least to "shame" them through well-publicized anticommunist demonstrations). The hurried recruitment of South African athletes, such as Zola Budd by Britain, is just one example of the lengths to which such attempts have gone.

Finally, apart from individual visiting athletes and coaches, few Western states have given much officially sponsored sports aid to developing countries. Quite the contrary, the pattern has generally been for promising foreign athletes (like other specialists) to be attracted away from their homelands to seek fame and fortune in the West. This, allied with the collaboration by some Western athletes, sports organizations and scholars with racist regimes such as South

Africa, is hardly likely to give moral leadership in the world or evince the sympathy of the Third World which may well see, with good cause, the communist states as more reliable champions of their cause.

Conclusion

Since the early 1950s, communist nations have striven for, and largely attained, sports supremacy at the Olympics and several other world championships. Not only has sport proved to be an effective means for them to compete peacefully with the West, and often to demonstrate in practice the "superiority" of the communist system, but they have also been able to use sport to generate popular sentiments of friendship toward them (especially in developing states) and smooth the way for proffered aid and treaty relations.

With their complete control of the sports system, communist leaders have been able to mobilize resources to achieve maximum efficiency in their sports challenge and, hence, perform what they believe to be important political functions. They have demonstrated that the highest realization of human potential can most effectively be achieved through the planned application of society's resources. They have attained this goal in sport (and in many other fields of human endeavor and excellence), and their achievements have been largely motivated by the deliberate, quite plausible intention of demonstrating the superiority of their system. In general, in the Western world, the priority attachment of sport to "cost-effectiveness" has resulted in elite development often being left to the physical and moral resources of the individual athlete and coach; such a system cannot compete seriously with countries that apply the resources of the entire society to develop excellence.

The future of world sport, particularly the Olympic movement, may well depend on whether the Western nations, whose sports systems are mostly fragmented and relatively autonomous of government control and whose profit-making commercial sport takes precedence over "amateur" events, will be reconciled to their increasingly weakened position in the world, especially in Olympic sport. Having lost their monopoly in most arenas, it may not be long before they forfeit their monopoly control of sports forums as well. This sporting demise of the West harbors the danger of political apartheid in world sport, including the abandonment of the Olympic Games (elements of this existed in the United States-inspired boycott of the 1980 Olympics, the United States' administration's successful attempts to keep communist athletes out of Los Angeles, and the imposing upon the Soviet bloc of South Korea as host nation of the 1988 Summer Olympics). Such a danger needs highlighting, for, as the former British sports minister, Denis Howell (1984), attests, "International sport provides the only occasion where the peoples of the world, especially the young people of the world, come together, compete with each other, and live together." In the increasingly perilous world in which we live, there may be precious few such opportunities left to humankind. In such circumstances, sport appears especially important in terms of prestige and moral leadership. A nation that neglects either one does so at the risk of losing more than sporting contacts.

References

Castro, F. (1962). In S. Castanes (Ed.), *Fidel, Sobre el deporte* (p. 91). Havana.

Castro, F. (1976). *El Deporto,* **3**, 9.

Clumpner, R. (1980). Socialist offshoots and the American model: Concern, implications, and possible decreations. *Proceedings of the North American Physical Education and Health Association*, p. 285.

Council of Europe, Committee on Sport (1977). *Rationalising sports policies. Sport in its social context: International comparisons*, p. 61. Strasbourg.

Honecker, E. (1976). *Report of the Central Committee to the Ninth Congress of the Socialist Unity Party of Germany*, p. 133. Berlin.

Howell, D. (1984). Sport and politics: An international perspective. *Comparative Physical Education and Sport*, **6**, 15.

Kultura i zhizn (1949, November 1). p. 5.

Pavek, B. (1983). Sociological observations of sports in the USSR and the United States. *Comparative Physical Education and Sport*, **5**, 6-27.

Rodichenko, V.S. (1970). *Rekordy, sobytiya, lyudi, 1969*, p. 105. Moscow.

Romanov, A.O. (1973). *Mezhdunarodnoye sportivnoye dvizhenie*. Moscow.

Sport v SSSR (1973). **6**, 2.

Sports Council (1984). *Annual Report 1982-83*, p. 16. London.

Sports Council (1982). *Sport in the community. The next ten years*, p. 40. London.

Teoriya i praktika fizicheskoi kultury (1968), **5**, 42.

UNESCO (1956). *The place of sport in education*, p. 57. Paris.

6

Mass-Sport Activities and Top-Class Athletics: Unity or Contradiction?

Edelfrid Buggel
SCIENTIFIC COUNCIL FOR PHYSICAL CULTURE AND SPORT
IN THE GERMAN DEMOCRATIC REPUBLIC
BERLIN, GERMAN DEMOCRATIC REPUBLIC

For many years, the relationship between mass-sport activities and top-class sports has been discussed in political, in mass media, and in sport scientist circles. Mass-sport activities can be defined as the whole-range concept of "sport for all" which reaches far into the compulsory physical education lesson in school. This relationship is not only of theoretical interest, but also provides insights into societal reality and into the actual development of physical culture and sport in a given country.

Two major concepts can be derived from this relationship. The first concept maintains that top-class sport and mass-sport activities are in strong contradiction. Once closely connected, the two have nothing more in common after the developments during the last few decades: that is, top-class athletics and mass-sport activities are now considered as being two different "worlds." The second concept, also featuring essential differences between top-class sports and mass-sport activities, points, however, to remarkable interrelations leading to positive results for both areas.

Why, then, are relations between top-class sports and mass-sport activities defined as being troublesome? Several reflections can be made in response to this question.

Principles for Physical Education and Sport

First, state and societal leading authorities of any country have to decide what roles physical education and sport principally play. Then decisions must be made as to how and to what extent mass-sport activities and top-class sports will be supported and promoted. Investments must be made, but to what extent? Will these investments be available for *any* citizen of a country regardless of social status, political attitude, religious creed, or color, or will they only be at the disposal of a privileged group of the population? These decisions are of high financial, material, and personal caliber and face *all* countries. *How* these decisions are made, for example, to whose advantage do they come into practice, depends on the economical, political, cultural, and other developmental levels of that country, and to the role physical culture and sport play in that country.

Influence of Science and Technology

The second reflection is of scientific origin. The scientific-technological revolution enforces a more effective integration of scientific fields and societal areas in the interest of progress. That phenomenon is much more strongly developed in top-class athletics, reaching up to the limitations of human capacities, than it is in mass-sport activities. For this reason, there must be a more differentiated specialization for coaches trained for top-class athletics as compared for the mass-sport teacher, despite a conforming profile in their basic professional training.

Organizational Systems

A third reflection concerns the organizational structures of mass-sport and top-class activities. Here, some essential, serious differences are found, particularly established by the even stronger and faster specialization of top-class sport events. An international trend shows that top-class athletics and mass-sport activities can rarely be brought together under one roof, for example, a sport team, a sport union, or a sport club. The concept of the two different "worlds" that top-class sports and mass-sport activities should represent obviously comes from this phenomenon.

Value Ranking

The last reflection concerns the values and rankings of mass-sport activities and top-class athletics: Has top-class sport a higher value than mass-sport (or vice versa), or are they of equal value?

This refers back to the first reflection but under another aspect. Values or rankings mean individual, team-bound, or societal motivations and assessments; they are the final representation of the essence of any societal phenomenon. Therefore, these values or rankings are always objectively and politically determined.

To define values always means to ask whether the development of top-class sports or mass-sport activities can, in fact, result in positive social effects or even include social conflicts; and whether social, political, racial, or other restrictions are existing in a country offering top-class or mass-sport activities to all. The same holds true with education through sports and with ethical values of sport. This means that top-class sports cannot have positive effects upon the athletes', coaches', or spectators' education or actions if these sports are ruled by professionalism and commerce.

In a socialist country, top-class athletics and mass-sport activities are equally ranked, and they are a unity despite all the differences between national development. Mass-sport and top-class athletics belong to the system of values in socialism, being values, and being worthwhile objectives of socialist morals.

First within that ranking system is a fundamental value of socialism: peace. This means that a policy of peaceful coexistence between states of different societal orders is the only alternative to a nuclear war. Thus, cooperation, based upon reason and objectivity, is necessary. This includes the necessity to respect other political and religious attitudes and concepts. Top-class and mass-sports can, and must, actively contribute to this task.

Historical View

Historically, the relationship between mass-sport activities and top-class athletics can only be slightly touched upon here. On the one hand, this relationship has undergone strong changes; on the other, some relations have shown to be pretty constant if only one thinks of Pierre de Coubertin's formula. According to that formula, 100 people have to participate in sports so that 50 achieve higher performances, leading to another 20 with even higher results in order to finally attain 5 top-class performances.

This formula has certainly not been perceived by de Coubertin as possessing scientifically significant proportions or as an exact basis for a purposeful policy in sport; we should, however, accept his main idea. Top-class performances spring from a given width; this idea was impressively shown by the top results at all the Olympic Summer Games from Athens in 1896 up to Moscow in 1980, and at the Olympic Winter Games from Chamonix in 1924 to Sarajevo in 1984—corresponding, of course, with the actual historical situation. We have to analytically investigate the national developmental programs for physical education and sport whenever we want to objectively assess whether Coubertin's formula can, or could, be implemented in a given country in relation to the question posed.

Sport in the GDR

If I were to make such an analysis for the German Democratic Republic (GDR), the following relevant principles of my country's sport concept should be cited as starting points:

- The effective role that physical education and sport are playing in an all-round and harmonious formation and education of *all* citizens in the interest of their health and well-being.
- The organic integration of sport into the conditions of labor and life, thus leading to close connections with economy, public education, health services, culture, and with other societal fields; the unity of the biological, social, and intellectual within the processes of formation and education.

From these premises, the daily-practiced unity of mass-sport activities and top-class athletics is fixed in the sport concept of my country and as part of real practice.

It should not be postulated that there are no contradictions or problems within the development of the two areas which are progressing as a unity. In accordance with dialectics, we understand them rather as being motives. Since 1945, but particularly since the formation of the GDR, physical education and sport have been considered to be one aspect of societal life, a stable component of our whole way of life following initiatives and guidance by the Socialist Unity Party of Germany. In all their fundamental documents, this party, our government, and our societal mass organizations (trade unions, youth or women's unions), there are—right up to the GDR's Constitution—principal, orientating, and concrete statements on the development of physical education and sport. Together, they form our national developmental program in which the sport organization of the GDR is defined as the main supporter in close cooperation with the State Secretariat for Physical Culture and Sport.

At the same time, the obligations are stipulated for the other state or societal authorities, such as for the construction and equipment of sport facilities, for free entry to sport facilities, for the sport medical care of participating people, and also for the instruction and training of sport teachers, coaches, and so forth. The ruling also includes free participation in group traveling at reduced fares, the continuous establishment and perfection of sport science and sport medicine in teaching and research; the regular postgraduate qualification of all those who work professionally in the fields of physical education and sport, and a short-time leave from the job to work as a voluntary sport official, judge, or referee, in the selection, recruiting, and promoting of athletic talents. At the same time, in this national developmental program, which is based upon my country's constitution and composed of all its corresponding laws, appointments, and decisions, a wide individual range of activities is offered for a lifelong, versatile, enjoyable performance and fitness-promoting engagement of every citizen in sports. These stipulations are defined as obligations for the authorities and as rights for the citizens who may utilize them if they wish.

This national developmental program forms the basis for a purposeful progress of sport in practice. All the experience and new requirements from actual sport practice react upon this concept, thus qualifying it and making it ever more precise. Thus, *real sport practice* is implemented in the GDR during the compulsory sport lessons at general schools, in universities, and in professional training schools for all pupils and students, as well as during the regular voluntary sport activities of 45% of the adults in the GDR. Real sport practice includes the following:

- The athletic Children and Youth Spartakiads held on school, town, county, district, and national levels, which are competitions and championships staged in 43 sports; these competitions annually invite about 90% of all the children and adolescents, again expressing the unity of mass-sport activities and top-class athletics.
- The 4 million citizens (e.g., 24% of the GDR population) who annually

reach the standards of the Sport Badge, a state standard of general physical fitness.

- The regular sport events in factories and living areas up to the national Gymnastics and Sports Festivals of the GDR, with 5 million citizens participating in them.

We wanted to show that top-class sport is no isolated domain in the GDR. It should be understood as a process leading from simple athletic results to performances that are close to the top or at world-level achievement level. Top-class sport exists this way in socialist societies in general, and in the GDR in particular, as an organic component of the total field of physical education and sport.

As early as 3 decades ago, the unity and the differences of mass-sport and top-class athletics have been realized in the German Democratic Republic and so training-methodological, sport-organizational, school-political and social consequences were drawn. Sport for all was always the basic political orientation, the mass-sport activity without social restrictions, promoted by the State and society in general, always seeking and promoting athletic talents. Therefore, more than 30 years ago, in 1951-52, the first Children and Youth Sport Schools were established. In 1954-55, clubs were founded to be centers for training youngsters and top-class athletes as well. One basic presupposition for doing so was, however, to change the social status of physical education lessons into a major subject in the 10th or 12th grade of the general schools. Marks in sport were of equal values compared with other major subjects. The ideal and social status of the sport teacher as well as that of the coach were increased by ranking them as full-accepted pedagogues, equalizing them with teachers in the fine arts or scientific subjects. Sport science and sports medicine could develop in depth and width in contents and on an institutional basis. All these items together established the real and solid basis of top-class athletics for training and competition with talents in that field.

A scientifically based planning of training and competitions, and a "sporting" atmosphere in the schools, at the working sites, and in territories, contributes to a sport-bound public opinion that only can flourish when a national sport concept exists; this concept is capable of developing in practice and essentially affects the way of life of a large percentage of pupils, apprentices, and students. Thereby not only are some single athletic talents found, but a wide reservoir is opened, and that again is the precondition for a small country to achieve high athletic results in many sports.

In such a sport-bound atmosphere or good "sporting climate," we often do not think of the adolescent's readiness, or of his or her parents, teachers, and professional instructors to meet the requirements put to a top-class athlete and to accompany him or her along this way. It is essentially shaped by the fact that the necessary athletic talent is highly regarded. A young athlete who cannot meet the expectations to be a top talent does not feel demoralized, but rather receives all the opportunities to continue his or her athletic interest in mass-sport activities. This is also an important aspect of the unity of mass-sport and top-class athletics.

A Nationwide Dimension

Having reflected on the relationships between mass-sport activities and top-class athletics at a nationwide dimension, that relationship can also be found in width and at the top in any given sport. The term width is applied here in a closer meaning. There are only empirical values on the relations between width and top in all the sport associations of different countries, as they always refer to talents who have to prove themselves on the various levels of excellence. That individuality of athletic perfection is only established within sports with a vast number of participants, that is, his or her competition against athletic rivals in his or her own sports club or with those from others during national or international events.

No one could speak of mass character upon lowest levels, as in long-jumping or running when it comes to sports with specialized requirements such as pole vaulting or hurdling. This may be explained by the proportions of basic and specific training or from the methodology of training. That means that the top level in special events in track and field results from the mass character of this sport in its basic events: running, throwing/putting, or jumping. This may be applied analogously to other sports.

To summarize, even in the sports themselves there must be a well-balanced width, that is, of mass-sport activities to find the talented youngsters in the basic events and to develop them specifically by proper training and competitive programs up to top-class performers.

The unity of mass-sport activities and top-class athletics is also expressed by the fact that there must be a certain variety of sports—according to the country's economic, political, geographical, demographical, climatic, anthropological characteristics—among which the athlete may make his or her choice, in which he or she may try his or her best and find satisfaction or even switch over.

From what we have said so far, there can only be a promotion of top-class level sports in accordance with Coubertin's ideals, and with socialist points of view within a comprehensive complex structure and development of physical education and sport.

We have, therefore, not only to look for basic proportions between mass-sport activities and top-class athletics, but also for social mechanisms, the existence and efficiency of which generally open possibilities to participate in sports.

Conclusion

When looking for the greatest moral, ethical, and psychophysical effects to be achieved by physical education and sport for the individual as well as for the society on the whole, there must be a unity of a country's mass-sport activities and top-class athletics "in the great and the small." It comes into reality by millions of people participating in mass sports and hundreds of thousands of athletes competing. That unity can only be achieved if physical education and sport are completely and equally integrated into other societal fields such as economy, politics, culture, public health, education, or defense, forming again a unity with them, even while differences are always considered. The results reached by physical education and sport in the GDR fully justify the conclusion that the societal conditions of a socialist state provide very good presuppositions for doing so.

7

An Analysis of the Organizational Structure of the Soviet Youth Sports System

Stephen C. Jefferies
UNIVERSITY OF ILLINOIS AT URBANA-CHAMPAIGN
URBANA, ILLINOIS, USA

The purpose of this paper was to identify key elements in the Soviet sports system which contribute to perennial Soviet athletic success.[1] Five elements were identified: (a) Soviet sports policy, (b) Soviet sports administration, (c) athletes, (d) coaches, and (e) training.

Soviet Sports Policy

Sport in Soviet cultural life receives official validation as a worthwhile human endeavor. State and Communist Party directives acknowledge the value of sport, especially as a means of promoting a favorable Soviet image abroad. Vydrin (1980) has argued that sport is an "important means of communist education." The Soviets believe that achievements in sport not only reflect individual skills and strengths, but they also reflect the skills and strengths of a society. A logical conclusion to be drawn from this belief is that the most successful sports nation must also possess the best social system.

The world is currently divided by two major politically antagonistic ideologies, and "battles" remain to be fought for extending their spheres of influence. The Soviets value sport as a powerful weapon to their political armory. The potential for sport to serve an an instrument of foreign policy

---

[1]The findings of the paper are based on the author's experience as an exchange scholar in the USSR.

is clearly recognized by the Soviet administration. The Soviets feel that international sport cannot be ignored, and that for matters of political expediency, sport must continue to be dominated by Soviet, or at least socialist, victories. Every Soviet athletic success is a victory for the socialist political system.

For years, the Soviets have effectively used sport as a strategy for exporting communism. Cuba, Vietnam, Cambodia, and Nicaragua have sport systems ideologically modeled on the Soviet social system. In Asia, Africa, the Middle East, and Latin America, this expansion continues undisputed. The Eastern bloc and Third World use sport achievements as a powerful vehicle for increasing their international visibility. Through generous offers of financial and technical assistance, "track suit" diplomacy has successfully extended Soviet influence abroad.

Sport is also viewed as a valuable means of regulating domestic behavior. Through sport, the authorities organize and integrate the Soviet people. It is often forgotten that the Soviet Union is not comprised of one body of people: fifteen major nationality groups and hundreds of minor nationality divisions constitute the USSR. The Soviet government faces major cultural and linguistic difficulties in attempting to harmoniously integrate many of these fiercely independent nationality groups. The regulation of sport and the organization of national competitions and championships is recognized by the administration as an effective means of domestic control. Emphasis is placed on the role of sport in developing "officially approved" values, attitudes, and behaviors in the younger population. Sport is also seen as an effective means of educating children to respect the mores of the developing society.

Soviet Sports Administration

The Sports Committee of the USSR, located in Moscow, controls every facet of the Soviet sports movement, and this Soviet system of centralized organization is efficient and productive. Within the confines of a single Moscow building are housed the heads and offices of every national sport-governing body. There are no competing groups within the same sport, nor are the interests of individual sports permitted to threaten the athletic interests of the nation. This centralized organization regulates all activity toward national goals, and the principal goal of Soviet sports policy is to maintain international domination in all Olympic sports.

The centrally organized Soviet sport system effectively overcomes communication problems due to the geographical and ethnic composition of the USSR. The USSR is the largest country in the world. The vastness of Soviet territory and the harsh climatic conditions present formidable obstacles to efficient communication. In addition, cultural and linguistic differences among the republics, and in some instances, among regions of the same republic, severely complicate the dissemination of news and information. This situation is both a strength and a weakness in Soviet sports affairs.

The diversity of national groups within the USSR has greatly enriched the nation's athletic resources as certain nationalities have traditionally excelled in specific types of sport. While the Soviet Union has benefited from the athletic contributions of its ethnic groups, the authorities have had to simultaneously reconcile ethnic differences in values and attitudes toward sport. As Riordan (1980) noted, physical culture has proved a very effective means of breaking down cultural barriers; however, it is doubtful whether individual republics, left to administer their own program of physical culture and sport, would have resolved to develop sport to the high level that currently exists.

While the Sports Committee of the USSR retains overall control, subordinating sports committees in the republics, regions, districts, and cities are responsible for the dissemination and practical application of national policies. Representatives of the surrounding national groups are ideally suited to implement Moscow's directives. In this way, official sports policy is seen as locally relevant. At the same time, throughout the entire USSR, sport is developed along a single, methodological path. Through this system, the Soviets claim they have been able to consistently develop outstanding athletes and simultaneously develop a popular mass-sports movement.

Although the Sports Committee of the USSR remains responsible for directing national sports policy, it would be incorrect to misinterpret the apparent rigidity of the Soviet sports system. Centralized organization is effective in maintaining compliance with minimal standards, but, clearly, the system would not be as effective if individual initiative was always subordinated to directives from a central, distant authority.

In practice, the system displays broad flexibility. Consider, for example, the area of sport research. The Sports Committee of the USSR first establishes a general plan and then delegates responsibilities to ensure there is no duplication of work. Investigators are then free to select specific research topics, and the critical concern is that work is productive. Practical applications rather than abstract theories are expected. The Soviet sports movement is validated on figures of participation and medals won by Soviet teams in Olympic and world competition. Research which contributes to the achievement of these goals is justifiable.

Athletes

The distinctive attraction of sport to young Soviet students is best illustrated by identifying differences in lifestyles between Soviet and Western athletes. This approach helps explain the quality and quantity of outstanding Soviet athletes; it may also explain why Western societies are unable to effectively cultivate talented, young athletes.

Two particular lifestyle characteristics strongly influence the leisure-time activities of young children. One is the availability of opportunities for recreation and entertainment. In the West, the bewildering panoply of leisure choices and activities occupies the free time of many children capable of outstanding achievements in various fields of endeavor, including sport. The availability of alternative sources of leisure activities increases with age; this, however, is not the case in the USSR. Although Soviet coaches are now becoming concerned about the influence of television, Soviet children currently face neither the quantity nor intensity of similar forms of Western entertainment.

A second major difference is that, in Soviet society, the productive use of free time is valued significantly higher than it is in the West. Soviet children are expected to take part in organized leisure programs offered by Palaces of Culture, the Pioneers, and other youth groups. The concept of free, unorganized, and unsupervised neighborhood play, often so highly valued in the West, is not encouraged in the USSR.

Soviet children enthusiastically elect to participate in sport. For physically able children, sport is an attractive option for "constructive" free-time activity, and Soviet children will dedicate years to pursuing a program of intense sports training. For these young children, the development of physical skills, the pride of being a team member, public recognition for athletic success, representative honors, and the opportunity to travel to competitions in other parts of the country are all factors which motivate their enthusiasm for sport.

As these children mature, additional incentives become increasingly important. For all Soviet athletes, the opportunity for international travel becomes a major inducement following the realization that few Soviets ever receive permission to explore beyond the Soviet borders. Representation at the national or international level presents athletes this rare opportunity. For those with sufficient ability, this chance becomes a great incentive to excel.

Outstanding Soviet athletes are honored for their achievements, and although they will never receive the financial rewards that accompany success in the West, they are assured of a financially comfortable future. Internationally acclaimed athletes are often awarded prestigious administrative positions or coaching responsibilities. For example, both Olga Korbut and Ludmila Turisheva now hold administrative posts in gymnastics.

Coaches

To become coaches, Soviet students with the necessary educational and athletic qualifications must complete a 4-year course in their chosen area of specialization in a higher educational institute. The majority of these students already possess outstanding practical skills, and many are present or past members of republican or national teams.

All Soviet coaches, regardless of their specialization or experience, receive similar training. This ensures consistency in content and methodology between all sports. After 4 years of training, these talented athletes complete their training and graduate as full-time professional coaches, fully acquainted with the latest developments in the theory and methods of coaching.

Most Soviet athletes who excel in sport, particularly to the level of republican or national representation, are destined to become future coaches or sports administrators. The time commitment they have made to their sport over the years, inevitably at some cost to other educational studies, makes the selection of a coaching career a very logical decision. Soviet athletes, however successful, will not be awarded promotional contracts or be able to use their athletic achievements as a vehicle for developing lucrative careers in other unrelated fields. The Soviet sports system, which has already profited from the success of these individuals as athletes, benefits again as these same individuals pass on their experience to the younger generation of athletes.

Soviet athletes have fewer career alternatives than Western athletes other than to become coaches, and financially coaching is not rewarding. It is true that working conditions are generally good and the activity is not unpleasant, but newly qualified coaches are given jobs which are among the most poorly paid in Soviet society.

However, one significant difference between coaching and most other Soviet professions is that the coach's salary depends on performance rather than on mere attendance. Successful coaching leads to promotions and corresponding increases in salary, but money is not the motivational force in Soviet society that it is in the West. Successful coaches in the West expect and receive enormous financial rewards, but in the USSR, even the most outstanding coaches receive relatively small salaries.

Recognition as a talented coach brings opportunities for raising one's status or rank in Soviet society, and with each increase in status, there is an expansion in responsibilities and opportunities. A coach may experience relatively little financial gain but profit inestimably from opportunities otherwise unobtainable regardless of profession or income. Coaches who discover and train outstanding athletes, regularly travel abroad for national and international competitions. As mentioned previously, these experiences are beyond the reach of most Soviet citizens.

Training

The final ingredient necessary for athletic success is a high-quality training environment. This includes the provision of necessary facilities and equipment and the creation of scientifically founded training programs.

A distinctive characteristic of Soviet sport is that sport has been brought to the people. Many of the boundaries or restrictions which might otherwise have limited participation have been removed. There are minimal fees for participation, and facilities are available within traveling distance of most Soviet homes. The Soviets claim that every region in the USSR has at least one sports school.

The widespread availability of local training centers should not be confused with their quality. The superb facilities constructed for the Moscow Olympics are not representative of the typical sport facility in the USSR. The Soviets have tried to make the most effective use of all available resources. In many cities, existing buildings have been renovated and converted into athletic facilities. In Leningrad, for example, the Winter Stadium, which houses the city's principal indoor track facility, was previously a training ground for the Tsar's horses. There is no comparison between the quality of athletic facilities that exist in the USA and in the USSR. There are, however, obvious differences between these two countries in availability and access to the existing facilities. The criteria in the USSR is solely that of demonstrating high-athletic ability.

In the USA, while physical ability is respected, the ability to meet membership dues is a more highly valued prerequisite.

One advantage the Soviets do enjoy, from the viewpoint of organization, is that two thirds of the entire population live in urban environments, which are concentrated around major cities. The greatest proportion of outstanding Soviet athletes either were born in a major city, or, as their ability became evident, transferred to an urban-training environment. However, although the cities may exist as centers for the development of talented athletes, it should not be overlooked that Soviet cities are inevitably very large, and travel (generally on public transportation) is a time-consuming affair. For this reason, within the cities, sports training facilities for the younger populations have generally been constructed to permit easy access. In most sports schools, the young athletes live close by.

The provision of over 6,000 sports schools throughout the USSR, with an estimated membership of 4 to 6 million young athletes, is an indication of the national commitment to a youth sports program. Simultaneously it is evidence of a Soviet belief that continued domination of international sport is dependent on the quality of their preparation of a sports reserve. The Soviets demonstrate a very aggressive policy of seeking and recruiting athletically gifted children.

Recruitment for serious sports training, depending on the sport, may begin with children of ages 4 and 5. Children who continue to demonstrate potential and who are able to sustain an increasingly intensified training program, attend the same facility until high school graduation at age 18 or 19. During this time, among the pressures that they must resolve, is the problem of successfully combining educational and athletic work. Young athletes of all countries face this dilemma. In the USSR, the problem is being officially tackled on a national scale by the introduction of special classes and sports boarding schools (Jefferies, 1984). Both innovations seek to harmoniously combine sport and education and remove from the individual the trauma of having to compromise one or other area. This unique Soviet solution is a promising attempt to overcome a major obstacle to conducting ongoing, developmental athletic programs.

The training opportunities enjoyed by young Soviet athletes cannot fully explain the ongoing, international success of the USSR in events such as the Olympic Games. The average age of Olympic champions is 25 (Chudinov, 1976). By this time, Soviet athletes have long since graduated from the children's sports school environment.

Upon graduation from high school, young Soviet athletes transfer to Schools of Higher Sports Mastery (SHSM), or, in the case of team sports, to one of the republican league teams. They will usually become either students or serve in one of the Soviet military organizations (KGB, army). In both cases, talented athletes are allocated sufficient time to continue training. Because all men must eventually complete a term of military service, there is a great incentive to enlist in the army and spend this time competing for the army athletic teams.

Students and military personnel receive payment for their training in these fields although their daily schedules revolve around the demands of athletics. During noncompetitive periods, time must be devoted to fulfilling career aspirations. A flexible curriculum permits graduation with either an academic degree or a military rank. Student athletes are officially given twice the usual amount of time (8 years) in order to graduate. In exceptional circumstances where athletes continue to be competitive for many years, it is possible to assign them coaching duties for which they, quite legitimately, receive payment.

Until recently, it was possible for the Soviet Union to enter identical teams in both professional and amateur international sports competitions. This was clearly unfair to nations who, according to their own definition of "professional" and "amateur," were forced to select from entirely separate pools of players.

Securing quality sports equipment in the USSR is another major problem, for Western-made equipment is not generally available. This is an area of concern to the Soviets who recognize the inferiority of their domestically manufactured products. Technological advances which have resulted in the production of improved sports equipment have had a major impact on the growth of athletic results. In events where differences and medals are calculated on the basis of fractional units, athletes must use the best available equipment. In order to remain competitive, the Sports Committee of the USSR arranges for the better Soviet athletes to be supplied with Western-made equipment. Soviet athletes would otherwise compete under very unfavorable conditions.

A final area for discussion is the training program itself. The Soviets have developed a general system and have applied this to all sports. Adherence to an officially regulated, age-based structure and methodological consistency in all training programs, regardless of specialization, is required. Within these broad organizational constraints, Soviet coaches operate freely. Individual initiative which produces valid results is respected, and new methods can easily be incorporated into the "official" system. This occurred with the specialist-class system, first introduced on an experimental basis in Moscow. In order to remain familiar with current training methods, Soviet coaches are encouraged to attend coaching conferences, and sports schools regularly receive conference papers and sports periodicals. The Soviets also carefully monitor foreign sports research and training reports and regularly implement this information into their own programs.

References

Chudinov, V.I. (1976). Biologicheski vozrast sportivnykh dostizheni kak osnova otbora i podgotovki reservov (Biological age of sports achievements as the basis for selection and preparation of reserves). In *Problemy otbora yunykh sportsmenov.* Moscow: All-Union Scientific and Research Institute for Physical Culture, pp. 14-16.

Jefferies, S.C. (1984). Sport and education: Theory and practice in the USSR, *Quest*, **36**, 164-176.

Riordan, J. (1980). *Soviet sport: Background to the Olympics.* New York: University Press.

Vydrin, V.M. (Ed.). (1980). *Sport v sovremennom obshchestve (Sport in contemporary society).* Moscow: Physical Culture and Sport.

8

The Evolution and Role of the Sports Councils in Britain

G. Bernard Wright
JORDANHILL COLLEGE OF EDUCATION
GLASGOW, SCOTLAND

For centuries, sport has had an immense appeal to people of all ages in Britain. Each sporting activity, as it has grown in popularity, has developed its own administrative structure. The diversity of sport in Britain can be illustrated by reference to statistics produced by the Sports Council and the Central Council for Physical Recreation (CCPR).

A Guide to Governing Bodies (1981), published by the Sports Council, provides a subject index which lists 92 different sporting activities, and the index of organizations identifies 193 governing bodies of sport. *The CCPR, A Guide: What It Is and What It Does* (1983) states that the Council consists of 240 governing bodies of sport and physical recreative activities.

Supporting and making provision for the growth and development of autonomous sporting bodies on this scale is a daunting task to face any central agency. Provision must also be made for members of the community who wish to participate in sport but without any link to the governing bodies.

Huw Jones (1968) suggested that the evolution of all social services in Britain have common characteristics:

> In Britain it is impossible to name any important social service that does not spring from voluntary effort; volunteers and voluntary organisations have stirred the nation's compassion, they have been the source of invention, they have provided the means of experiment and exploration; they have been the pattern makers and the advocates.

Many of the features outlined by Huw Jones can be identified in the evolution of the sports councils, a complex and fascinating phenomenon involving outstanding individuals, professional associations, voluntary bodies, governing bodies of sport, social factors, and political initiatives.

The Central Council for Physical Recreation—CCPR

The CCPR, from its inception, was a dynamic and influential organization. It was a powerful influence in leading successive governments toward increasing expenditure and concern for sport and recreation which led to establishing the sports councils. The formation of the CCPR was an act of great vision and faith on the part of Phyllis Colson. The contribution this remarkable woman made to the creation, growth, and administration of the CCPR was immense. Miss Colson realized that a coordinating council was necessary if facilities and opportunities for sport and recreation were to be improved throughout the country. The Physical Education Associations supported her in an approach to the Board of Education who were surprisingly enthusiastic but predictably unable to offer financial support.

Miss Colson did not delay but immediately set herself the task of recruiting a team of influential and distinguished members: The King and Queen agreed to be the Council's patrons; the Prince of Wales, vice patron; and Lord Astor, the president. The inaugural meeting of the Central Council of Recreation and Physical Training, as it was first named, took place at the conference room of the board of education on the afternoon of July 4, 1935. The CCPR began its work with a great deal of goodwill but no financial resources. It survived with the assistance of donations from professional associations and trusts until 1937 when it received the first statutory grant from the board of education.

A report from the British Medical Association's Physical Education Committee, published in 1936, provided a great stimulus for the CCRPT. The report was emphatic and uncompromising in its criticism of the existing provision for physical education and recreation for schoolchildren and for adults. This report specifically encouraged authorities and voluntary organizations to make use of the CCRPT in the provision of appropriate training courses for leaders. At this time, demands for improved resources and facilities for physical education and recreation increased. Comparisons with other European countries added pressure for government action and culminated in 1937 with the Physical Training and Recreation Act and the appointment of a National Advisory Council with 22 subsidiary area committees. The scheme was supported by an allocation of £2m to be spent over 3 years. Although there were serious reservations concerning the philosophy underlying this legislation and the organizational structure designed for its implementation, the bill was generally welcomed.

The National Fitness Council (NFC) clearly envisaged that it would absorb the CCRPT within its organization, but this initiative was resisted. Although the NFC succeeded in encouraging the development of new facilities, it was not considered to be an effective organization. It is significant to note that the general disillusionment concerning the effectiveness of the NFC was not forgotten. When the debate began concerning the establishment of an "executive" sports council, the weaknesses in the National Fitness Council were recalled. The NFC closed at the outbreak of war in 1939.

The CCRPT was active during the war years, organizing conferences and courses to develop trained leaders and to provide fitness and recreation. Despite financial constraints, the Council continued to grow during post-war years.

In 1944, the Council changed its name and subsequently became the Central Council for Physical Recreation—CCPR. In 1944, the CCPR received an invitation to extend its activities into Scotland, and, in 1947, received a similar invitation from Nothern Ireland. The CCPR's sphere of influence then encompassed Britain. In 1953, the Scottish section sought autonomy and became the SCPR.

The contribution the CCPR made to the community in Britain was substantial. This can be illustrated by referring to the major role played by the CCPR in the establishment of the National Sport Centers which can be considered a tribute to the ambition, vision, courage, and entrepreneurial skills of the senior staff of the Council. The statutory financial aid to the CCPR steadily increased from 1937/38 = £1,000, to 1954/55 = £80,000, and 1971/72 = £556,118.

The Wolfenden Report—Sport in the Community (1957-60)

In the summer of 1957, the CCPR announced the appointment of the Wolfenden Committee. The report was presented to the CCPR in September 1960, was published immediately, and contained more than 50 recommendations. The most important was the need for a Sports Development Council of 6 to 10 persons, reponsible to the lord president of the council or directly appointed by the chancellor of the exchequer. The committee decided unanimously that there was little hope of sport being given a substantial change of status unless a new body, independent of the Ministry of Education, was established with direct financial support from the government.

Political Reaction

The Wolfenden Report created immense public interest and support. No government or political party could ignore this demand for new initiatives. The report became the focus for political debate as each party considered how it could provide a policy commitment which would appeal to the voting public. A Conservative party committee's report, "The Challenge of Leisure" (1959) advocated the establishment of an "independent" Sports Council with an income of £5m a year. The Labor party published *Leisure for Living* (1959) which declared the party's policy to be the formation of a Sports Council *within* the Ministry of Education.

Minister With Special Responsibility for Sport

The first important political movement came in 1962 when Lord Hailsham was appointed Lord President of the Council and Minister for Science, in addition Minister with Special Responsibility for Sport. This appointment increased revenue, but although pressure was mounted in the House of Lords and the House of Commons, Quintin Hogg (Lord Hailsham had renounced his Peerage in 1963) resisted all arguments for the establishment of a Sports Development Council.

The First Sports Council—
The 'Advisory' Sports Council—1965

At the general election in 1964, a Labor government was returned to power, and the Prime Minister, Harold Wilson, fulfilled its election pledge to create a Sports Council. Mr. Dennis Howell was appointed to undertake this task. Dennis Howell recalls that, at the time of his appointment, he reminded the Prime Minister that he had supported the Wolfenden Committee's recommendations and had spoken against the establishment of a Sports Council. Harold Wilson replied that he was aware of Dennis Howell's views and that was precisely why he was being given that post. The Prime Minister said that as he was aware of *all* pitfalls, he would be better able to avoid them. On February, 3, 1965, the Government announced it had decided to establish a Sports Council to advise them on matters relating to the development of amateur sport and physical recreation services and to foster cooperation among the statutory authorities and voluntary organizations. Mr. Howell, as minister responsible, would be chairman and the members of the Council would serve in a personal capacity.

This was an exciting development. Politicians, civil servants and everyone involved in sport watched closely and waited to see if this new "Advisory" Sports Council could work effectively. The minister set about organizing the new Council with energy and enthusiasm. Walter Winterbottom, who had succeeded Miss Colson at the CCPR, was seconded as director general. Apart from the personal qualities and experience he could bring to this new post, his appointment was clearly intended to ensure the fullest cooperation and support from the CCPR. The Sports Council quickly established four committees from its own members to consider development in specific areas: sports development and coaching, research and statistics, facilities planning and international. The next significant move came when Dennis Howell was promoted from Under Secretary at the Department of Education to Minister of State at the Ministry of Housing and Local Government, later to become the Department of the Environment. The Sports Council moved with him, and coincidentally, another recommendation from the Wolfenden Committee, to remove responsibility for sport from education, was fulfilled.

Further Political Initiatives

As the general election approached in 1970, the status of the Sports Council once again became an important political issue. The Conservative party pledged, in their election manifesto, to make the Sports Council "independent." Opinions were polarized. The main arguments could perhaps be summarized as follows.

In favor of retaining an Advisory Sports Council

1. The presence of the minister as chairman made advice, executive, and political action one process. The full cooperation of the civil service was facilitated.

2. Good working relationships were established with the CCPR and the governing bodies of sport and those would be disturbed by any change.
3. An Executive Sports Council with a responsibility for distributing grants would be inhibited in its relationship with government due to its dependence upon funding. The Council might also tend to become dictatorial in its relationships with governing bodies.
4. The record of the Advisory Sports Council justified its continuance without change of structure.

In favor of establishing an Independent Sports Council

1. The Minister should not be chairman because his presence could inhibit discussion and unduly influence decision making.
2. The structure of an Advisory Sports Council was far too complicated with too many agencies involved—rationalization was essential.
3. Sport must have a direct grant of funds and not be dependent upon government departments with other priorities.
4. The direct responsibility for distributing funds would give the Sports Council much more influence. Discussions with local authorities and governing bodies would, therefore, be much more meaningful.

A Royal Charter—The Executive Sports Council

The Conservative party returned to power in 1970. Eldon Griffiths was appointed Joint Parliamentary Secretary of State at the Ministry of Housing and Local Government and Minister for Sport. The new minister announced, in the House of Commons on June 10, 1971, that the government had decided to "enhance the status of the Sports Council, to give it executive powers and widen its responsibilities."

Implications for the CCPR

As many authoritative voices had predicted, the new Executive Sports Council could not continue to work in the same way with the CCPR. Mr. Eldon Griffiths recommended that they should amalgamate. This inevitably created considerable concern among the members and staff of the CCPR. It had to be recognized, however, that in its willingness to cooperate fully with the Advisory Sports Council, the CCPR had made it virtually impossible for it to return to its previous position. After much debate and consultation, the CCPR agreed to transfer its property, assets, and staff to the control of the Executive Sports Council. Many, including the previous Minister, advised against this decision. Nevertheless, at an extraordinary meeting of the Governing Bodies of Sport in 1971, members declared the need for the CCPR to continue its role as a "standing forum" where all national and governing bodies of sport and recreation might be represented. The president of the CCPR, The Duke of Edinburgh, spoke forcefully in opposition to the total integration of the CCPR within the Sports Council. The CCPR, therefore, continued in England with its objectives being redefined. The transition was achieved in Scotland and

Wales quite amicably with provision for governing bodies to retain a forum built into the structure through a Standing Conference of Sport.

The Role of the Sports Councils

The Sports Council has been described, in political terms, as the "Cabinet of Sport" with the CCPR (and the Standing Conference in Scotland and Wales) as the "Parliament of Sport." The Royal Charters, granted on December 22, 1971, clearly defined the roles of the Sports Council. Scotland and Wales had their own charter, and the position of Northern Ireland was defined in the Recreation and Youth Service Order of 1973. The following extracts give a clear indication of the responsibilities involved.

> In furtherance of its objects the Council shall have the following powers:
> (a) to develop and improve the knowledge and practice of sport and physical recreation in the interests of social welfare and the enjoyment of leisure among the public at large in Great Britain, and to encourage the attainment of high standards in conjunction with the governing bodies of sport and physical recreation;
> (b) to foster, support or undertake provision of facilities for sport and physical recreation;
> (c) to carry out itself, or to encourage and support other persons or bodies in carrying out, research and studies into matters concerning sport and physical recreation; and to disseminate knowledge and advice on these matters;
> (d) to collaborate with foreign and international bodies in the furtherance of the foregoing to secure the benefits of relevant experience abroad;
> (e) to make grants or loans upon and subject to such conditions and otherwise as the Council shall deem fit in the furtherance of the foregoing providing always and notwithstanding the foregoing that the Council shall attach to any loan made by it such conditions as may be prescribed from time to time by the Lord Commissioners of Our Treasury;
> (f) to carry on any other activity for the benefit of sport and physical recreation;
> (g) to advise, co-operate with or assist Departments of our Government, Local Authorities, the Scottish Sports Council, the Sports Council for Wales, and other bodies, on any matters concerned whether directly or indirectly with the foregoing;
> (h) to establish and/or act as trustee of any charity the objects of which are in accordance with any of the Council's objects.

In simple terms, the Sports Councils would claim to be able to offer advice, information, facilities, and funds. The funds made available to the Sports Council (England) from the government (grant-in-aid) have steadily increased from £3.6m in 1972-73 to £28.02m in 1982-83. The Council calculates that its £28m in 1982-83 generated £149m of public and £43m of voluntary investment.

The role of the Sports Councils can best be described in their slogan which was introduced in 1972—"Sports for All." No other organization has been able, realistically, to claim so great an ambition. In their admirable publication, *Sport in the Community—The Next Ten Years* (1982), the Sports Council identify their priorities for the next decade. The strategy is built around three themes: a primary one of promoting participation, and two secondary ones of providing facilities and encouraging excellence.

Dynamic organizations are constantly adjusting and changing their emphasis according to specific needs. This key personnel also stamp their personality and individual philosophy upon the policy and strategy of any organization. This is clearly apparent in the Sports Council. The nature for the relationship between the Council and each successive minister for sport is an interesting study in itself. One can readily understand that accountability to government for financial expenditure is essential; nevertheless, one can question the reality of the "independence" of the Sports Council when political pressure can determine the appointment and retirement of officers.

Any agency which distributes funds is bound to be criticized. One of the most frequent criticisms of the Sports Council is that it spends too much of its income on its own staff and administration; during 1982-83, the Sports Council (England) employed an average of 565 personnel. The response to this argument is that these provide a service and professional expertise for the benefit of sport. Another closely related concern is the potential growth of bureaucracy and the increased problems of communication which would follow. It is essential that the "Cabinet of Sport" should ensure ease of communication be retained with the "Parliament of Sport" and also with the general electorate who provide all their financial resources.

In less than 2 decades the Sports Councils have made a very substantial contribution to the development of sport in Britain. Its resources, however, are relatively meager when addressed to total needs. The success of the Sports Councils must be judged against their ability to work in partnership with government, local authorities, governing bodies of sport, and voluntary organizations. The Sports Councils must provide the leadership and motivation necessary to make "sport for all" a reality in Britain.

References

British Medical Association. (1936). Report of physical education committee. London: B.M.A.

Conservative Party. (1959). *The challenge of leisure*. London: C.P.C.

Department of the Environment. (1975). *Sport and Recreation*. London: H.M.S.O.

Evans, H.J. (1974). *Service to sport*. London: Pelham.

House of Lords Select Committee. (1973). *Sport and Leisure*. London: H.M.S.O.

Jones, R.H. (1968). *Voluntary effort in the welfare state*, The Berl Wober Memorial Lecture, The corporation of Glasgow Health & Welfare Committee.

Labor Party. (1959). *Leisure for living*. London: L.P.

Mcintosh, P.C. (1972). *Physical education in England since 1800*. London: Bell & Sons Ltd.

McNair Committee Report. (1944). *Teachers and youth leaders*. London: H.M.S.O.

Morgan, A.E. (1939). *The needs of youth*. London: O.U.P.

Morgan, A.E. (1943). *Young Citizen*. London: Penguin.

Rodgers, H.B. (1978). *Rationalising sports policies: Sport in the social context*. Strasbourg: Council of Europe.

The Royal Charter. (1971). *The Sports Council: The Scottish Sports Council: The Welsh Sports Council.*

The Scottish Sports Council. (1972-83). *Annual Reports*. Edinburgh: Scottish Sports Council.

The Sports Council. (1981). *Sport: A guide to governing bodies*. London: The Sports Council.

The Sports Council. (1982). *Sport in the community: The next ten years*. London: The Sports Council.

The Sports Council. (1972-83). *Annual Reports*. London: The Sports Council.

The Welsh Sports Council. (1972-83). *Annual Reports*. Cardiff: Welsh Sports Council.

Wolfenden Committee on Sports. (1960). *Sport in the community*. London: CCPR.

SECTION C
Canada: A Bureaucratic Model

9

Canadian International Sport Policy: A Public Policy Analysis

G.A. Olafson and C. Lloyd Brown-John
UNIVERSITY OF WINDSOR
WINDSOR, ONTARIO, CANADA

> Because of the nature of international sporting competition, and the new significance attached to it, it is inevitable that sooner or later our national government must take a hand in a matter so closely bound up with Canada's place in the world.
>
> Report of the Task Force on
> Sports for Canadians, 1969, p. 7.

During the past 23 years, the Canadian government has gradually evolved its sport policy, partially in part as a reaction to international political events. The focus of this paper is an examination of "Policy Statements which may be in the form of decisions, decrees, licenses or statements the authority of which is drawn from enabling legislation."[1] Our methodology involves an extensive analysis of statements and pronouncements of official policy makers as formal inputs in the policy process. House of Commons Debates, which are reflective of the official policy and attitudes, will be examined by reference to two models. Institutional Relationships: A Generalized Regulatory Policy Process (Brown-John, 1981); and, Government Legislative Involvement in Organizational Structure of Sport Systems (Olafson, 1982, 1983a).

Since passage of *The Fitness and Amateur Sport Act* (1961), the federal government has had at its disposal a vehicle for the development of its fitness sport delivery system. With completion of the following documents, *Task Force on Sport for Canadians* (1969), *A Proposed Sport Policy for Canadians* (1970), *A National Policy on Amateur Sport* (1979), and *A Challenge to the Nation* (1981), the federal government opened the door to increased influence on Canadian international sport policy.

---

[1] Brown-John, Lloyd C. Canadian Regulatory Agencies, p. 55.

Public Policy

The public policy process in Canada is not entirely unlike that of most other liberal democratic Western democracies. Policy outputs, be they related to sports or foreign policy, are, in one manner or another, a product of an interactive process referred to as *pluralism*." This means simply, that what government does, *or* does not do, is a consequence of action-reaction relationships between interactive and usually competing groups in society. All groups implicitly acknowledge the unwritten rules of the political game, all groups support the existence and maintenance of the political system, and all groups concede the legitimacy of the outcome. They may not agree with it, but, short of revolution, they accept it as legitimate. Furthermore, because what government does by way of public policy outputs is definitive (e.g., in the form of a law), government is often described as making policy decisions in an authoritative and allocative manner. Simply stated, that means, that especially in a parliamentary system such as Canada, that what Parliament does or what the government does, acting on behalf of Parliament and the Crown, is final. Thus government becomes the final arbitrator between competing social demands and values, and, in the process, where necessary, allocates public resources (money) accordingly.

Lest one assume arbitrariness, democratic governments must seek reelection periodically; hence, there is a well-defined tendency to seek compromise in the development of policy. As parliamentary democracies are highly influenced by bureaucratic norms, there is tremendous pressure, both for bureaucratic solutions to public policy problems and for solutions which may be best described as "satisfying."

Innovative policy changes emerge from many sources and reflect the product of a process whereby interests have competed and conflicts have been resolved. In the area of sport policy in Canada, especially in respect to Canada's international status in sport, two major elements came into confluence during the 1960s. First, there was the widespread and frequently embarrassing realization that Canada's international competitive skills were on the decline. Specifically, Canadian hockey teams had fallen from global prominence, and Canadian athletes were being overwhelmed at international meets, especially the Olympics. Members of Parliament, faithfully tuned to their constituents' outrage, pressed the federal government to do something about Canada's alleged shameful performances.

Second, there was a growing political reality for Canada which emerged ultimately in the decision to reject Taiwan's participation in the 1976 Montreal Olympics in favor of the People's Republic of China (PRC). This decision reflected the essentially bureaucratic origins of Canadian foreign policy. For several years prior to the decision, Canadian diplomats had sought to distance themselves from the Americans and the malaise into which the United States had descended over Vietnam. American foreign policy in the Far East had become increasingly more repugnant for Canadians, and one clear means of inserting a distance was to make a definitive decision in favor of the PRC over Taiwan. Moreover, for years, mounting Canadian wheat sales to the PRC had demonstrated that Canada's future economic interests were more closely linked with the PRC than with Taiwan. The Canadian government's attempt to opt for a "two-China" policy failed, and, given choice and reality, Canada opted to reject Taiwan in favor of the PRC. Whether Canadians broadly supported the policy decision or not was immaterial at the time, as it was a foreign-policy decision derived within the inner sanctum of the External Affairs Department, and it reflected the career diplomats' perception of where long-term interests rested.

Sport Policy

Sport policy in Canada had been an emerging concept incorporating several complex dimensions. We can hope to capture only a small hint of those complexities in this paper.

Discussion in the House of Commons on sport policy generally has focused upon either success or failures in Olympic competition or on our attitudes toward certain foreign governments and their activities or policies (e.g., South Africa and apartheid).[2] The government endeavored to side-step some controversy by shifting policy decisions in respect to participation with South Africa to "sports associations in Canada."[3] Thus, while the federal government increasingly was becoming more involved in linking foreign policy to sport policy, in 1968 it still obscured responsibility by assigning it to sport organizations in Canada.

Trudeau's emergence as leader of the Liberal party and an ensuing federal election led to a promise to appoint a task force to investigate amateur sport in Canada. Subsequently, on August 2, 1968, a three-member task force was appointed consisting of Harold Rea, a business consultant; Paul Des Ruisseaur, a sports medicine specialist; and Nancy Green, a world champion skier.

A month later, in the speech from the throne, the government noted that it had undertaken and was "pursuing a thorough review of our external and defence policies."[4] This review of Canadian foreign policy ultimately became important in terms of relations with China and the subsequent "fall-out" surrounding the participation of athletes from Taipei in Montreal's Olympics.

The next significant event in the development of a sport policy was a document entitled, *A Proposed Sports Policy for Canadians*, presented to the Canadian Amateur Sports Federation on March 20, 1970. This document suggested that the government was focusing proposed policy on the development of a mass participation-based policy; in fact, the document clearly stressed pursuit of excellence.[5] Thus, began the development of policy formulation directed toward achieving excellence in international sport. In introducing the policy, the Minister indicated that the policy was workable, but that "in the long run, the Canadian people themselves will have the most to do with the final shape of the policy."[6]

---

[2]See for example. Canada, House of Commons Debates, Second Session, March 1 and 8, 1968, pp. 7161 and 7408.

[3]Canada, House of Commons Debates, Second Session, March 1 and 8, 1968, p. 7408.

[4]Canada, House of Commons Debates, First Session, September 12, 1968, p. 8.

[5]The reader is directed to pages 31-45 of a Proposed Sport Policy for Canadians.

[6]Munro, J. (1970), p. 47.

On March 16, 1970, the Minister tabled the proposed policy. Several days later, the Parliamentary Secretary to the Minister, in reply to questions in the House noted, ''Sport policy for Canadians is designed to increase participation of all Canadians in sports and recreational activities so that all can derive the greatest benefit.''[7] Citing as a justification of the foregoing, he referred to priority ratings for sports based on the criteria of participation, potential for competition, nature of the activity, sports scholarships, and achievement awards recognizing the ability of young Canadians. In concluding his remarks, the Parliamentary Secretary stated:

> The Department of National Health and Welfare is well on its way to implementing the sports policy for Canadians, a policy that will benefit not only the top athletes who will represent Canada in the summer Olympic Games in Montreal in 1976 but will also be of benefit to the physical well-being of all Canadians.''[8]

The foregoing is illustrative of the growing bureaucracy associated with the sport delivery system in Canada. The continued development of system coupling, which is evidenced by the increase of binding legislation, is indicative of this trend. Additionally, the *Task Force Report* and *The Proposed Sport Policy*, in combination with the House Debates, contribute to an evolving sport policy.

By May, 1971, the sport policy received added impetus with the presentation of a report by the Minister to the National Advisory Council on Fitness and Amateur Sport which created Sport Canada with a mandate ''to enhance Canada's world sport image and to strengthen national unity.''[9]

As the foregoing was evolving and the formation of a sport/recreation bureaucracy was taking place, the Canadian government engaged itself in the process of recognizing the People's Republic of China. During the routine proceedings of the House on Tuesday, October 13, 1970, the Secretary of State for External Affairs, announced:

> The successful conclusion of our discussions in Stockholm. . .concerning the establishment of diplomatic relations between Canada and China is as follows:
> 1. . . . .
> 2. The Chinese government reaffirms that Taiwan is an inalienable part of the territory of the People's Republic of China. The Canadian government takes note of this position of the Chinese government.
> 3. The Canadian government recognizes the government of the People's Republic of China as the sole legal government of China.[10]

In answer to several speakers, the Minister noted that

> Both Peking and Taipei assert that it is not possible to recognize simultaneously more than one government as the government of China. Accordingly, the authorities on Taiwan and the Canadian government have each taken steps to terminate formal diplomatic relations.[11]

[7]Canada, House of Commons, Debates, Second Session, May 26, 1970, pp. 7371-7372.

[8]Canada, House of Commons, Debates, Second Session, May 26, 1970, p. 7372.

[9]Munro, J. (1971), Sport Canada—Recreation Canada, p. 25.

[10]Canada, House of Commons, Debates, Third Session, October 13, 1970, p. 49.

[11]Canada, House of Commons, Debates, Third Session, October 13, 1970, p. 50.

With the diplomatic recognition, the first incident associated with the Taiwanese, was the removal of their flag from the Pavilion at the British Columbia Trade Fair. The Prime Minister, in answer to several speakers replied, "It is not really a matter of courtesy. . .We recognize only one China."[12] Thus, the Canadian policy became known as the One-China Policy.

Consistent with this policy was Canada's decision to support the admission of the People's Republic of China to the United Nations. During the House question period of October 5, 1971, the Secretary of State for External Affairs, stated:

> The Canadian Government will vote in favour of the Albanian resolution and will vote against all procedural motions which would prevent the United States taking a clear decision on the matter.[13]

With the 1976 Olympic Games having been granted to Canada and with this change in External Affairs policy, the stage was set for the "Taiwan Incident" of the Montreal Olympics—and another chapter was written regarding the intervention of the federal government in establishing Canadian international sport policy. Several weeks prior to the Montreal Olympics, Otto Jelinek attempted to gain the support of the House on the matter of leaving, "The handling of the rules and regulations, including participation, in the hands of the International Olympic Committee where they rightfully belong."[14] On first presentation, the motion failed to gain the necessary unanimous support. Later in the sitting of July 5, a member noted that according to the International Olympic Committee (IOC) rules, "Pre entry must be accorded to teams of all National Olympic Committees."[15] In reply to this point, the Minister indicated, in quoting from a letter sent to the IOC on November 29, 1969, that "All parties representing the National Olympic Committees and national sport federations recognized by the IOC will be free to enter Canada."[16] Debate on the issue continued with the Prime Minister noting, "This problem has been in discussion with the IOC for more than a year. They apparently have not seen fit in one way or another to solve this problem."[17] The central problem of this debate was Canada's refusal to "allow Tai Pei's 1976 Olympic team to enter the country under passports reading, "Republic of China."[18] The Minister consistently replied to queries from the opposition by stating that "Provided they come as representatives of Taiwan. . .they may gain entry."[19] Over the next 2 days, the opposition repeatedly questioned the government on the issue and, responding to the questions in the House, the Prime Minister always replied, "The government is right on this particular issue."[20] Debate in the House concluded on July 12, 1976, when P.E. Trudeau noted:

[12]Canada, House of Commons, Debates, Third Session, June 10, 1971, p. 6562.

[13]Canada, House of Commons, Debates, Third Session, October 5, 1971, p. 8516.

[14]Canada, House of Commons, Debates, Third Session, July 5, 1976, p. 15001.

[15]Canada, House of Commons, Debates, Third Session, July 5, 1976, p. 15005.

[16]Canada, House of Commons, Debates, Third Session, July 5, 1976, p. 15005.

[17]Canada, House of Commons, Debates, Third Session, July 5, 1976, p. 15006.

[18]Kanin, D.B. (1981), A Political History of the Olympic Games, p. 78.

[19]Canada, House of Commons, Debates, Third Session, July 5, 1976, p. 15008.

[20]Canada, House of Commons, Debates, Third Session, July 8, 1976, p. 15159.

All we are saying, and it seems to me this is a policy that would have the support of any member of the House regardless of his party provided he believes in a One China policy, is that we will not let athletes come into Canada under false representations and to pretend that they represent a country, China, that they do not represent. That is all we are saying.[21]

Thus Canada "merely made an appropriate (in terms of previous Olympic policy and diplomatic conduct) demonstration of its foreign policy"[22] and thereby added another chapter in the emergence of its international sport policy.

Conclusion

We have illustrated that sport policy and the involvement of government in Canada is very complex and is becoming increasingly more bureaucratic. As Canada's international reputation, as perceived by Canadians, suffered from the apparent humiliation of defeat in several areas of international sport and competition, Canadians, especially their Parliamentary representatives, reacted. This reaction forced the government to define a "sports policy" and to commit public funds to that policy.

Internationally, the role of Canada in world affairs has been slowly emerging. Part of this role has included the attempt to define for Canada a position distinct from that of the United States. The decision to opt for the People's Republic of China (PRC) over Taiwan at the 1976 Olympics was a major policy shift, which reflected both the economic reality of Canada's relationship with the PRC and, undoubtedly, the sentiments of Canadians. In practice, as suggested earlier, the decision was largely bureaucratically based and reflected long-standing sentiments among Canada's foreign service personnel who sought to distance themselves, both from the Americans and from the Chinese, who had traditionally been aligned with America. It is probably safe to say that the Olympic decision paid off handsomely for Canadian farmers as it was one more demonstration of Canada's affinity with its largest wheat customer.

References

Brown-John, C. (1981). *Canadian regulatory agencies*. Toronto: Butterworths and Co.

Kanin, D.B. (1981). *A political history of the Olympic games*. Boulder, CO: Westview Press.

Munro, J. (1970). *A proposed sports policy for Canadians*. Ottawa: Department of National Health and Welfare.

Olafson, G.A. (in press). Structural variation and sport policy: A comparison of Canadian and British sport systems. *Proceedings of Congress on Sport and International Understanding*, Helsinki.

---

[21]Canada, House of Commons Debates, Third Session, July 12, 1976, p. 15249.

[22]Kanin, D.B. (1981). *A political history of the Olympic games*, p. 78.

Olafson, G.A. (1983, November). *Interorganizational theory: A review of the concept and its applicability to the research of sport organizations*. Paper presented at the Meeting of the Canadian Association for Sport Sciences. Kitchner, Ontario.

Olafson, G.A. (1983b, June). *Sport policy research: The application of interorganizational theory and network analysis*. Paper presented at the Meeting of the Canadian Political Science Association, Vancouver.

10

The Role of Canadian Provincial Governments in Sport

Eric F. Broom
THE UNIVERSITY OF BRITISH COLUMBIA
VANCOUVER, CANADA

Canada, the second largest country in the world, yet with a relatively small population of slightly under 25 million, is a federated state with a federal government and 10 provincial governments, each of which is fully autonomous. The two territories are governed from the national capital but are presently seeking a greater degree of self-government.

In 1867, the British North America Act (BNA Act) awarded certain jurisdictional responsibilities to federal and provincial governments and, despite major changes in conditions in the intervening century, these responsibilities have remained relatively unchanged and jealously guarded by the two levels of government. This unwillingness to adjust jurisdiction with changing conditions has hampered cooperation between the two levels of government, as has a consistent pattern of voter preference which, for the most part, elects different political parties federally and provincially.

Sport and physical recreation, the subject of this paper, were not mentioned in the BNA Act, but in the second half of this century, the seeking for political recognition through sport has in no way reduced the struggle for primacy in this jurisdictional area. As in other spheres of Canadian political life, federal and provincial policies and practices in sport and physical recreation have, in large part, been out of tune.

The inability of the federal and provincial governments to cooperate, with very few exceptions, except for intermittent periods of uneasy coexistence, has been and is the major obstacle to attaining the ultimate potential of Canadian sport. This paper will examine the role of the Canadian provincial governments in sport and physical recreation.

Sport and Physical Recreation's Historical Development

Prior to the 1930s, provincial governments' involvement in amateur sport was virtually nonexistent, apart from the small grants to the organizations in charge of Canada's participation in the Olympic, Pan-American, and Commonwealth Games. Sport, in this period, was outside the realm of governmental social policy.

In 1934, the province of British Columbia became the first government in Canada to promote sport and recreation in anything other than a haphazard manner. Motivated by welfare considerations during the Depression, the program, originally designed for the thousands of unemployed men in relief camps in the province, later expanded in the war years to encompass the whole community. The program, formally designated, "Provincial Recreation Program," and popularly known as "Pro-Rec," functioned until 1953. Once federal funds became available in 1937, it was used as a model for similar programs in Alberta, Saskatchewan, Manitoba, and New Brunswick.

In 1943, the federal government passed the *National Physical Fitness Act* in response to the high-rejection rate of military recruits because of low physical fitness and established the National Council on Physical Fitness to Advise the federal Fitness Branch on the administration of the Act. An important Branch program, and one which finally caused the withdrawal of the federal government, was cost-sharing, or matching grants, to the provinces which assisted the development of provincial fitness and recreation programs.

The initial reaction of the provinces ranged from supportive to cautious: British Columbia and Alberta used the federal funds to assist established programs; Saskatchewan and Manitoba both passed Physical Fitness Acts in 1944 and established divisions to administer their programs; Prince Edward Island, Nova Scotia, New Brunswick, and Ontario established programs, although the latter two entered the cost-sharing program only after a considerable delay in 1947 and 1949, respectively, and Quebec never did participate.

Eventually, federal officials came to regard the Council, which was largely made up of provincial government representatives, as a provincial body which was determined to extract more money from Ottawa (West 1973:38). After 11 years of frustration for both sides, the federal government, without consultation, unilaterally terminated the Act in 1954. For the remainder of the decade, programs in a few provinces such as Ontario and Alberta matured, expanding in budget and services offered, but such was not the case in other provinces. By 1960, most provinces were in need of renewed federal stimulus if their sport and recreation programs were to expand.

When, in 1961, the federal government introduced the *Fitness and Amateur Sport Act*, one of the three major thrusts of the ensuing program was cost-sharing grants to the provinces. It was originally intended that the funds allocated annually to the federal-provincial agreements should be 50% of the total Fitness and Amateur Sport budget. This level of allotment was made in the first 2 years of the agreements, with $500,000 in 1962-63 and $1.0 million in 1963-64 being made available. However, as the total budget increased, the allocation to this program remained fixed at $1.0 million annually. From 1962-63 to 1967-68, nine provinces and two territories participated in the program, and Quebec entered in 1968-69.

In 1970, the federal government, in the belief that the program had accomplished its objectives of stimulating greater provincial involvement in sport and fitness, once again without consultation, unilaterally terminated the program. As in 1954, the federal government thought it was receiving too little recognition for its contribution. The provinces, on the other hand, balked at the necessity of obtaining federal approval of expenditures. At a time in Canadian history when provincial governments sought a greater measure of control of their own destiny, this was perceived as federal infringement of provincial prerogative (Baka, 1978:515).

The provinces were particularly dismayed because the unilateral federal action occurred at a time when, after several years of difficult negotiations, the program appeared to be running smoothly at last. Relations between the two levels of government became increasingly strained, and provincial mistrust of cooperation with the federal government was increased.

There can be no doubt that the two federal-provincial cost-sharing programs, 1944-54 and 1961-70, greatly assisted the provinces in developing both structures and programs in sport and fitness, but the method of their termination has caused long-lasting resentment among the provinces.

Whereas in 1954 termination of federal assistance initiated a decline of programs in most provinces, in 1970 the provinces quickly filled the funding void, and the ensuing decade was characterized by widespread expansion of provincial government sport and recreation programs.

During the 1970s and 1980s, the range of programs and services offered by provincial governments has shown great similarities. The differences have been in extent rather than kind with Ontario, Quebec, and Alberta surpassing other provinces in annual budgets on a per capita basis.

Provincial Sport and Recreation Departments

As a general rule, provincial governments' sport and recreation departments play a facilitating rather than a providing role. In line with this principle, financial assistance to community sport, directed through municipal recreation structures, is offered by all provinces. A major area of emphasis of most provinces during the 1970s, more particularly British Columbia, Alberta, and Ontario, was financial assistance to municipalities toward the capital costs of sport and recreation facilities.

Grants to provincial sport associations for clinics, conferences, and competitions are a major program in all provinces and showed a dramatic increase during the 1970s. All provinces give high priority to leadership training, and, in addition, to funding training programs for volunteers. Most provinces also provide assistance to sport governing bodies for the hiring of full- or part-time administrators, technical directors, and coaches. Similarly, all provinces have assisted the establishment and development of provincial sport federations and award regular, substantial grants to enable these bodies to provide a range of services for their members' sport associations.

In the 1970s most provinces became more active in the promotion of physical fitness. A variety of funding patterns emerged: Some provinces grant-aided autonomous agencies such as Action B.C. and Shape Up Alberta; other provinces appointed fitness consultants within their sport departments; and Ontario, in 1978, established a Fitness Services Branch.

Services to special groups, especially for the disabled population, was another area in which provincial governments became active in the 1970s. Alberta was an early leader in this field, and most provinces strongly supported Provincial Games for the Disabled. These services gained momentum in all provinces in 1981, the International Year of Disabled Persons.

During the 1970s, financial support of Provincial Games assumed a top priority among almost all provincial government sport programs. All provinces, with the exceptions of Nova Scotia, have Provincial Games. Some provinces hold both Winter and Summer Games each year, while others hold such Games in alternate years. The Northwest Territories, the Yukon Territory, Quebec, and Newfoundland cooperate every 2 years to organize the Arctic Winter Games. These multisport competitions, which attract a high level of media coverage, serve as a political showcase.

The biannual Canada Games hold a special interest for all provinces. In 1967, when the Games were inaugurated, provincial governments were quick to use the potential for political exposure. What began as a friendly competition between provinces rapidly became events in which provincial identity could be expressed through sport. To some provinces at least, winning became very important. The provinces provide teams with additional financial support in order to ensure that athletes representing them are well prepared, competitive, and dressed in distinctive uniforms. Provinces have shown great willingness to equally fund the capital and operating expenses of a Canada Games with the federal and municipal governments when the festival is within their province. In addition to providing an ideal level of competition for aspiring young athletes, the Games offer opportunities to politicians for public exposure at federal, provincial, and municipal levels. As a result they have been well supported by all three levels of government and are one of the most successful programs in the country.

Provincial interest in high-performance sport was stimulated by the award of the 1976 Olympic Games to Montreal, and several provinces established special programs to assist their athletes. Quebec, for example, in 1972, designed its Mission '76 program, with a goal of "30% representation in the Canadian team at the forthcoming Olympic Games," and a budget totalling $3,050,000 (Mission [Quebec] '76 booklet). Alberta established an Olympic and Commonwealth Development Plan with $250,000 to help its athletes prepare for the 1976 and 1978 Games. Several other provinces, including Ontario, Manitoba, and Saskatchewan, instituted their own schemes. A major problem was the inability of the provinces to integrate their programs with the federal government Game Plan, into which they had entered as partners in 1973. The provinces had no say in Game Plan administration, and this was politically unacceptable (Baka, 1978:489). Thus, the provinces withdrew from the federal Game Plan in 1975.

Almost all provinces provide grants to increase opportunities for their athletes and coaches to experience high-level training. British Columbia, for example, established a "Road to the Olympics" program in 1982 which offers financial aid to provincial sport-governing bodies where national teams, or sport development centers, are located in the province. At present, five sports (boxing, rowing, soccer, track and field, and women's field hockey) receive such grants.

Sport development centers, or sport training centers, which are frequently associated with a university to incorporate coaches' training and research, have been debated in Canada for 20 years. Clearly, the size of the country made a national center impractical, and federal support of provincial centers was politically unpalatable. The provinces are now initiating some development. In 1981, Ontario funded a prototype center for track and field sprint events at York University in Toronto and in 1983 awarded $200,000 to six provincial sport associations to develop and operate seven sport development centers at colleges or universities.

All 10 provinces have programs of financial awards to assist athletes in striving for excellence. British Columbia was among the leaders in this development, and initially the awards were small in number and value and were confined to university students. By the mid-1970s, the programs had developed into High Performance Athletes Assistance Programs similar to the federal government program, usually, but not always, with the intent of assisting athletes in attaining Sport Canada carded status. Much duplication still occurs. Quebec, Ontario, and British Columbia have the largest budgets for these programs, with those of the Maritime Provinces remaining relatively small.

In addition to the High Performance Athlete Assistance Program, the three western provinces established programs of University Sports Awards. The British Columbia program, which started in 1980, makes available 550 awards of $1,000 each annually. Alberta and Manitoba established similar programs in 1981, the former with awards of $1,000 to university students and $500 to junior college students, the latter with awards ranging from $600 to $1,000. The total budget for High Performance and University Awards in British Columbia in 1983-84 was a little over $1.0 million.

With the expansion of provincial government activity in the sports field during the 1970s, all provinces and territories supplemented general budget appropriations with lottery revenues. On the understanding of a federal withdrawal from lottery operation after the Olympic Lottery in 1976, the provinces planned to expand their own lotteries. They were incensed by the federal government's unilateral decision to remain in the lottery field, and, with the exception of Quebec, were extremely negative to Loto Canada and its objective of paying off the Olympic facilities debt. This uneasy alliance of federal and provincial governments in the lottery field continued until December 1979 when the short-lived Conservative federal government placed lotteries exclusively under provincial jurisdiction in return for an annual payment from the combined provinces which now approximates $35 million.

The reelected, Liberal federal government, anxious to share in the massive revenue, reentered the gambling field on May 1, 1984, through a sport-betting pool. Sport Select Baseball, which requires a winner to correctly predict the results of baseball games, and later hockey and football games, is not, according to the federal Minister, a lottery because playing the pool requires the element of skill. Nine provinces, the exception being Alberta, which will receive $200 million from the Pool revenue toward the capital and operating costs of the 1988 Winter Olympic Games in Calgary, have challenged the scheme in Federal Court, alleging that it violates the 1979 agreement. The National Baseball Association has also taken legal action to stop the pool from operating a betting scheme based on baseball scores.

With the exception of Saskatchewan, where the provincial government awarded the lottery license to Sask Sport, the provincial sport federation, lotteries are administered by provincial government agencies. Total spending on the 15 different games offered by the various government lottery corporations has climbed to more than $1.3 billion a year, and roughly 30% of that total will find its way into government coffers. Revenues from the lotteries are allocated to amateur sport, fitness, recreation, culture, heritage, and other areas at the discretion of each provincial government. In general, sport is the major beneficiary.

Provincial sport-governing bodies receive in excess of 75% of their operating funds from provincial governments, as do the national associations from the federal government. Associations recognize the potential danger of the situation, but very few seem able to reduce the level of dependency.

Over the years, federal and provincial ministers and sports leaders have proclaimed that the task of developing sport in Canada to its highest level, meaning not only excellence but also mass participation, would be severely hampered, or even impossible, without the full cooperation of the two levels of government. Yet full cooperation has not occurred.

Sport Today

It is now 50 years since a provincial government first promoted sport in a serious manner, and almost 25 years since that watershed year of 1961 when both federal and provincial governments became heavily involved in sport. However, Canada still lacks a national plan to integrate the efforts of both federal and provincial governments. The federal Green Paper, *Toward a National Policy on Amateur Sport* (1977) was intended to remedy this deficiency, but it was developed without provincial input. A major criticism of the paper was that the lack of federal-provincial cooperation might result in a federal policy but not a national policy.

The subsequent federal White Paper, *Partners in Pursuit of Excellence: A National Policy on Amateur Sport* (1979) in title, if not in development, acknowledges the necessity of the two levels of government working together. The paper was presented as a draft plan which represented a first attempt to coordinate the national effort in sport and to define, as clearly as possible, the functions appropriate to every facet of the system (1977: 24). Unfortunately, the White Paper was released in the middle of a losing federal election campaign, and any momentum it might have generated was lost.

Despite this setback, the federal-provincial ministers responsible for sport and recreation in 1982 approved a *Blueprint for High Performance Athlete Development*, the ultimate objective of which was to ensure Canada's best possible ranking at international sports events. The document acknowledged the need for a greater degree of cooperation and coordination between and among the two senior levels of government and delineated areas of responsibility for each level of government and areas of shared responsibility (1982:2).

Politics intruded on provincial sport in three major ways. First, the long-standing inability of the federal and provincial governments to cooperate has made sport a political battleground. Examples of cooperation include the following: the federal-provincial cost-sharing agreements between 1944 and 1954, and 1962 and 1971; the Canada Games since 1967; and a few minor programs. They are more easily forgotten by the provinces than incidents of noncoopera-tion, including the termination of the cost-sharing programs in 1954 and 1971; Game Plan in 1975, the Green Paper, *Toward a National Policy for Amateur Sport* in 1977; and the lottery confrontations of 1976, 1978, and 1984.

The Canada Games stands out as the only long-lasting, successful, cooperative venture. Its longevity is a tribute to its ability to provide political exposure to all three levels of government: federal, provincial, and municipal.

Second, the dramatic increase in the last decade of provincial government interest, and, therefore, funding in high-performance sport has occurred at the expense of recreational sport. Elite sport is high profile and through media coverage gains the exposure and recognition governments desire.

Finally, the continued financial dependency of provincial sport governing bodies on government makes them vulnerable to coercion if the government so wishes. Sport and government now have a symbiotic relationship, but the political will is in a position to dominate and influence the future directions of sport.

References

Baka, R.S.P. (1978). *A history of provincial government involvement in sport in Western Canada*. Dissertation, University of Alberta.

Broom, E.F., & Baka, R.S.P. (1979). *Sport and governments in Canada*. Canadian Association for Health, Physical Education and Recreation, Sociology of Sport Monograph Series.

Canada (1977). *A working paper: Toward a national policy on amateur sport*. Ottawa: Fitness and Amateur Sport. (Minister Iona Campagnolo.)

Canada (1979). *Partners in pursuit of excellence: A national policy on amateur sport*. Ottawa: Fitness and Amateur Sport. (Minister Iona Campagnolo.)

Canada (1982). *Blueprint for high performance athlete development*. Ottawa: Sport Canada.

Quebec (1974). *Sport and Recreation* (Special Edition). Education Quebec.

West, J.T. (1973). *Fitness, sports and the Canadian government*. Materials prepared for the Fitness and Amateur Sport Branch.

11

Political Diplomacy in a Canadian Sport

Pamela G. Gilverson
UNIVERSITY OF ALBERTA
ALBERTA, CANADA

What makes one pressure group more successful in achieving its goals than another? A case study approach allows this researcher to investigate two theoretical concepts pertaining to Canadian pressure groups in an effort to identify some of the internal politics which underlie nationalistic pretentions of "idealism" in amateur sport. Pross's theoretical framework of pressure groups and Simeon's concept of resources as indicators of power provide useful referencs for this exploration. A comparative analysis of the structures and political resources of the Canadian Marathon Canoe Racing Association (CMCRA) and the Association Quebecoise de Canotage Long Parcours (AQCLP) provide the case material. From the evidence of this study, it is argued that political resources, as indicators of power, contribute to short-term successes of groups.

Although sport organizations tend to perform functions that are more bureaucratic and service-oriented than influential, it is argued here that they do fit into the mainstream of the Canadian political system as pressure groups. A pressure group also referred to as an interest group, is an organization whose members act together to influence public policy in order to promote their common interest (Pross, 1975:2).

Pressure groups do not act independently of their environment, and, according to Pross (1981), most pressure groups are chameleons; in other words, they are groups who readily adapt their structures and behaviors to best fit the policy process. Pross suggests that pressure groups have advantages over individuals when they are attempting to influence the system. Most importantly, pressure groups have some type of organizational structure to support them which may allow them to share costs, deploy talents, and generally have access to more political resources. Recognizing this relationship between the levels of organization or structure and their behavior, Pross (1975) introduced his typology to arrange such groups into some sort of meaningful pattern. Groups can be defined along his continuum, registering anywhere from issue-oriented at one extreme, to institutionalized at the other. Institutionalized pressure groups consist of the following characteristics (Pross, 1975:10):

- They possess organizational continuity and cohesion.
- They have extensive knowledge of those sectors of government that affect them and their clients and enjoy easy communications with those sectors.
- There is a stable membership.
- The operational objectives are concrete and immediate.
- The organizational imperatives are generally more important than any particular objective.

Issue-oriented group characteristics would be the reverse of those identified above (i.e., their organizational continuity would be limited and noncohesive). Issue-oriented groups usually form to lobby on a particular issue and do so within a limited organizational structure. They generally disband when the issue is resolved. The lack of commitment to future activity affords issue-oriented groups more freedom, creativity, and flexibility.

Increased attention has been paid to the idea that government officials, the bureaucrats, are instrumenting policy change and development and, as a result, attempt to control interest groups (Pross, 1975; Bella, 1981; Anderson; 1982). The increased complexity of the government has necessitated hiring specialized professionals who, as Bella (1981) indicates, play an active role in having policies appear meritorious in the public eye. Pross also asserts that bureaucracy within the pressure groups will structurally adjust to better accommodate government policy. Sport Canada, the bureaucratic machinery of government, provides extensive resources of funding and consultative services to sport-governing organizations. The government relies heavily on its ability to stimulate, and in some cases, even create interest groups within the various sports. Thus, a symbiotic relationship with the sport groups ensures the survival of Sport Canada.

Simeon pursues the idea that political and other resources are indicators of power. In his analysis of public policy, he: suggests that we explain what governments do by reference to the distribution of interests in the society and the resources available to these interests (Simeon, 1976:569-569).

Using three case studies, Simeon showed how political resources, coupled with strategies and tactics, affected the outcomes through a process of negotiations. He found money to be the most striking and effective resource. The most subtle play was effective in strategy or composite negotiations occurring simultaneously. Simeon identified costs of spending resources and suggested that the best bargaining occurs when the political resources are evident but not necessarily spent.

The Canadian Marathon Canoe Racing Association

CMCRA is a recently organized federal group. A symposium held in 1979 marked its beginning and, since then, it has held four annual national championships and six annual general meetings. Most of the meetings have not been funded by the federal government leaving the provincial associations to assume the expenses. The early objectives of the association are stated as broad generalizations indicating what the organization hopes to accomplish. A mission statement developed at a planning meeting summarizes the original objectives of the association:

> To encourage the development across Canada of a broad base of marathon canoe and kayak races, and to establish a national and international team program dedicated to the pursuit of excellence.
>
> (CMCRA, 1983)

A national sport audit was conducted by the provincial representatives from several provinces following the 1983 planning meeting. The audit summary was presented alongside CMCRA's application to the federal government for funding in December, 1983. The audit revealed a list of 2,645 Canadian paddlers in 142 marathon-type races in one season. A total of $74,527 was estimated to have been spent on marathon canoeing that year. The organization is very young and has a volunteer executive of only three persons and a budget of $2,068 (expenditures).

CMCRA has been negotiating with the Canadian Canoe Association (CCA) to become a "technical arm" of that association. Throughout the negotiations, CMCRA has been able to "piggy back" some of CCA's resources and services. These have included a partnership in the national newsletter, circulation of correspondence through the CCA office, and assistance with the preparation of funding applications and financial assistance for representatives of CCA restructuring meetings. The 1984 annual general meetings of both associations witnessed a historic restructuring of CCA which now has two technical arms: one for sprint and one for marathon racing.

Prior to May 15, 1980, marathon canoeing had been one of three equal partners (marathon, flatwater, and white water) which formed a single canoe organization. The lion's share of the funding was received by flatwater, the only Olympic canoeing discipline. A new association, AQCLP, was formed, and it concentrated on political and sport-related activities rather than organizational detail. The Quebec team coach became one of the key actors in this new association in its funding negotiations. Quebec hosts numerous canoe festivals each year, the largest of which is the Shawinigan Canoe Classique which originated in 1934 to commemorate the tercentenary of the city of Three Rivers and the death of a priest who was thrown over the Shawinigan Falls (Cote, 1984). It has since developed into one of the most prestigious canoe races in the world—one for which the Quebec government provided a grant of $50,000 in 1983.

CMCRA's initial budget submission dates back to 1979—its first year of organization. To date, it has received no funding from Sport Canada despite its repeated annual submissions. Contacts between the CMCRA officials and the Sport Canada consultant have increased over the past 2 years; for example, the current CMCRA President has made numerous visits to the Sport Canada and CCA offices.

Marathon canoeing, as a high performance sport, is more advanced in Quebec than in other provinces. Quebec has sent teams to both the national and world championships. In order to support annual representation by Quebec athletes at the world championships, the Quebec coach has sought funding and support from Sport Canada by working through AQCLP and sending letters to CMCRA to arrange political negotiations with the Minister of Fitness and Amateur Sport. Concurrently, CMCRA was negotiating with CCA to attain sanction for its athletes to compete internationally. The Quebec coach began independent negotiations with CCA to name Quebec as the only official marathon affiliate to their organization. These lobbying tactics, lead by the Quebec coach, intensified and, this resulted in the Quebec government reimbursing their athletes' travel to the 1982 world championships. A further tactic was a budget submission by AQCLP to Sport Canada requesting $111,800 for its athlete-development program which was rejected. In the meantime, Jean Chretien's office (Minister of External Affairs) contacted Sport Canada to ask why the Quebec athletes were not being accommodated. Chretien and the Quebec coach were neighbors with summer cottages on the same lake, and the Quebec coach, an unsuccessful politician, had run against Chretien in the Shawinigan riding. A negative response to this request went through the bureaucratic channels and suggested that AQCLP follow Sport Canada guidelines for funding submissions. By the summer of 1983, CCA had agreed to sanction the two Quebec paddlers at the world cup but without financial support. Upon returning home with the silver medal, the athletes received $5,000 from Quebec to reimburse their travel, and a subsequent lobby of Chretien's office resulted in some support for Quebec athletes traveling to the Canadian championships in 1983.

CMCRA's objectives were established as long-term, multiple, broadly defined, and collective in the sense that they were developed on a nation-wide basis. Applying the objectives of CMCRA to Pross's theoretical framework suggests that the organization would be characterized as becoming institutionalized; however, the association does not have the resources to meet its objectives, and, when one considers its finances, it becomes clear that spending reflects mere survival of the organization and does not begin to meet the stated objectives. Pross also suggests that interest groups act like chameleons, changing to suit government policy. This appears to be the direction of CMCRA with its restructuring change to become a "technical arm" of CCA. Given the organizational feature of the CMCRA and its inoperable objectives, it would appear that it scores low on both counts of Pross's continuum.

The Association Quebecoise de Canotage Long Parcours

AQCLP, by its structure and organization, is an issue-oriented group with its issue being to get funding for its best athletes to compete internationally. The organization was formed in a period of crisis, and all of its actions reflect attempts to resolve this issue. It does not have objectives established toward developing itself as an all-encompassing umbrella organization for marathon canoeing. The organization itself appears to be loosely structured. There were no signs of formal documentation such as minutes, a constitution, or briefs that were accessible to the researcher; however, there were numerous newspaper articles and evidence of the political tactics used to lobby at both the ministerial and bureaucratic levels. According to Pross's framework, such issue-oriented groups are short-lived and tend to disappear once their issue is resolved. This would appear to be the case with AQCLP. It experienced many small successes through its short history, and these are reflected upon in the following analysis.

CMCRA continues to work toward its goal of acquiring Sport Canada funding. Thus far, it has been largely unsuccessful. Simeon would argue that the reason for its lack of success is its lack of resources, in other words, its lack of power as an organization. CMCRA's budget reflects this lack of resources, and the structure outlined earlier reinforces this point. The result is a "catch 22" situation for a new sport-governing organization in its developmental stages. The organization has struggled for 3 years, unable to increase its resources to develop new ones, and, without some external assistance, it may remain a fledgling group, or, as Pross suggests, it may disappear altogether. However, CMCRA is now in a position to increase its resources with its link to CCA. Already it has increased its ability to communicate to its membership with the use of a joint newsletter. Two CMCRA board members have been elected to the board and are now included in that budget for travel to the new board meetings.

AQCLP used a number of political resources to achieve its goal and in many ways was successful. Its overall budget was considerably larger than CMCRA's as a result of its lobbying strategies and tactics. It is argued here that AQCLP had more political resources at its disposal than did CMCRA. The media took up AQCLP's issue and followed its actions extensively, thus increasing the profile of the sport in the province. Chretien was called upon to pressure Sport Canada to give AQCLP money for its athletes. The Shawinigan International Canoe Classique is a popular festival which has received support from both the provincial and federal governments over the years. The provincial government has contributed substantially to this event. Other resources, including the number of racers and races in the province, the level of public interest, and the political experience of the Quebec coach add to this extensive list. There is little doubt that these resources contributed to the many successes of AQCLP; however, according to Pross, AQCLP would need to use these resources toward institutionalization if it were to be powerful within the Canadian political system. Instead, the group appears to be fading in the way that many issue-oriented groups do when they have attained their objectives.

Conclusion

The original question posed was, "What makes one group more successful in achieving its goals than another?" This paper revealed that political resources, coupled with effective strategies and tactics, yielded short-term successes.

AQCLP fitted Pross's issue-oriented categorization of his continuum while CMCRA scored low on the items but showed signs of moving in an institutionalized direction. CMCRA was not, however, successful in achieving its short-term goal of acquiring Sport Canada funding. In this instance, the issue-oriented group attained more successes than did the institutionalized one. It was the efforts of a politically astute individual, the Quebec coach, and the resources he was able to draw upon which resulted in a series of successes for AQCLP. This case supports Simeon's contention that political resources contribute to the success of groups, perhaps to the extent of being even more important than the "institutionalization" concept identified by Pross.

References

Anderson, J.E. (1982). Pressure groups and the Canadian bureaucracy. In K. Kernaghan (Ed.), *Public administration in Canada, selected readings: Fourth edition*, Toronto: Methuen.

Bella, L. (1981). *The politics of the right-wing 'welfare state'*. Unpublished doctoral dissertation, The University of Alberta.

CMCRA. (1983). *Minutes of the planning meeting*. Ottawa, Ontario.

Cote, J. (1984). *St. Maurice International Canoe Classique*. Summary paper presented to the CMCRA Annual General Meeting, Ottawa, Ontario.

Pross, A.P. (1975). *Pressure group behaviour in Canadian politics*. Toronto: McGraw-Hill Ryerson.

Pross, A.P. (1981). Pressure groups: Talking chameleons. In Whittington and Williams (Eds.), *Canadian politics in the 1980s* (pp. 221-242). Toronto: Wettmen.

Simeon, R. (1972). *Federal-provincial diplomacy; the making of recent policy in Canada*. Toronto: University of Toronto Press.

Simeon, R. (1976). Studying public policy. *Canadian Journal of Political Science, 9*, 548-580.

PART II

Some European and Imperial Problems

12

Play Up! Play Up! And Win the War! The Propaganda of Athleticism in Britain, 1914-1918

Colin R. Veitch
UNIVERSITY OF ALBERTA
ALBERTA, CANADA

> A lexical definition of *propaganda* reveals it to be any systematic, widespread dissemination or promotion of ideas, doctrines [or] practices to further one's own cause or to damage an opposing one. (Gusalnik, 1976; 1139).

In his examination of British involvement in international propaganda following the First World War, Black (1975: ix) expands this definition, illustrating that it is the media of popular communications that hosts this "conscious, organised attempt to influence [the individual's] attitudes, beliefs or actions." L.B. Brown (1973: 12) demonstrates the importance of propagandist manipulation to a country in a state of national crisis by pointing out that "social power rests with those who can control and implement an ideology, whether by persecution and torment, or by education and propaganda."

Sports and Games as Propaganda

Recent research directed at the British press during the First World War has ignored or overlooked the use of sports and games in the propaganda process. Accordingly, drawing on pictures, photographs, captions, prose, and poetry gleaned from several of the British wartime journals and periodicals, this paper will reveal how the military efforts of the British soldiers on the Western Front were continually portrayed by using the language and imagery of sport. In particular, it will show how the British press under scrutiny made flagrant political capital from the depiction of the German race as a sportsless, and thereby cultureless, civilization. It was implied that sports and games allowed the Briton access to significant elements of racial and cultural superiority, the possession of which would ultimately guarantee him a military victory over a barbaric, inferior foe. This ideology, reduced to its simplest formula, perpetuated the tenuous logic that sports and games provided the British soldier with the biological, physical, and moral qualities necessary to defeat his German counterpart. Thus it was that, even after the disastrous Somme campaign had ground to a halt with the loss of more than 400,000 British casualties, one popular periodical was able to make light of the setback and educate its readers as to the *real* victory that had been won in Flanders as

> When it came to a sheer test of manhood on fairly equal terms, the German veteran was not a match for the British recruit. The Briton's advantage resided largely in his athletic habit of body and his sportsmanlike spirit. (*The Great War. The Standard History of the All-European Conflict,* vol. 8, 1917: 48)

The equating of success in sport with victory on the battlefield was by no means a 20th century phenomenon. As has been clearly demonstrated over recent years by Mangan (1981) and others, such a conviction constituted the essential military component of the tenets of "athleticism," the educational ideology which evolved in the British public schools of the 19th century and advanced the popular notion that young men's characters could be beneficially shaped and molded through the pursuit of sport—in particular, team games. While this powerful social code still held sway in the years prior to the First World War, it should be emphasized that it was not the only belief structure which appears to have influenced the British wartime press to celebrate sports and games as crucial elements for the manufacturing of an allied victory in the war.

As Travers (1979: 276) has shown, British military tacticians immediately prior to the war were stressing that the way to overcome an opposing army's superior weaponry and technology was simply to "build" a better soldier. Hence, the British army laid increasing value on extending participation in sports and team games to the junior ranks in the years prior to 1914, believing that such activities would develop manliness, discipline, courage, loyalty, and capacity for self-sacrifice in the common soldier. These attributes, it was believed, would be sufficient to carry the troops through a frontal assault on a heavily armed enemy and secure victory (Veitch, 1984: 54-57). Interwoven with these two ideological strands was one other crucial factor—an underlying, social Darwinistic conviction that the British sportsman-soldier was racially superior to his German counterpart. This element spurred the most caustic racial polemics of the war as the British press strove to depict the two nations as culturally and biologically alienated: thus divorcing Great Britain from the evidently abhorrent notions of Germanic *Kulture* and the philosophical dogma of Neitzsche and Bernhardi which espoused the biological necessity of warfare. Frequently, British attempts to disassociate themselves from such theorizing was based upon equally questionable assumptions which related the German national character, with all its deficiencies, to a paucity of organized games in the German citizen's life.

The influence of these three elements—military theory, athleticism, and a mutated, games-oriented form of social Darwinism—on the shape of British sports propaganda directed at the home population, can be traced in three distinct areas in the literature: the depiction of German and English national character; the portrayal of the wounded soldiers from the war; and the descriptions of the British and Allied armed forces, both at battle and at rest behind the front lines.

Sports in the Press

As has been noted, the British press attempted to portray the German people as inhumane, warmongering barbarians for the benefit of their readers. The frequent "atrocity stories" that appeared during the war are but one element of this propaganda process. Another common contribution to this manufactured image was the German's alleged disregard for sport. Much was made of the Germans predilection for dueling as opposed to the vigorous and manly team games of football, rugby, and cricket played by their English counterparts. F.H. Swift (*The Contemporary Review, 110*, 1916: 465-473), in an examination of the cultural values surrounding the *Mensur* or student-fencing bout, noted that it was "not only one of the most brutalising activities devised by a nation, but it shuts out of student life wholesome sports."

Other critics took these quasibiological theories to quite preposterous lengths. One in particular advanced the notion that the German racial somatotype adversely affected his golf swing (Graeme, *The English Review,* vol. 29, 1919: 241). Another journalist wrote of the German soldier being "massive in limb and body, but he suffered from a national defect. His neck was short, and this in a fighting man is fatal" (Goodchild, *Everyman,* 5 November 1915: 46). Quite the most outrageous and blatantly racist views of Germany are offered up for public consumption by *The War Illustrated,* however. One notable double-page spread contrasts a picture of an emaciated, dejected-looking German soldier with that of his cheerful British counterpart, adding the caption, "Health, buoyant spirits, good temper and gay gallantry—all that make up 'moral'—is stamped upon this English Tommy's face, with its laughing eyes and row of spendid teeth." (*The War Illustrated,* January 27, 1917: 564-5; hereafter cited as *WI*). The propagandist purpose of this "double feature," together with its blatant disregard for the truth, is confirmed in an article by Captain Brown of the Royal Army Medical Corps, who wrote, following the war, that the universal opinion among his fellow doctors was that the standard of physique among the British recruits was deplorably low—lower even, than that among German prisoners of war—and that "The number of physical defects and disabilities [was] legion" (*The English Review,* vol. 28, 1919: 242-250). Another passage extended this national comparison still further, commenting of the German soldier, "His face is fully expressive of all the savagery and 'frightfulness' associated with the exponents of 'higher civilization,' so called ...compare his physiognomy with the frank, open countenance of the Briton." (*WI*, vol 2, 1915: 1)

These shameless, racist accusations were contrasted with pictures and illustrations of the patriotic response to the war of Britain's finest manhood—

the sportsmen. Several volunteer battalions were recruited in Britain, their ranks comprising only skilled sportsmen and athletes, and these units received copious coverage in the wartime press (Veitch, 1984: 63-75). They were portrayed as an inately superior military force, stoically marching away to do their duty in "the greater game" of war (*WI*, November 21, 1914: 336; vol. 1: 630).

It is evident from this brief survey that convenient, social Darwinistic adaptations to support the national purpose were not exclusively the preserve of the German race but were a prominent part of the written British response to the outbreak and progress of the war. Sport played an important part in this theorizing, for it allowed an athletic distinction to be drawn between two nations who shared the same racial and linguistic heritage, and who had both been placed at the summit of the civilized world by the 19th century evolutionary anthropologists (Bolt, 1971: 1-29). Sports and games were, therefore, convenient agents of cultural diffusion which could be manipulated to enhance the Englishman's national character and simultaneously account for the German nation's lapse into military barbarism.

The use of sports and games to identify racial strengths and weaknesses in the British and German troops was extended to an analysis of the allied armies, too. To varying degrees, the soldiers of these forces were portrayed as national sporting stereotypes, which increased both the image of allied and military unity and reiterated the concept of their physical supremacy over the German forces. Team games, reputedly the source of so much British imperial vigor and success, were shown to be no longer the exclusive preserve of the elegant Englishman, but a popular and equally beneficial training ground for the troops of both Belgium and France (*WI*, 1914: 79; 1915: 158). In perhaps what is the most unprecedented visual statement of allied unity, a photograph shows a British officer congratulating the captain of a French soldiers' soccer team after they had *beaten* a team of British cavalrymen (*WI*, 1916: 315).

Both the Canadian and Anzac soldiers were invariably depicted as rugged sons of the Empire, hardened to war by a life on the very outposts of the Crown's colonies and dominions. Strong, determined men who would brook no nonsense from the Germans, the latter brigades are aptly represented by one "Giant Anzac, a powerful athlete, 6'4" in height," who caught a German by the hips during one midnight raid and threw him bodily over the parapet. (*WI*, 8 July 1916: 492). Canadian soldiers were deemed to have other soldierly skills which stemmed from their lives as hunters and trappers in a land that was evidently still beyond the realm of British comprehension; several issues of *The War Illustrated* show a Canadian sniper at work, and one in particular accounts for the soldier's proficiency with the rifle by the fact that he has "brought his knowledge of game hunting in the Far West to the greater work of beating the enemy on the plains of Flanders' (*WI*, 22 July 1916). By far, the most romanticized nation, in sporting terms, however, were the Italians. Far away from the mud-locked subterranean passages that played host to the trench warfare of the Western Front, the Italian Alpini were characterized by the British press as adventurous mountaineers, boyishly foiling the attempts of the Austrian forces to drive them from their traditional eyries in the Dolomites. Lithe, fit, and innovative in their tactics, artists' impressions abound of the troops on skis or roped together, climbing a sheer precipice to attack the unsuspecting Austrian outposts. One picture showed the readers an

> Amazing incident on the Alpine front. Alpini succeded in lassoing an Austrian *mitrailleuse* gunner, bringing him down the mountainside with his weapon, a triumph of skill and strength, and by no means an unusual occurrence in the Alps. (*WI*, 1 April 1916: 154).

It should not be overlooked that, at no time, were the German or Austro-Hungarian forces assigned any form of press coverage that equated positively with sports and games. To have shown them as having the ability and capacity to play, and play games which were considered unequivocally English, would be to undermine the entire image of German inhumanity and physical and moral inferiority which was clearly such a major part of British wartime propaganda.

As well as serving the cause of allied unity, images of sports and games were also used to display the British soldier's hearty resolution in the face of adversity. Notably prominent was press coverage of wounded British troops recuperating with athletics and games, no doubt intended to reassure the increasing number of British families being blighted by the news of an injured relative or friend. Several items emphasized that, despite his physical wound, the quintessential, sporting spirit of the Briton had survived the worst that his enemies could throw at him. Injured soldiers are repeatedly shown playing football, (*WI*, vol. 2, 1915: 19) and a "Grand International Final" featured soccer and baseball matches between French, Canadian, and British soldiers (*WI*, vol. 2, 1915: 344). A later item showed a wounded New Zealander playing tennis, which was described as "A Spartan cure for shrapnel injuries" (*WI*, vol. 3, 1915: 189). It is notable that all of these examples utilized the medium of film to convey their impact to the reader. As one researcher in World War I propaganda notes, "The effect that actual war scenes could add to the printed word was unlimited. It was a prevailing assumption of the time that the camera could not lie" (Sanders, 1975: 135).

Without doubt, sports found favor among certain sectors of the British press during the war years as an exemplary medium for the portrayal of British and allied superiority over their enemies. This process, advocating as it does notions of British superiority based upon incomplete and misleading athletic, military, racial, and biological ideologies of dominance, can be seen as a functional manipulation of the British reading public to maintain enthusiasm and national unity during the war. Throughout the years of 1914-1918, the treatment of sport in the wartime press reinforced and sustained a palatable image of violent and indiscrimatory death among the nation's youth, while simultaneously attempting to reduce the ideological complexity of war to a simplistic absolute: British sportsmen will triumph over the savage Huns on the field of battle, whatever the cost. To refine this propagandist message still further, one could do no better than adapt the topical example of Winston Smith's haunting vision of the Ministry of Truth's slogan in Orwell's *1984:* War is Sport; Athleticism is Mastery; Defeat is Victory; Ignorance is Strength.

References

Black, J. (1975). *Organizing the propaganda instrument: The British experience.* The Hague: Martinus Nijhoff.

Bolt, C. (1971). *Victorian attitudes to race.* London: Routledge & Kegan Paul.

Brown, E. (1919). *The physique of the nation.* The English Review, **28**, 242-250.
Brown, L.B. (1973). *Ideology.* Harmondsworth: Penguin.
English Review, **28**, 242-250.
Graeme, (1919). *The English Review,* **29**, 241.
Graeme, (1919). *The German insanity,* The English Review, **29**, 239-246.
Goodchild, G. (1915, November 5). *Everyman,* 46.
Gusalnik, D. (Ed.). (1976). *Webster's new world dictionary.* New York: William
Collins and New World Publishing.
Mangan, J.A. (1981). *Athleticism in the Victorian and Edwardian public school.*
The emergence and consolidation of an educational ideology. Cambridge: Cambridge
University Press.
    Sanders, M.L. (1975). Wellington House and British propaganda during the First
World War. *The Historical Journal,* **18**, 119-146.
    Swift, F.H. (1916). The making of a gentleman in germany, *The Contemporary*
Review, **110** (July-December), 463-473.
    Swift, F.H. (1916). *The Contemporary Review,* **110**, 465-473.
    Travers, T.H.E. (1979). Technology, tactics and morale. Jean de Bloch, the Boer
War and British military theory, 1900-1914. *Journal of Modern History,* **51**, 264-286.
    Veitch, Colin R. (1984). *Sport and war in the British literature of the First World*
War, 1914-1918. Unpublished master's thesis, The University of Alberta, Canada.
    The War Illustrated (1917). pp. 564-565.

13

The Lion, the Eagle and the Kangaroo: Politics and Proposals for a British Empire Team at the 1916 Berlin Olympics

Ian F. Jobling
UNIVERSITY OF QUEENSLAND
ST. LUCIA, QUEENSLAND, AUSTRALIA

An examination of proposals to send a British Empire team to the 1916 Berlin Olympic Games provide interesting insights about the role of sport in British-American and British-Australian-Imperial relationships. The first part of this paper will be confined to a brief consideration of the significance of sport when the athletic supremacy of the British "lion" was being threatened by the American "eagle." The outcome of this sporting rivalry between two powerful antagonists had ramifications which affected the relationship between Britain and her former colonies. The second dimension of this paper will be to consider the implications of the Empire Team proposals on the recently independent "kangaroo" of the Commonwealth of Australia which was experiencing ambivalence in its relationships with Great Britain and the Empire.

The Lion and the Eagle

The 1908 Olympic Games in London were organized in less than 2 years (British Olympic Council, 1908; Cook, 1908a). The preparation prior to the opening in July 1908 was commendable, but there was one aspect of the organization which, as time would tell, was significant. As reported in *The Times,* London in July 1908, the management of the Games was exclusively controlled by the individual British sporting associations: "They provide all the officials, and are responsible for the proper conduct of the competitions." This factor was one of many which strained British-American sporting relationships (*Revue Olympique,* 1908; Howell & Howell, 1978) with accusations and bitterness culminating with Theodore Cook of the British Olympic Council publishing a 50-page statement entitled, "A reply to certain criticisms made by some of the American officials" (Cook, 1980b) in which Cook stated "The American papers have been flooded with reports from those who accompanied the American team...as to the unfairness, discourtesy, and dishonesty with which the Americans had in every respect been treated."

The extent of the discord between the British and Americans is highlighted through a study of the reports of events during and after the Games in the presses of the respective countries, and also in a publication by Burlford (1910) titled *American Hatred and British Folly.*

A significant point of argument was the British use of a "point system" of 5 for first place, 3 for second place, and 1 for third place. In contrast to their outright success in both the medal count and point-score system in 1908, Britain did poorly at Stockholm in 1912, being outscored by both Sweden and the United States. The official report of the 1912 Stockholm Olympics (Begrall, 1913) included many tables of results, one of which was a comparison of the Swedish and the English method of calculation of points; neither was flattering to Great Britain (see Table 1). However, when the medals won by Great Britain and her "colonies" were combined, the disparity was not so great. In September 1912, the British press published a table depicting the Empire tally (see Table 2).

The rivalry for medal supremacy at both the 1908 and 1912 Olympic Games strained British-American sporting relationships. Soon after the 1912 Games began, a leading article in the *New York Times* on July 9, 1912, suggested that "something really is the matter with Englishmen since they are no longer masters of the playground...the saying that Waterloo was won on the playing fields, once a boast, is now a bitter prophecy." The comments of James E. Sullivan, 1912 U.S. Olympic commissioner and a vehement critic of the British organization of the 1908 Olympic Games (Lucas, 1977) would have further rankled many Britons. The British *Sporting Chronicle* of August 9, 1912 reported that Mr. Sullivan said, "We are hoping to do still better in Berlin at the next Olympic meeting in 1916, as our training, although it has reached perfection, could be still better perfected."

Table 1. Comparison of scores

Nation	Swedish system 3-2-1 points	English system 5-3-1 points
Sweden	136	208
USA	124	188
Great Britain	76	111

Some British sporting officials and commentators were so disappointed about their lack of sporting success that proposals for Great Britain's withdrawal from the Olympic Games were promulgated and published. The tone of the arguments presented in some cases were related to the different character of British sport and sportsmanship (*Revue Olympique*, 1912). For example, *The Sportsman* of London (August 7, 1912) reported:

> America has adopted in her sports, at any rate in international sport, her own great business axiom—'beat the other fellow, fairly, if convenient, but beat him,' and we must accept the fact that our ideas of sportsmanship differ from theirs.

It was in this athletic climate that the idea of a British Empire Team, first promulgated by the Australian, Richard Coombes, was renewed for the 1916 Berlin Olympic Games.

Proposals for a British Empire Team

Coombes proposed his idea of a British Empire Team following an inter-empire sports championship held in 1911 as part of the Festival of Empire in London to commemorate the coronation of George V. During the celebration dinner which concluded the sports carnival, Lord Desborough, a member of the British Olympic Association, announced that arrangements were being made for the Australasian, Canadian, South African, and British teams to train together and to go to the 1912 Stockholm Olympics as an Empire team (*Referee*, Sydney, 1911). An example of how such a team might work was outlined by Coombes, who was Australasian representative on the International Olympic Committee and President of the Australasian Athletic Union, through his pseudonym ("Prodigal") when writing in Sydney's *Referee*:

Table 2. The Empire tally

Nations	Entries		Points		Order
1. United Kingdom		┌526	111 ┐		III
2. Australasia*	773 ─	│ 59 ┐	├ 177½		
3. Canada		│ 74 ├	─66½┘		
4. South Africa		└119 ┘			
5. France		┌508	50 ┐		VI
6. Austria		│250	8 │		
7. Bohemia	875─	│167	0 ├─ 32		VII
8. Hungary		└458	24 ┘		
9. Sweden		882	208		I
11. USA		572	195		II
16. Russia		369	9		
	593			85	
17. Finland		224	76		IV

*(Australia and New Zealand)
Note. From *Sperling Chronicle*, Manchester, September 21, 1912.

The scheme, then, is that the Colonies—Australia, New Zealand, Canada, and South Africa—will select their teams and the whole contingent be brought together in London, say, a fortnight before they are due to leave for Stockholm. The British team will also be concentrated in London as far as possible, and then the whole army will train together under the care of responsible coaches and trainers, and be got into the best possible condition for the descent on Sweden...This is surely the very ideal of Empire—the forces of the Mother Country and her children, and Colonies, congregating on the shores of Britain to concentrate the forces of the Empire, and then voyaging to the battle-ground of Stockholm to challenge in friendly warfare the best of the world's athletes.

Although the short notice prevented an "official" Empire Team being organized and entered in time for the Stockholm Olympics (*Referee,* Sydney, April 24, 1912), the seeds had been sown for this idea to germinate after Britain's dismal performance at these Games, particularly against her archrival, the United States of America.

Curiously, the Empire team idea may have been rekindled by the success of swimmer "Duke" Kahanamoku. In a letter to the *New York Times* (July 13, 1912),

Equality asked: Can anybody tell me why when a Hawaiian gentleman, with a totally unpronounceable name, wins an Olympic event points are scored in the United States column, but when a white British subject residing in South Africa, Australia or Canada accomplishes a similar feat the points won are not credited to Great Britain.

However, it was following a letter from Arthur Conan Doyle, published in *The Times* of London on July 19, 1912, that the idea of a British Empire team for the Berlin Olympics of 1916 gained momentum. Doyle's suggestions were editorially supported by *The Daily Mail*:

However much the cult of athletics may be disparaged, victory in the Olympic Games is now regarded throughout the world as a test of national virility and energy. That being so, we must neglect no proposition to achieve success and to prove to foreign people that the British Empire is far from being in a state of decay but is very much alive.

The editor of the *New York Times* reacted to Doyle's suggestions by stating, on July 21, 1913, that,

There is occasion for irony in the fact that the persons, who at first made light of the British failures at Stockholm on the grounds that it was more important 'to play the game than to win,' are now eager to take up a scheme which they hope will disposses the United States from its proud pre-eminence and head of the list of scores with a pan-British total of victories.

Further credibility to the idea was given when the British Olympic Association's official report to the Stockholm games, published in September 1912, referred to the united Empire team's prospects but hinted at possible difficulties pertaining to "the definition of a 'nation.'" (*Times,* London, September 19, 1912).

The role and attitude of Australia, as one of the Empire countries embroiled in the socio-political struggles between the British Lion and the American Eagle, is worthy of consideration. When Conan Doyle's suggestion was published, the London *Times* expressed the following as an attitude of all the former British colonies:

> The glory which accrues to the individual dominions is but moderate in amount, and the sentimental satisfaction, which each derives from its separate represen- tation cannot be great. Certainly the colonials themselves feel that it would be vastly better to be associated with a powerful empire team, the flag of which everybody at the games knows and respects, and to help keep that empire in its place at the head of the nations.

Was this sentiment accurate in respect to Australia's attitude, or were there expressions of independent nationalism which were in conflict with devotion to Great Britain and the Empire?

The Kangaroo—Attitudes Toward the Lion and the Empire

The Commonwealth of Australia was established in 1901 but unlike in America, it was not after a revolutionary struggle by triumphant colonies over a defeated Motherland (Crowley, 1974). In 1901, more than 98% of the Australian popula- tion was of English, Scottish, Welsh, or Irish descent, and 18% had actually been born in Great Britain (Souter, 1978). The historical, economic, political, and social bonds to Great Britain remained strong. Economically, Australia's trade was mostly with Great Britain, and almost three-quarters of the capital invested in Australian joint-stock companies and public bonds was British; even the coins in usage bore the likeness of Britannia and Queen Victoria, and the monarch was Australia's head of state (Crowley, 1974; Souther, 1978). There' was no national anthem, and the flag, the result of a public competition with 30,000 entries, incorporated the Union Jack with the Southern Cross. It was regarded by the *Bulletin* of September 28, 1901 as,

> That bastard flag…a true symbol of the bastard state of Australian opinion, still in large part biassed [sic] by British traditions, British customs, still lacking many years to the sufficiency of manhood which will determine a path of its own.

In these early years of the Commonwealth, Australia relied on Great Britain for its defense. Prior to Federation, the Australian colonial governments had sent volunteers to the Boer War, and the Commonwealth government con- tinued to encourage this to the extent that more than 16,000 Australian volunteers had served with the British army in South Africa between 1899 and 1902. *The Sydney Morning Herald* stated that the "Lion's cubs had rallied to the dam" (February 20, 1902), and Prime Minister Edmund Barton ex- plained to Federal parliament, "The bond of Empire is not one only of mere patriotism but also one of self-interest" (Australia *Parliamentary Debates*, Jan. 14, 1902).

Australia's allegiance to the concept of Empire was becoming increasingly significant by the end of the first decade of the 20th century. On May 24, 1905, the late Queen Victoria's birthday, was proclaimed as the inaugural "Empire Day" which became an annual public holiday. As Sir John Foster Fraser wrote in his book, *Australia: The Making of a Nation* (1910), "There is loyalty in

Australia, but it is loyalty to the Empire, not Great Britain." This distinction may have seemed subtle at the beginning of the federation but, by the time of the Festival of Empire in 1911, when the native-born population of Australia had risen to 83%, there were signs that this sentiment was becoming stronger, especially in that significant sociocultural aspect—sport.

Sport and Australian Identity

Sport, and particularly success in sport, had already become important to Australians by the first decade of the 20th century (Jobling, 1981). Defeating England in cricket was an occasion for national celebration (Mandle, 1973) as were victories in rowing. Success in the earlier multination, multisport events had also made Australians proud of such sportsmen as Edwin Flack, Freddy Lane, "Snowy" Baker (Jobling, 1980) and, of course, of the gold medal performances in 1912 by the mens 4 × 200m freestyle relay. The first and second placings of Fanny Durack and Wilhelmina Wylie, respectively, in the inaugural Olympic 100 meters freestyle for women at Stockholm were wildly acclaimed in Australia (Jobling, 1982). Even in sport, however, the affinity to the Empire was strong, and *The Sydney Morning Herald* of May 12, 1912, published an article under the heading," The Bond of Sport—Athletics and Imperialism," which perhaps expressed the attitudes of Australians:

> Manly sport has played no mean part in binding the Empire together. Friendly competition in sport has drawn the various parts of the Empire closer as the years have gone by, and if in other respects the Empire is the greatest the world has ever seen, it may also be claimed for it that it stands in the forefront in the world of sport. . .As an integral part of the British nation Australia has helped to uphold the Empire's supremacy in sport as well as in other ways.

As stated previously, Richard Coombes is regarded as having initiated the idea of forming an Empire team for the Stockholm Olympics during the 1911 Festival of Empire (*SMH*, September 13, 1911; *Referee*, Sydney, September 29, 1911). As editor of the *Referee*, Coombes was able to ensure that the idea was given prominence, and many columns over the remaining months of 1912 were utilized to present both his and other views. The Australian daily press also presented divergent opinions (*S.M.H., Age*, Melbourne). In early August, the *Sydney Morning Herald* expressed that there was "a sentimental argument in favor of the linking up of the athletes of the Empire," but the practicability of the scheme was questioned (August 8, 1912). The view that Australia would not like to lose its separate identity in the Olympic Games was frequently expressed, but this was sometimes qualified by the comment that, for example, "they would sacrifice this if there was a real prospect of benefiting the Empire" (*Referee*, Sydney, September 4, 1912). Robert C. Reid's comment is of interest:

> It seems quite a mistake that the various Empire units should compete against one another—they should, as you put it so aptly, be standing shoulder to shoulder in the firing-line at the Olympiads. (*Referee*, Sydney, September 25, 1912)

The arguments pertaining to the inappropriateness and unpracticability of the scheme were many and varied: It was unsportsmanlike; it placed difficulties on an athlete to "peak" for Empire selection trials and maintain that form for the Olympic events; there was the expense of sending athletes to London who might then not compete in Berlin; and the difficulty of representation of an Empire Council was a serious concern (*Referee, S.M.H., The Leader*). An example of the last criticism was succinctly expressed in this way, "Anyone with any experience of the governing bodies of sport in England will immediately forecast the clash between their conservatism and impertinent unconventionality of the colonies." (*S.M.H.,* October 30, 1912).

It would seem, however, that a most significant reason for Australians not supporting the scheme was related to the matter of loss of identity (*SMH.,* September 20, 1913). This view was most clearly, and realistically expressed in the *Sydney Morning Herald*:

> At present any competitor sent from Australia competes in the Games as an Australasian, and any victory credited to him is recognized by the hoisting of an Australian flag. Apart from all questions of loyalty to the Empire, there is a narrower local patriotism for Australia, which is certainly gratified by the present system, which is also a tremendous advertisement to this continent. And in this advertisement lies the Australian council's main hope in financing an Olympic team. (October 30, 1912)

Although Richard Coombes and *The Referee* continued to press the relative merits of the "Empire scheme" throughout 1912 and early 1913, the enthusiasm of sports officials and commentators in other parts of Australia and the Empire dwindled (*SMH,* January 8, 1913; *Referee,* Sydney, March 26, 1913; June 18, 1913). Although the matter was revived in September 1913 when Britain announced its British Olympic fund (*SMH,* September 1913; *NYT,* September 19, 1913), it was also made clear that the British athlete had politely turned aside the proferred help of the Dominions in the effort to recover the prestige formerly enjoyed (*SMH,* September 19, 1913). The decision of the British Olympic Association was clarified in a letter from its secretary to Hugh D. McIntosh, the sporting entrepreneur in Australia who had offered to raise 5,000 pounds to devote "to the training of Australasian athletes who might afterwards be tried out against British athletes before an Empire team was selected" (*Referee,* Sydney, Sept. 10, 1913). The BOA secretary wrote that the question of an Empire team "has been settled by the International Olympic Committee that Great Britain and the overseas dominions shall compete separately" (*Referee,* Sydney, September 10, 1913).

Although this author has been unable to confirm from perusal of minutes and reports of the IOC that this question was even discussed, it is clear that Australian sporting officials and commentators dismissed the idea from this time. Even *The Referee* launched itself into a program of fund-raising for the preparation and expense of sending a prestigious Australian team to Berlin in 1916 (*Referee,* September and October, 1913). Despite the many economic, political, and historical ties with Great Britain which would remain for many more decades, an Australian cultural identity was emerging, especially one related to sport. The renowned poet, Henry Lawson, stated that Australia was a "land where sport is sacred," and in so doing had echoed and heralded the sentiments of many others (Jobling, 1981) including Richard Twopeny, who had written in his book *Town Life in Australia,* "the principal amusements of the Australians are outdoor sports of one kind or another" (Twopeny, 1883).

Summary and Conclusions

The proposals for a British Empire Team were promulgated at a time when the role and significance of success in sport was used as a weapon in the political, economic, and cultural rivalry for supremacy between Great Britain and the United States. Principally through the commitment and zeal of Richard Coombes, in his dual role as Australasian representative on the International Olympic Committee and editor of the leading Australian sporting weekly, *The Referee,* Australians became aware of the importance of success in international sport and its relationship to fostering a national identity. Although experiencing the ambivalence of being legislatively but not economically, politically, or culturally independent of Great Britain, an examination of these proposals for an Empire Team provided an interesting insight into early postcolonial relationships.

An analysis of the documents, reports, articles, and opinions highlighted many factors about such proposals and their possible impact on relationships between former colonies and Great Britain, as well as between Great Britain, the British Empire, and the United States. There were many impracticalities of the scheme which would have made it difficult to implement, but it is clear that, although nationalism and imperialism beat side-by-side in many Australian hearts, when it came to sporting contests against Great Britain or other countries, the opportunity for a patriotic and victorious "kangaroo" to emerge became paramount. Australians were seeking an identity, and sport was becoming an avenue for achieving it.

References

American ambitions. (1908, December). *Revue Olympique*, 179-187.

Australia *Parliamentary Debates.* (1902, January 14). (Hansard).

Bergrall, E. (Ed.). (1913). *The fifth Olympiad: The official report of the Olympic Games of Stockholm 1912.* Stockholm: Wahlstrom and Widstrand.

British Olympic Council. (1908). *The fourth Olympiad: The official report of the Olympic Games of 1908.* London: British Olympic Association.

Bulletin, Sydney, September 18, 1901.

Burlford, T.F. (1910). *American hatred and British folly.* London: T.R. Burlford.

Cook, T.A. (1908a). *The cruise of the Branwen.* London: Ballantyne and Co.

Cook, T.A. (1908b). *Olympic Games of 1908 in London: A reply to certain criticisms.* London British Olympic Association.

Crowley, F. (Ed.) (1974) *A new history of Australia.* Melbourne: Heinemann.

Daily Mail, London, July 1912.

England's duty. (1912, November). *Revue Olympique*, pp. 166-170.

Fraser, J.F. (1910). *Australia: The making of a nation.* London: Cassell.

Howell, M.L. and Howell, R. (1978). The Olympic movement restored: The 1908 Games. In Landry, F. & Orban, W. (Ed.) *Philosophy, Theology and History of Sport and Physical Activity*. Book 8, Congress Papers. Miami: Symposia Specialists.

Jobling, I.F. (1980, May) The crumpled laurel wreath: International sports in disarray. Australia and the Olympic Movement 1894-1936. *Proceedings of the Sports Sciences Section of the 50th ANZAAS Congress, Adelaide.*

Jobling, I.F. (1981). The 'Sporty' Australians: Women and sport in Australian history. *Medicine and Sport*. Basel: Karger.

Jobling, I.F. (1982). *Australian women at the Olympic Games: Swimmers not runners, 1912-1928.* Proceedings of the Sport Sciences Section of ANZAAS, Sydney: Macquaine University, pp. 86-99.

Leader, Melbourne, October, 1912.

Lucas, J. (1977). Early Olympic antagonists—Pierre de Coubertin vs James E. Sullivan. *Stadion III.*

Mandle, W.G. (1973, December). Cricket and Australian nationalism in the Nineteenth Century. *Journal of Royal Australian Historical Society, 59*, 235-246.

New York Times, New York. July 9, 1912; July 13, 1912; July 21, 1913; September 10, 1913; October, 1913.

Referee, Syndey, September 20, 1911; September 29, 1911; April 24, 1912; September 25, 1915; March 26, 1913; September 10, 1913; October, 1913.

Souter, G. (1978). *Lion and kangaroo—Australia: 1901-1919, the rise of a nation.* Sydney: Fontana Books.

Sportsman, London, August 7, 1912.

Sporting Chronicle, Manchester, August 9, 1912; September 21, 1912.

Sydney Morning Herald, Sydney. February 20, 1902; September 13, 1911; May 12, 1912; August 8, 1912; October 30, 1912; January 8, 1913; September 30, 1913.

Times, London, July, 1908; July 19, 1912; September 19, 1912.

Twopeny, R.E.N. (1983). *Town life in Australia*. London: Elliot Stock.

14

Sport, Physical Culture and Political Action in Germany During the Weimar Republic 1925-1933

Horst Ueberhorst
RUHR-UNIVERSITÄT BOCHUM
FEDERAL REPUBLIC OF GERMANY

The military collapse of Germany in November, 1918, struck at deeply the national self-confidence of most Germans, because still in the spring of 1918, high-raised victory hopes were widely spread. The force which had united Germany in 1870-71 was in the Prussian army, and democracy lacked prestige and authority in Germany. Real power remained with the nobility and the industrials, who despised parliamentary government. Now, as a consequence of the long war and the defeat, the physical and psychic forces of the people were exhausted and the masses declared the nobility and the industrial bourgeoisie guilty for the national catastrophe. Unresisting, the Kaiser (emperor) and the princes yielded their thrones. Not a hand stirred to defend a monarchy which had lost all credibility. Nevertheless, by the revolution of 1918-19 the social proportions in Germany were changed less fundamentally than expected. The continuity of elites and its social recruitment is far more characteristic at the period of transition from the Empire to the Republic than changes in government and ruling style.

When Germany became a Republic, power fell to the Social Democrats. Their majority had long since abandoned the revolutionary notion of earlier years and saw its mission in transition from the old to the new form of state, but in the first years the Weimar Republic had to fight for survival: The communists had to contend with the Spartacus-Upheaval in Berlin, 1919; the Kapp-Putsch of the Rightists in 1920; communist riots in the Ruhr district and in central Germany in 1921-22; separatism in the Rhine province and Hitler's Beer-Hall-Putsch in Munich in 1923; and, in the same year, culmination of inflation and occupation of the Ruhr, the industrial center of Germany, by French troops. Each of these crises could have meant an end to the Weimar Republic. Already at the beginning of parliamentary life after free elections, the new government was faced with a severe dilemma: The allies decided not to stop the starvation-blockade before the peace-treaty of Versailles was signed. It was an extremely difficult decision the government was forced to make: Not signing the treaty meant no dismissal of German prisoners of war, the continued occupation of German territory, increasing unemployment, starvation, and death. On the other hand, signing the treaty meant, stirring up national passions, decaying of the new democratic state-institutions, and the increasing danger of civil war.

In spite of all the troubles and turbulances during the formative years of the Republic, the government had remarkable success in improving the living conditions of the working class by increasing social expenses, by enlarging social housing construction, by ameliorating public health service, social help, and security. Art, science, and education, including physical education, flourished also. Impulses from the prewar reform-movement were still alive.

The progressive governments of the Weimar Republic supported the gymnastic and sport movement as well. The liberal and socialist parties had always favored subsidizing physical exercises. Now—not at least alarmed by warning doctoral reports—there was a universal agreement of the importance of sport as a form for social hygiene. Young people streamed into gymnastic and sports clubs. In 1919, at their first convention at Leipzig after the war, the Labor Turners recognized the growing importance of sports and renamed their Federation: Arbeiter-Turn-und Sportbund (Workers Gymnastic and Sport Association). This federation became an important cultural factor of the Weimar Republic in the twenties.

The "Reichsausschul für Leibesübungen" (DRA), the National Committee of Physical Exercises—the umbrella organization of bourgeois sports—developed a clearly formulated program of action under General Secretary Carl Diem and President Theodor Lewald.

- A sports-ground law proposing 5-square meters of sportsground and 1/10 of a square meter of gymnasium space for each head of population and one indoor pool for each 30,000 citizens.
- Daily sport lessons in all schools. This demand was strongly supported by align "Reischsschulkonferenz" in 1920.
- Gymnastic and sports duty for youth. This would be a substitute for compulsory service in the army.
- Support for gymnastic and sport societies by suspending them from paying taxes and by reducing travel expenses for sport groups. Although the laws could not be realized because of lack of finances, they had a strong impact on the whole sportive life and a strong influence upon local authorities. From 1924-1928, these measures created a boom in building sport facilities.
- Reischsjugendwettkämpfe, or national youth competitions, held for both sexes yearly, comprised of running, jumping, and throwing the ball or the shot put, were introduced and became very popular. The provincal govern-

ments supported these track and field events and were willing to cooperate with the DRA. More than 1 million youngsters participated in those games in 1928.

• In 1921, a Gymnastic and Sports Badge was introduced on Diem's initiative and later institutes of physical education evolved as a result of student agitation. The German College of Physical Exercises was founded in 1921 in Berlin. The institutes of physical education and the German College of Physical Exercises were coeducational. In fact, postwar Germany saw a greatly increased participation of women in life outside the home: Women succeeded in infiltrating men's institutions and organizations; the German Gymnastic Union (DT) and the Labor Sports Movement admitted women on equal terms with men. The Labor Turners, especially, encouraged women to enter their organizations and to take over, if possible, leading positions. The Labor Sports Movement was supervised by the ZK, the Central Commission for Labor Sport and Bodily Hygiene, and divided in different sport sections.

Up from 1925, it seemed that the Republic had a real chance to become stable and would master further crises. The foreign policy of Gustav Stresemann regained political equality for defeated Germany through the pact of Locarno (1925) and accession to the League of Nations (1926). Along with the political pacification came the economic recovery. How then could the German democracy finally fail in 1933 and Hitler come to power? To answer this important question, the following major events must be analyzed which reflect the weakness of democracy in general and of the Weimer Republic in particular.

Youth Searching for a "Better Germany"

In October 1913 youth groups demanded to shape their own lives, formally proclaiming at their annual meeting at the Hohen Meissner mountain: "The free German youth is determined to shape its own life, to be responsible of itself and guided by the innate feeling of truth. To defend this inner liberty they close the ranks."[1] Ten months after this meeting, they met again at the battlefields and in the trenches of World War I, coming from classrooms and lecture halls. Thousands were already killed at Langemarck/Flanders in 1914, when German student-volunteer companies attacked the British by frontal assault. The myth of Langemarck was to act as a profound influence upon Germany's youth and created the demand of obedience and readiness for self-sacrifice for one's comrades. The activists among the youth movement later could be found in the Freikorps and the "Stahlhelm" (steel helmet), in militant organizations, and among social revolutionaires of both the Left and the Right. The front-line experience prevented for most of them an integration into a peaceful, orderly, and bourgeois life. For social and political reasons the Weimar Republic never became their home.

---

[1]Koch, H.W. (1972). *Hitler Youth: The duped generation*. New York: Ballantine Books, Inc., p. 10.

In 1922, Hitler called for creation of a youth movement of the NSDAP, the Nazi party; however, after the failure of the Beer-Hall Putsch in Munich 1923, it took until 1926 before Kurt Grube built up the Hitler Youth. Outside the Hitler Youth the National Socialist Student Movement was founded, and at the end of 1928, was led by Baldur von Schirach, who used this as a base of power from which he had hoped to bring about the fusion of all nationalistic youth groups. Thanks to Hitler, von Schirach not only became the leader of the NS Student Association, but when he was only 26 years old, was appointed "Reichsjugendführer" of the Hitler Youth at the end of 1931, the same year Ernst Röhm was appointed Chief of Staff of the SA, Hitler's brown-shirts, a paramilitary party troop. The Hitler Youth (HJ) as an organization in its own right was put under the supreme SA leadership. In 1932 the Papen government assisted the Hitler Youth to enter the "Reichs Committee of German Youth Associations" (RJK), a paramilitary association, which had previously turned down the HJ's application for membership; von Shirach now tried to make the Reichs Committee an instrument of the Hitler Youth.

Paramilitary Training in the Reichs Committee (RJK)

What were the origins and aims of the Reichs Committee? As early as 1924, army officials conducted experiments substituting several types of sport training for military instruction, which embraced such useful skills as physical conditioning, marching, map reading, marksmanship and gymnastics, that is, basic military training. An ambitious plan had called for a network of military sport camps. When Groener became defense minister in 1930, he wanted to establish a state-sponsored physical fitness and military sport program for young men. This military sport project would function as a substitute for the forbidden compulsory service. Also, he hoped to gain control of the different youth groups and to provide some meaningful activity for thousands of unemployed youth, who were left by default to the extremists. But prior to 1932 the government did not succeed in establishing the Reichs Committee (RJK). The RJK, as its president General von Stüpnagel said, should have the following functions: (a) to train and certify military sport instructions, (b) to foster cooperation among all the organizations active in this area of sport training, and (c) to organize and operate a number of camps for training prospective military sport instructors.[2] SA Chief Röhm urged his SA commanders to send as many "storm-troopers" (SA men) as possible to the instructor-training courses, which enjoyed government subvention. He also appointed one of his leaders to serve as liasion-officer. Thus, instead of what the government had hoped, that the RJK act as a counter balance to Hitler's growing influence over jobless and disappointed youngsters, the Republic trained its own gravediggers. General von Schleicher fervently worked in vain to enlist the Social Democrats, at this time second to the Nazis in electoral strength (Communists were not allowed to join the RJK). The Social Democrats (SPD) had already formed the "Iron

---

[2]BA, NS (1932, September 16). 231124, OSAF, 2509/32. (BA = Bundesarchiv)

Front,'' after he had recognized above all the growing fascist threat as epitomized by the combative SA. The SPD newspaper *Vorwärts* denounced the formation of the RJK as "the militarization of youth programs" and led the party attack against the new youth agency.[3] With von Schleicher's resignation as chancellor at the beginning of 1933, the RJK fell into the hands of the Nazis, who wasted little time in converting it to their purposes. Röhm made clear his desire for the RJK. At a conference of SA, army, and Stahlhelm leaders in July 1933, Hitler announced the disbanding of the RJK and the transfer of its functions to the SA. Expanding the RJK's 16 schools to over 200, the SA for 2 years provided—in conspiracy with the Reichswehr—over 300,000 young men destined for the Wehrmacht, the future German army.

The Iron Front and the Final Decline of the Republic

How could this happen? Was the danger of Fascism recognized in time by the Workers Sport Movement and was there a real chance to stop the decline of the Republic? Only a modified answer can be given on this important question by looking backward to the year 1930, which marks the turning point in the history of the Weimar Republic and signals her final phase. At the general elections of September 1930, the National Socialists had significant success and increased their votes from 800,000 to 6.5 million. It is true that from this time onward, the Social Democrats recognized the danger that threatened the Weimar Republic, namely radicalism from the Right, but failed to see the dangerous situation that grew up from tolerating an antiparliamentarian presidial cabinet ruling through emergency decrees. Soon it became apparent that the creation of Brüning's presidial cabinet was an important step in reducing the power of the parliament. As a consequence, the interior political disputes were displaced from parliament to the streets, where more and more bloody clashes occurred. To end the growing terror and to defend democratic principles against increasing threat of Nationalism, the Iron Front was founded on December 16, 1931. It was also a reaction to the building up of the nationalistic "Harzburger Front" (SA, Stahlhelm, and radical Conservatives). The new republican organization, the Iron Front, was to demonstrate the close connection between the Social Democrats (SPD), the Free Labor Unions, the "Reichsbanner" (a paramilitary Republican troop) and the democratic Working Sport Organizations. But at this time, the workers sport movement was already split (since 1928 the majority followed democratic SPD-leaders; the minority followed Moscow-oriented communist leaders) because the Red Sport International would not accept anything less than communist domination of the entire movement. So from the beginning, the Iron Front was faced with a dilemma: It had to defend the threatened Weimar Repubic against two enemies—the National Socialists (Hitler Party) and the radical Conservatives, and the Communists. SPD leaders were branded by Communists as being Social Fascists and by the Nazis as "November Criminals" (Novemberverbrecher), those who

---

[3]*Vorwärts*, (1932, September 15).

in November 1918 should have stabbed—to put it metaphorically—the dagger into the back of the brave fighting army.

In 1932 there were seven (!) elections which excited the masses. All were started in a period when the world-wide economic crisis reached its peak and shook the whole foundation of the German society. As Stampfer, a social-democratic historian pointed out, the sense for democracy got lost; elections did not lead, as they should, to a reasonable period of stabilization but became a source of continuous unrest and troubles. It was the destruction of democracy by the tools of democracy.[4] The economic crisis produced a social-political and cultural crisis. As a result, the disappointed, unemployed, and starving masses turned to Hitler, expecting from him salvation in their need. Hitler, who in July 1932, could double his votes in comparison with the elections from 1930, now openly demanded the chancellorship. As president Hindenburg refused to accept this, new riots broke out. Terrorism escalated to a civil-warlike situation.

The Iron Front was willing to fight for the maintenance of the Republic. The *Labor Sports Journal* (ATZ) clearly indicated the political problems at ths time. It is really impressive how clearly and realistically the ATZ pointed out the consequences of the Nazis coming to power.

> "Freedom lost—all is lost. Then the leaders of the working class will come under the brutal rule of men who do not want the salvation of the state but the supression of the proletarians!"[5]

For the first time after the war, the necessary connection between labor sport and military fitness was underlined. The following resolution from the Conference of the Socialistic Labor Sport International (SASI) is cited:

> "The labor class can be successful in its fight against Fashism only by creating its own defensive formations."[6]

And:

> "Shoulder to shoulder with the comrades from the Reichsbanner and the Free Labor Unions we have to fight for a free German Republic, for the most liberal constitution of the world, for the rise of the German people, against Fashism and Capitalism."[7]

The executive board of the Labor Sports Movement stated July 9, 1932: The only chance for successful defense against Nazi assaults will be a cooperation with the Iron Front.

Just how long could the readiness to fight be kept alive? The younger generation, as far as they were organized in the Iron Front, was willing to fight, but the SPD believed that it could master the crisis by parliamentarian methods. Instead of indicating that the Republican would have to fight, it protested mainly through verbal declarations and gave up its last chance to resist against acts of violence. So working youth lost their confidence in the leadership of the Social Democrats. Today we know that the Iron Front was not the "invincible bulwark of the Labor Movement" as it had been declared, but a "giant with

---

[4]Stampfer F. (1947). Die ersten 14 Jahre der Deutschen Republik. (The first 14 years of the German Republic.) Offenbach, p. 611.

Arbeiter—Turnzeitung (ATZ). (1932)[5], p. 26; (1932)[6], p. 52; (1932)[7], p. 128.

feet of clay.''[8] At no time did the Republicans succeed in building up the Iron Front as an operational and fighting unit. As a result of this failure, the working youth, as well as the whole Democratic Workers Sport Movement, became paralyzed and made no effort to prevent the agony of the Weimar Republic.

Conclusion

This does not mean that there was no real opportunity to resist. One chance was given at Papen's coup d'etat (20.7.1932) in Prussia, the dismissal of Prime Minister Braun and the Minister of Interior Affairs Severing, the last big social-democratic bulwark in the German ''Reich.'' Armed resistance was a risk, but probably the only chance to stop the process of self-destruction of the Republic. An unexpected, determined demonstration of civil war preparedness by the Iron Front could have been a decisive power factor in the political game.

The masses did not recognize this coherence because the speakers at the big meetings of the Iron Front used strong words and suggested a misleading feeling of strength and power. To some extent, this is also true of the leaders of the Labor Sports Movement. During this time, the leader especially believed in the idealism of the labor youth and encouraged them to join the Iron Front in order to strengthen the forces against reaction and National Socialism. They accused the Communists as well as the Nazis and proclaimed that the split of the working class, caused by the Communists, had weakened the Weimar Republic. So what potentially could have prevented the coming to power of Hitler—a proletarian united front—was not realized because of different ideological positions. This is why the SPD was forced to a ''two-front-war'' against Nazis and Communists in a civil-warlike situation, which only could have been mastered by determined resistance.

Furthermore, for ideological reasons, the labor sports organizations were opposed to the bourgeois sports organizations, although they both had fully recognized the growing importance of sport and physical education in the Weimar Republic.

On January 30, 1933, Hitler became Reich chancellor. Apart from members of his own party, there were several conservatives in his cabinet who hoped to tame him. But soon Hitler rid himself of his allies. Already in 1933 an Empowering Act, approved by all middle class parties, gave him practically unlimited power. He banned all parties but his own, the trade unions were smashed, basic rights virtually removed and press freedom abandoned. Thousands disappeared without trials in concentration camps. Hitlers position was enhanced by his big foreign policy successes.

The ''Führer''-principles were advanced in most organizations, even in sport. An appointed ''Reichssportführer'' started to press German sport into a new ideological concept. His main idea was to strengthen the German youth by paramilitary exercises and to create a fighting spirit, which Hitler could use to achieve his goals.

---

[8]Rohe, K. (1961). Das Reichsbanner Schwarz, Rot, Gold. (The Reich's banner black, red, and gold.) Frankfurt: M. p. 414.

So in conclusion, the Weimar Republic failed mainly because of the half-hearted defense of his supporters. Authoritarian structures of the bourgeois sport organizations made it easy to shape German sports up from 1933 after a national-socialistic model. The Weimar Republic was destroyed because democracy and state ruled by law had not taken root in years of the Republic, so that their removal meant little to the majority. What mattered much more was that within a few years, Hitler succeeded in doing away with unemployment. Hitler could build up his dictatorship by exercising both ruthless terror and by rising antidemocratic feelings of the masses. Thus, he first undermined, and then he totally destroyed democratic structures.

By knowing this, the history of the Weimar Republic can be a warning example for all democracies.

15

Strange Bedfellows and Cooperative Partners: The Influence of the Olympic Games on the Establishment of the British Empire Games

Katharine E. Moore
THE QUEEN'S UNIVERSITY OF BELFAST
BELFAST, NORTHERN IRELAND

Although the discussion of another multisport festival at an Olympic Congress may initially seem out of place, it is the intention of this paper to examine and highlight the long-standing relationship between the Olympic Games and the establishment of the British Empire Games. While the sheer size and scope of the Olympic Games has tended to overshadow the British Empire Games, we must return to the late 19th century to look at the origins of both movements, and will begin with a sketch of the two men who presented grandiose plans for multisport competition to the world during the 1890s.

The name of Pierre de Coubertin is well-known throughout the sporting world. His dream of founding the modern Olympic Games has been documented by several authors, including Eyquem (1976), Lucas (1981), MacAloon (1981), and Mandell (1976), and his untiring efforts can only be referred to briefly in this paper. In marked contrast, the name of J. Astley Cooper will no doubt produce a blank stare or a puzzled look because virtually no substantiated material about this man has ever appeared in print in English. Yet it was Cooper, 3 years before Coubertin convened his Congress at the Sorbonne, who publicly suggested that a multisport gathering be held in conjunction with an exhibition of culture and industry praising the Anglo-Saxon race. This ambitious festival suffered from a lack of a definitive name, but, for the duration of this paper, it shall be called the Pan-Britannic Festival. The connection between these two men and their respective sport festivals has not been studied in any detail, and, therefore, is the starting point for this paper.

Pierre de Coubertin

John MacAloon (1981) succinctly summarized the successful formula utilized in establishing the modern Olympic Games: "Coubertin's drive and personality, the resources of money, prestige, and social contacts he commanded, and his total investment in his identity as a sports entrepreneur and reformer were essential to his success." Coubertin's attempt to host a conference in 1892, designed in part to discuss the Olympic Games, was less than successful, so he increased his traveling, speaking, and writing, and was able to recruit enough international interest in, and support for, his idea so that the 1894 Sorbonne Congress signaled the start of official planning to hold the first celebration in Athens in 1896. But what had inspired Coubertin to act when he did? Although no direct link has yet been found, it is likely that Coubertin was aware of Cooper's proposals and may even have seen the Pan-Britannic Festival as a potential rival to his Olympic Games. Coubertin had visited England on several occasions and was convinced that manly sport was the solid foundation of the British Empire as well as a large reason for the dominant position of Britain within the world during much of the 19th century. He suggested the revival of the Olympic Games as early as 1887 (Mandell, 1976) and was impressed with his visit to the Much Wenlock "Olympic" Games in 1890. Coubertin made a point of being familiar with athletic affairs in England.

J. Astley Cooper

In 1891, J. Astley Cooper began his far-reaching media campaign to promote what he broadly termed the "Pan Britannic and Anglo-Saxon Festival." He began cautiously with an anonymous article titled "Many Lands—One People" in the July 1891 edition of the periodical, *Greater Britain*, and then he awaited the response of the public, which was extensive and generally positive. In fact, the debate about Cooper's proposal remained a topic of discussion in newspapers and periodicals throughout the Empire until early in 1894. Cooper's suggestion that a periodic celebration of culture, industry, and athletics be established was widely supported in theory, but a major problem plagued the movement from the beginning: Who should be eligible to attend? There is no doubt that Cooper intended the athletic participants to be men of suitable background, "the flower of the Race" (Cooper, 1893), or, as Mandell (1976) described them, "white and well-born."

Where the participants would come from was another question. From the outset, Cooper included Americans in his plans, no doubt recognizing a rising political and athletic power in the world, but causing confusion because the name "Pan-Britannic" implied members of the British Empire alone. Canadian officials were less than pleased that their American neighbors were invited to join in; as one newspaper put it, "His [Mr. Cooper's] scheme may be either racial or imperial; it cannot be both without implying a menace to the Empire" (*The Gazette*, 1891). In an attempt to appease his critics, Cooper finally suggested that his scheme should have two sections: one, labeled "Britannic," open only to subjects of the Queen and Empress; and the second, "Anglo Saxon," a contest between the winners of the Britannic section and the best representatives of all-American (*Referee*, 1892).

The second major problem of the Pan-Britannic Festival concept, one which contributed directly to its demise, was the question of leadership. Cooper's initial reluctance to attach his name to the scheme may seem surprising, but it is evident that certain protocol had to be followed in British sport in the late 19th century, a time when competition was very much controlled by the upper class, and when small groups of men exerted tremendous power over the evolving sporting associations. Cooper clearly saw himself as the promoter of his ambitious scheme, not as its actual administrator.

One of the few examples of an offer of legitimate, practical support for the establishment of the Pan-Britannic Festival came, paradoxically, from the United States. A World's Fair was being held in Chicago in 1893, and J.E. Sullivan, Secretary of the Amateur Athletic Union of the United States, wrote to Cooper suggesting that he incorporate his Pan-Britannic idea into the celebration. Cooper politely but firmly refused the offer, stating that he believed the periodic gathering should be held in England, "the cradle of the English-speaking race" (*Referee*, 1892). This rebuff undoubtedly antagonized the Americans, and may, in fact, have paved the way for the positive reception of Coubertin at the Fair.

By the beginning of 1894, Cooper's proposal was losing momentum. It still labored under the absence of an official name and a lack of definite leadership. The fact that it was often referred to in the press as an "Olympic" festival indicated that public identification with the ancient Greek ideals was widespread, although not an entirely accurate connection in this case. Another suggestion, clearly defined and unmistakably led by Coubertin, benefited from this historical link.

Although Lucas (1981) calls the Sorbonne Congress "the Great Camouflage of 1894," by June of that year Coubertin had recruited enough tangible support for his Olympic Games to go ahead with definite plans for 1896. As Redmond (1981) has noted, there is no doubt that Coubertin's festival was perceived as more international and democratic in nature than Cooper's, but of equal importance is the fact that it was visible and apparently highly organized. Cooper was an imperialist dreamer who wrote extensively but did little in the practical promotion of his ideas; Coubertin was an active idealist who wrote, spoke, traveled, and spent money tirelessly in the pursuit of his vision.

Once Coubertin's plans were laid out in detail following the Sorbonne Congress, Cooper and his Pan-Britannic idea faded into the background, assisted and kept there by the modest but continuous celebration of the Olympic Games. Cooper (1908) referred directly to the 1908 Olympic Games in a somewhat bitter piece of writing as "nothing more nor less than a sideshow to the Franco-British Exhibition." In the same article, Cooper hinted that he might have been more than indirectly responsible for Coubertin's activities when he said,

"I do not know how far the widespread discussion in the Press of my English speaking Olympic Games scheme inspired Baron de Coubertin," but it is difficult to imagine the two men not knowing of each other's plans. The fact that Cooper's idea was first put into wide circulation, predating Coubertin's, has not been a well-advertised or closely examined aspect of Olympic history.

The Olympic Games

The London Olympic Games highlighted serious problems between Britain and the United States and may have provided some incentive to include an athletic meeting in the 1911 Festival of Empire celebrating the coronation of King George V. This festival lasted several months and included a modest sporting contest featuring male athletes from Australasia, Canada, and the United Kingdom competing in athletics, swimming, wrestling, and boxing. Following the conclusion of the Festival of Empire, serious planning was undertaken to enter a British team in the 1912 Olympic Games, a suggestion put forward by Richard Coombes of Australia and James Merrick of Canada. This proposal reflected the very ideal of Empire:

> The forces of the Mother Country and her children, the colonies, congregating on the shores of Britain to concentrate the forces of Empire, and then voyaging to the battle-ground of Stockholm to challenge in friendly warfare the best of the world's athletes. (*Referee*, 1911)

However, preparations could not be completed in less than a year, and the Empire countries competed individually in the 1912 Olympic Games. Less than 2 years after that, the Empire, along with much of the world, turned its attention to a different battleground and another, more deadly, brand of warfare.

The Olympic Games of the 1920s provided Empire officials with the opportunity to meet and discuss future plans for a separate competition. Track and field officials took the initiative and organized a series of post Olympic meetings between a British Empire team and the American Olympic team in 1920, 1924, and 1928. The increase in domination of sport by the Americans became more obvious as the decade wore on, and competition which excluded that powerful country was an attractive prospect for several Empire countries. Bobby Robinson, manager of the Canadian track and field team, came to the 1928 Games in Amsterdam with concrete promises of support for Empire countries which would compete in Hamilton, Canada, in 1930. The Olympic Games proved to be a crucial model for Robinson in the development of the concept and format of the British Empire Games, and he stressed that although the British Empire Games would have some similarities to the Olympic Games, the "family" atmosphere would make them unique.

The fact that the 1932 Summer Olympic Games were staged in Los Angeles proved to be a large stumbling block to establishing the British Empire Games. Many Empire countries were concerned about the expense of sending two teams to compete in North America in 2 years: Hamilton in 1930, and Los Angeles in 1932. But, over time, even the most skeptical Empire sportsmen were convinced by generous travel subsidies offered to assist countries in getting to Hamilton. The promise of free accommodation and food was also a good incentive, particularly in the midst of a world-wide economic depression.

The First British Empire Games opened in Hamilton, Canada, on August 16, 1930, with 11 countries marching in the official ceremony. Forty years after it was first publicly suggested, the Empire hosted its own multisport competition on a large scale, but the Empire had changed considerably during those 4 decades. Several dominions, including Australia and South Africa, had been federated and were much more independent of the mother country, and Britain's own status on the world scene had significantly altered. If the Empire had not actually declined in world power, at least it had been overtaken by other countries, and the British Empire Games provided a morale boost. The increasing success of the Americans in the Olympic Games was no doubt an additional incentive to initiate separate Empire competition. Perhaps of greatest importance to the British Empire Games, Bobby Robinson and the city of Hamilton were devoted planners and practical administrators, and they made a long-standing idea a reality.

Conclusion

This paper began with a brief examiniation of the connection between Pierre de Coubertin and J. Astley Cooper and their respective movements. Very little analysis of the circumstances surrounding the suggestion of a Pan-Britannic Festival has been undertaken. In addition, this significant movement has largely been overlooked by Olympic historians. The notion that the establishment of the modern Olympic Games may be linked in some way with Cooper's idea has been presented, and even though conclusions are still tentative, some may be put forward here. Although a direct connection between Cooper and Coubertin has yet to be discovered, their two proposed festivals did influence one another, and may, in fact, have been rival plans. As has been discussed, Coubertin had certain advantages in his favor—social position, money, and a freedom to travel and personally recruit support for his Games. Cooper, on the other hand, was a voluminous writer who appears to have done very little in a practical vein to advance his own cause. Their proposed sporting ventures took very different paths after 1893. Cooper's idea was almost forgotten prior to 1911 when the Festival of Empire included sport, and not until 1930 did a realization of a portion of his ideas take place, albeit dramatically altered after 40 years. Coubertin's Olympic Games have been successfully hosted 18 times since their inception and are a unique event of the 20th century.

An attempt has been made to show how the Olympic Games influenced the establishment of the British Empire Games. While these two sets of Games certainly are separate entities, an examination of their relationship has shown continuing interaction from 1891 to 1930 and invites further investigation from both Olympic and British Empire historians.

References

Anonymous (1891, July 15). Many Lands—one people: A criticism and a suggestion. *Greater Britain*, 458-462.

Cooper, J.A. (1893, July). The Pan-Britannic gathering. *The Nineteenth Century, XXXIV*, **197**, 81-93.

Cooper, J.A. (1908, June). Olympic Games: What has been done and what remains to be done. *The Nineteenth Century, LXIII, CCCLXXVI*, 1011-1021.

Eyquem, M.T. (1976). The founder of the modern games. In Lord Killanin, & J. Rodda (Eds.), *The Olympic Games: 80 Years of People, Events and Records* (pp. 138-143). New York: Collier Books.

The Gazette (1891, December 11). p. 4. Montreal, Canada.

Lucas J.A. (1981). The Genesis of the modern Olympic Games. In J. Segrave, & D. Chu (Eds.), *Olympism* (pp. 22-32). Champaign, IL: Human Kinetics.

MacAloon, J.J. (1981). *This great symbol: Pierre de Coubertin and the origins of the modern Olympic Games*. Chicago: University of Chicago Press.

Mandell, R.D. (1976). *The first modern Olympics*. Los Angeles: University of California Press.

Redmond, G. (1981). Prologue and transition: The "Pseudo-Olympics" of the nineteenth century. In J. Segrave & D. Chu (Eds.), *Olympism* (pp. 7-21). Champaign, IL: Human Kinetics.

The *Referee*. (1892, December 30). p. 3. Sydney, Australia.

The *Referee*. (1911, September 27). p. 9. Sydney, Australia.

16

Sport, Culture, and Postcolonial Relations: A Preliminary Analysis of the Commonwealth Games

Brian Stoddart
CANBERRA COLLEGE OF ADVANCED EDUCATION
BELCONNEN, AUSTRALIA

A considerable amount has been written on the connections between sport and international relations (Loy et al., 1978; Riordan, 1978; Trainor, 1978; Baka & Hoy, 1978; Espy, 1979; Strenk, 1979; Kanin, 1981; McNab, 1981; Whannel, 1983; and Mechikoff, 1984). As transnational sports gatherings such as the Olympic Games apparently become "more political," the output increased with an overwhelming emphasis on a search for ways in which the trend might be reversed. Upon reflection, much of the extant scholarship is superficial, both sociologically and politically, lacking in systemic significance because of its concern with sport as a culturally isolated issue. One indication of this low-level analysis is the fact that, in many cases, key terms such as *politics* and *international relations* remain remarkably obscure. What emerges, as a result, is a simplistic notion of sport having *symbolic* importance only; as the introduction to Lowe et al. (1978) states, sport possesses no *intrinsic* political value of its own. This restricted analysis makes it increasingly difficult to produce a deeper understanding of sport's growing international significance and complexity. What is required is further development of an understanding about the power of sport in relation to cultural capital and cultural values. These values, in themselves, exercise considerable political impact through the distribution of power resources as indicated by some recent studies (Gruneau, 1982; Gruneau, 1984; Whannel, 1983; Tomlinson & Whannel, 1984; Stoddardt, 1981; and Manning 1981).

This is an interpretive essay rather than purely empirical research; it is from a nonpolitical scientist as, indeed, is much else in the field, one of its deficiencies. By way of case study, it sets out to show some fundamental relationships between the Commonwealth Games and the international community which has constituted them. The argument begins from the proposition that the Games are postcolonial sports festivals which gather an array of countries with but one common bond—the heritage of a long-impotent, political, and cultural imperial power (Stoddart 1982b). Pardoxically, though, the Games show little sign of the atrophy which logically they should; on the contrary, they are growing. Although theoretically the every-4-year meetings should occasion considerable tension between quite different state systems, practically they do not. The area of investigation of these paradoxes lies in the culture of the Games. A natural starting point arises with two deficiencies in scholarship shared by the Games and international sports relations generally.

History of the Games

First, the Games lack a thoroughly analytical and interpretive account of their history. Material does exist, though not as much as might have been expected. What there is, remains largely descriptive and isolated from the cultural-political environment which produced the Games (*The Story of the British Empire Games* 1950; *Australia at the Commonwealth Games* 1978; *An Official History: The Friendly Games* 1978). As a result, or even because of that, the accounts are founded upon massive assumptions about the intricate social bases on which the Games were predicated. That in itself leads to the second principal deficiency—the basically undynamic quality of work on the Games which follows wider examples of superficial analysis such as Caldwell (1982). Such work lacks a vital systemic approach which would locate sport as a central institution rather than a peripheral one in the evolution of the Commonwealth. An associated point here has been an unwillingness at the theoretical level to recognize a distinction between functions of sport internationally.

At the risk of considerable oversimplification, an initial objective of international sport, including the Commonwealth Games, was to emphasize positive, creative relations between countries (Stoddard 1982a; McHenry 1980). At the root of the philosophy was an unstated assumption that sport lay completely outside the regular run of economic and political affairs. If relations in those mainstream areas were fragile, they might be strengthened through sport which was a nonthreatening commodity. (It is this view in which much of the current work remains—sport with no intrinsic power of its own.) However, along the way, sport was increasingly resorted to for negative, destructive purposes to express disapproval of or dissatisfaction with particular international actions or policies. Because much of the thinking has been caught in the positive mode, this negative use of sport internationally has been labeled as, "Bringing politics into sport."

Put simply, perceived positive acts such as cricket tours promoting goodwill, ping-pong diplomacy reopening Chinese-American relations, or sports stars bringing attention to small countries are all seen in an approving light;

in contrast, the *fedayeen's* use of the Munich Olympics to score a political point, the use of international sport to blockade a South African political regime, and boycotts of Olympic Games because of wider political circumstances are generally regarded in a disapproving way. This is a sterile approach which fails to see sport in the shape of any other bargaining resource at the international level: uranium, oil, military power, or cultural exchange. At the risk of being unkind, many analysts of sport and international relations have wanted to see a duality with sport as an important social and political institution, yet without the obligations which such importance would ordinarily attract. In the field of sport and politics, as in other areas of sports' analysis, romantic attachments to idealized visions of sport's construction have been inimical to intellectual progress.

As opening day of the 1982 Commonwealth Games in Brisbane demonstrated, such a dual position has become increasingly difficult to defend in the face of practice. In the main stadium, the Australian prime minister, along with many of his senior colleagues (and, for that matter, a number of his political opponents) were beginning a 2-week campaign of gaining as much public goodwill as possible from a visible association with leading popular athletes. A few weeks earlier, at a handing over of monies to Commonwealth Games officials, the prime minister dwelled on the political nature of the government's interest in sport, yet denied the rights of alternative groups to the same usage—"Nobody really wanted to hear much" about boycotts (Prime Minister of Australia, 1982). This duality flowed into opening day. While the prime minister was reaping his political harvest inside the stadium, outside it, the Queensland police, given special powers by legislation for the duration of the Games, began arresting aboriginal demonstrators protesting their lack of landrights from federal and state governments which had spent upwards of $40 million on the holding of an athletic festival (Preston, 1982). It was a perfect demonstration of the divided thinking about positive and negative usages of international events, a thinking which failed to consider the dynamic evolution of such events. In the case of the Commonwealth Games, the basic equation is quite simple: As the formal, political ties with the imperial power have declined, the informal cultural ones have been strengthened to maintain a strong power relationship and a particular vision of social order.

The Festival of the Empire

The forerunner of the present Commonwealth Games developed in the context of the Festival of Empire in 1911 to mark the coronation of King George V (Blanch & Jenes 1982; *Australian Foreign Affairs Record*, 1982). It was the apogee of the British Empire, but, importantly, the origins of its decline were also well set. Not only was George crowned King, he was affirmed as Emperor of India, the jewel in the crown where imperial servants were establishing a new government seat in New Delhi to run the country. Formal British political control seemed set even if some mild political concessions had been accorded Indian political hopefuls. Elsewhere in the Empire, the situation seemed similar: The Australian states had joined in federation with a reaffirmed, strong British connection in areas such as foreign policy and foreign loans; and the Union of South Africa had emerged from the Boer War, which at one stage had threatened an area of empire unity, but whose unity was now back in affirmed status. The Dominions Act had advanced the political tutelage of the majority white-power satellites in Canada, Australia, South Africa, and New Zealand; even so, the political links between them and the imperial power were scarcely weakened; the political links emerged naturally from a cultural homogeneity. In the Afro-Asian states British power seemed paramount; even though nascent political opposition movements did exist, they posed little threat to British control. The Festival of Empire concept of a sports gathering in 1911 was not repeated then before World War I, which in a number of ways, re-affirmed the basic political links between Britain and its acolytes. Sport did play a major role, however, in reestablishing postwar relations in the form of the interallied games which took place in 1919. The prevailing atmosphere there was to return to prewar normality in political relations even though a number of fundamental alterations in the imperial relationship had occurred, psychologically, if not formally.

It was significant, then, that the British Empire Games began in 1930 after a decade of quite fundamental political change in the empire's structure, though most accounts are noncontextual and miss the point (McLaughlin, 1978). Sym-bolically, the Statute of Westminister gave further freedom to the white-dominated Dominions even though some of them did not ratify it immediate-ly. The rise of political labor parties in these areas began to gather quickly through the 1920s, often associated with an antiimperial sentiment not infre-quently originating in a pro-Irish stance. By 1930, the economic patterns of empire were becoming dislocated, with Britain recalling empire loans to rescale her budget, and conferences reworking the nature of imperial trade with the client states becoming more strident in their demands. In Afro-Asia, nationalist movements seeking political concessions were in various stages of develop-ment, led by India where Gandhi's reaccession to the Congress party sparked the most serious challenge to imperial political authority yet—a mass civil disobedience movement which dragged on over 4 years. Other significant developments were emerging in east and southern Africa and in the Caribbean. The 1930 Games in Hamilton, Ontario, took place at a time of change in political relationships, and the importance of that was signaled in 1934 when London itself staged dominant power sought to reestablish an authority by way of culture in the field of sport which, in that context, was already subject to a contradictory heritage.

Dominant Powers and the Games

The events chosen for competition at the imperial sports gatherings, from the start emerged from what the dominant power saw as appropriate, and which had been exported to the major satellites from late 19th century Britain (Mangan, 1981). While they all sprang from 19th century ideals of prepara-tion for public and imperial service, they also carried a sense of being separated from political issues even though, in reality, it was far from the case. Around this point in the late 1920s to early 1930s, some nations were given formal recognition of their imperial endeavors to become test-playing cricket powers: That is, cultural power was beginning to bind where political authority was loosening. A vocabulary of imperial sporting standards began to arise in support of the growth, and transgressions of the standards was viewed very dimly (Sissons & Stoddart, 1984). This whole pattern continued in some ways in 1938 when Sydney ran the Games; it was the city's 150th anniversary of its foundation, and the celebration was as much of its cultural identity with Britain as of its nature as an independent center. Officials were quick to stress the emphasis on loyalty to the imperial ethos; there arose the concept of the Games as a family of nations meeting to share common ideals.

This emerged right from the start in 1930 when athletes took a formal oath asserting that they were, "Loyal subjects of His Majesty, the King Emperor" and competing, "For the honour of our Empire." If anything, however, the Second World War saw as much change to that ethos as the First World War had achieved, perhaps more. In 1941, Australia switched its war focus from the British to the American domain as a result of the Japanese thrust into the Pacific, and, as the change was formulated by a political labor leader, the impact upon imperialist thinking was even more solid than it might have been. The switch was more psychological than actual, in the public arena at least, but it did undercut the mental political dependence upon Britain. Cricket relations sought to quickly reestablish the prewar condition not with all that much success. Australia could scarcely have the Games again after 1938, but the staging of the first postwar Games in Auckland certainly centered them in the right geographical region as far as the move went to reset cultural identity. Even so, the 1950 meeting did see the beginnings of change: Nigeria was admitted to membership, the first of a flood of new states until the late 1960s.

The basis for that was the flowering of independence movements throughout Africa and Asia, beginning with India and Pakistan in 1947, and culminating in the African and Caribbean changes of the 1960s. Along the way, though, the movements were generally peaceful: The British were stunned by the savagery of Hindu-Muslim conflict on the Indian subcontinent; the Mau Mau revolution of the Kikuyu in Kenya; and the inroads of communism which led to the Malayan emergency of the 1950s. Beyond that, however, the political shapes taken by the new states were not uniformly those which might have been wished for by the former imperial power. While India became the world's largest democracy, other states showed tendencies toward one-party systems at best and Marxist aspirations at worst. Starting from the psychological blow of losing India, the British empire lost its political authority remarkably quickly. In the Games sense, the end of that process was marked with their holding the games in Kingston, Jamaica, in 1966, still the only nondeveloped nation to stage them. Between that time and 1950, however, a significant change began. By 1954, there was a new monarch whose accession to the throne had a sports-cultural mark, the dying empire's conquering of Mount Everest in the form of New Zealand's Edmund Hilary and Nepal's Tenzing Norgay. By 1958, the new postcolonial phase of cultural relations saw the end of South Africa as a Games competitor, the logical outcome to pressures built as early as 1934 when Johannesburg lost the event because of South African domestic policies. With the Jamaica Games came the dropping of the word "Empire" from the governing body's title, a significant alteration.

By 1966, the major face of the British decolonization process was ended, and a new postcolonial phase had begun. The key question, of course, was how colonial relationships might be carried into that new phase in the absence of the overarching political authority which had existed earlier. The answer lies, essentially, in an interpretation of the cultural power of which the Commonwealth Games were a major part—ritual and communication have been two central agencies by which the imperial ethos has survived much longer into the postcolonial age than might have been anticipated.

Royalty and the Games

Royalty has been at the heart of the Games with Queen Elizabeth II, particularly, placing great stress on the meetings as a central occasion for the family of nations with otherwise little in common. The elaborate nature of the delivering of the Queen's message by way of runner, with the last bearer handing the message to its announcer in the midst of a large crowd and Commonwealth representatives, is as much cultural communication as the exchange of pure information. Linguistically, the message itself invariably refers to the ideals, attitudes, conventions, and values of a past political authority rather than postcolonial realities. It was significant that in 1958 the Queen chose the occasion of the Cardiff Games to announce that her eldest son would become Prince of Wales, formal heir to the throne. Since then, he has been a central figure in a number of Games, a careful grooming for monarchical continuity. Nor does the ritual stop there. Key meetings, such as that of the 1982 Commonwealth Games Federation gathering to consider New Zealand's future participation prospects, are generally held in London, symbolic center of the old empire. The Games flag itself, of a Crown surrounded by chained satellites, is reminiscent of the old order, and in Brisbane, the military involvement in proceedings recalled the deterrent presence of British forces in many earlier colonial settings. In fact, as the Games have developed, the ritual aspects based upon imperial memories have multiplied, a direct relationship between cultural power and the decline of formal direct authority as a number of sources both theoretically and directly suggest (Real 1975; *The Story of the British Empire Games* 1950; *Australia at the Commonwealth Games* 1978). The Games are a central feature of postcolonial continuity and are given a credibility, which, currently, far outweighs their importance in purely athletic terms, It is not that the Games have become more or less political; it is just that the constituted circumstances of their political context have altered substantially. The emphasis upon communication confirms that.

Cultural and Economic Dependency

For the 1982 Games, the official state broadcaster, the then Australian Broadcasting Commission, was allocated $20 million by the federal government for coverage by television and radio. This use of funds has been found in other Games' settings and has been indicative of the cultural significance afforded to the event. It has been a simple extension of the financial support given by governments in recent times out of all apparent proportion to the athletic value of the meetings, as indicated by Baka and Hoy (1978). Nor has that expenditure been held there; the Australian government used the 1982 venue to announce an athletic scholarship scheme to enable attendance by developing Commonwealth nations' athletes at the Australian Institute of Sport. This in itself was a natural extension of the Commonwealth youth and economic development programs which arose to replace the former political connections. That is, cultural and economic dependency had succeeded formal political subordination.

In this general area, complex developments have occurred since 1966, and most of them proved difficult to resolve, both for the dominant, cultural force and for its former colonial states. Generally, the problem runs this way: For Britain and its major supporters, the increasing decolonization process created difficulties of controlling the evolution of the Commonwealth Games machine. For African and Asian states, the difficulties concerned their very participation, particularly if their new political forms were reformist rather than conservative. Put crudely, as by the Marxist-Leninist Ugandan intellectual, Dan Nabudere (1979), the cultural practices of the imperial bourgeoisie and their successors in independence simply reflected the needs of the colonial state. Put more subtly by Patrick Marnham (1980) and Orlando Patterson (1969) to name two, so long as people in those developing nations judge their progress in all areas against the standards of the former cultural power, they will remain in a dependent condition—and sport is not exempt from that generality. In fact, the Commonwealth Games perpetuate that.

In 1982, as earlier, athletes from developing nations arrived at the Games to swim in pools twice as long as those to which they were accustomed, to ride untried racing cycles on curved and banked tracks never previously encountered, or to run on artificial surfaces not available in their home countries. As suggested in a perhaps overstated way by Hart Cantelon (1982), those who have succeeded athletically in the developing nations have also been exposed to other aspects of the dominant culture imbibed from the imperial past. Be that as it may, struggling nations such as the Solomon Islands, Kiribati, and Papua-New Guinea, to take the South Pacific examples, are spending considerable proportions of scarce funds to attempt to match forces with those of the more affluent members of an artificial Commonwealth (*Australian Foreign Affairs Record*, 1978).

Conclusion

The complicated postcolonial condition helps explain the very curious history of the Commonwealth's position on South Africa (Archer & Bouillon, 1982; Tatz, 1983). What is interesting about it is not so much the damage inflicted upon South African sport by postcolonial states (which might be expected to be hostile toward the race relations conditions of southern Africa) as the very lack of a powerful front and, indeed, the weakening resolve. While New Zealand has made no secret of its attitudes about wanting to reciprocate sport with South Africa, and Australian sports officials adopt much the same attitude, African and Asian states have been much more docile on the issue in the Commonwealth setting than they have more widely. The reason, basically, is that the shared culture of sport as transcending other differences is a very strong postcolonial artifact in the Commonwealth context. Cricket bolsters that, incidentally. For a while, the powerful state of West India cricket allowed its government's antiapartheid stand to have some influence, but then some players went to South Africa taking the "sport-is-outside-politics" line, and thereby weakened the official position. Marnham and Patterson would see the genesis of that only too clearly in the inherited cultural practices of a decline, imperial political power. Two important spinoffs from this are worth mentioning because, like so much else about the Commonwealth Games, they have wider application.

First, the positions of governments on this cultural unity matter are becoming less tenable as the emphasis upon winning becomes greater. It is no longer easy to sustain the myth that to compete in the friendly family games is, in itself, a worthy objective. As the Australian prime minister put it in 1982, Australians want to be in the "business" of winning, not just competing. For that reason, vast amounts of public money are being poured into top-level sport. For a number of the major Commonwealth powers, the problem now is to run a modern line of sport development in an anachronistic, largely uncompetitive, postcolonial setting. It is almost as difficult for them as it is for most of the new African and Asian nations.

Second, the athletes remain largely ignorant about the evolved social and political context in which they find themselves. They fail to see that their battles with officialdom are not always the result of simple obstinacy and blind faith in outmoded rules; frequently, the disputes arise from the officials' faith in a system based upon a false concept of shared views. One area where that has become increasingly complex in recent years has been the emergence of the black athlete whose heritage is in the former empire in areas such as Britain and Canada. The black athlete's sports' fame and place in the sporting family of nations has not always been matched by a general acceptability into and or success in the host nation (Cashmore, 1982).

This has been, fundamentally, part of the working out of former relationship patterns after the demise of the dominant political and economic power. As Britain reordered it defense arrangements to west of the Suez Canal by the early 1970s and reviewed its immigration policies following the influx of West Indian and East African peoples of imperial descent in the late 1960s and early 1970s, the Commonwealth Games became a significant force in attempting to mantain unity in a former colonial empire. Sport, in that sense, will never be recognized in its full political strength as long as it is abstracted from its historical and cultural context. For that reason, the symbolic removal of the word "Empire" from the organizing body's title in 1966 and the further disappearance of the word "British" by 1974 did not signify concessions of political equality so much as the fully fledged reliance upon the cultural power of the Games. In 1982, then, it must have been most satisfying for the organizers of this cultural imperialism to hear the cheers reserved by the Brisbane crowd for the Falkland Islands' participants in the Brisbane Games: Two shooters come from the war with Argentina in which most Commonwealth countries pledged support for Britain even though there were no political grounds for doing so. The bonds of empire had definitely not disappeared along with the simple trappings of formal authority.

References

An official history: The friendly games (1978). Edmonton, C.G.F.

Archer, R. & Bouillon, A. (1982). *The South African game: Sport and racism.* London: Zed.

Australia at the Commonwealth Games, 1911-1978: Edmonton (1978). Sydney: Vaucluse.

Australian Foreign Affairs Record (1982). **53**, 7.

Baka, R. & Hoy, D. (1978). Political aspects of Canadian participation in the Commonwealth Games. *CAPHER Journal,* **44**, 4.

Blanch, J. & Jenes, P. (1982). *Australia's complete history at the Commonwealth Games.* Sydney: Blanch.

Caldwell, G. (1982). International sport and national identity. *International Social Science Journal,* **92**, (XXIV, 2).

Cantelon, H. (1982). The reproductive and transformative potential of sport: Comparative analyses utilizing the Weberian concepts of domination and rationalization. In J.C. Pooley and C.A. Pooley (Eds.), *Proceedings of the Second International Seminar on Comparative Physical Education and Sport.* Halifax: Dalhousie.

Cashmore, E. (1982). *Black Sportsmen.* London: RKP.

Espy, R. (1979). *The politics of the Olympic Games.* Berkeley: University of California Press.

Gruneau, R. (1982). Sport and the debate on the state. In H. Cantelon and R. Gruneau (Eds.), *Sport, culture and the modern state.* Toronto: University of Toronto Press.

Gruneau, R. (1983). *Class, sports and social development.* Amherst: University of Massachussetts Press.

Kanin, D. (1981). *A political history of the Olympic Games.* Boulder: Westview.

Lowe, B. et al. (1978) *Sport and international relations.* Champaign, IL: Stipes.

Loy, J. et al. (1978) *Sport and social systems: A guide to the analysis, problems and literature.* Reading MA: Addison-Wesley.

McHenry, D. (1980). The use of sports in policy implementation: The case of Tanzania. *Journal of Modern African Studies,* **18**, 2.

McLaughlin, M. (1978). Hamilton hosts the first British Empire Games—August 23 to August 30, 1930. *CAPHER Journal,* **44**, 4.

McNab, T. (1981). The international scene. In B. Tulloh (Ed.), *Biosocial aspects of sport.* London: Galton.

Mangan, J.A. (1981). *Athleticism in the Victorian and Edwardian public school: The rise of an educational ideology.* Cambridge: Cambridge University Press.

Manning, F. (1981). Celebrating cricket: The symbolic construction of Caribbean politics. *American Ethnologist,* **8**, 3.

Marnham, P. (1980). *Dispatches from Africa.* London: Cape.

Mechikoff, R. (1984). The Olympic Games: Sports as international politics. *JOPHER,* **55**, 3.

Nabudere, D. (1979). *Essays on the theory and practice of Marxism.* London: Onyx.

Patterson, O. (1969). The ritual of cricket. *Jamaica Journal,* **3**, 1.

Preston, N. (1982). The Commonwealth Games: An area for social conflict. *Social Alternatives,* **2**, 4.

Prime Minister of Australia. (1982, July 24). *Media release.*

Real, M. (1975). Super bowl: Mythic spectacle. *Journal of Communication,* **25**, 1.

Riordan, J. (Ed.). (1978). *Sport under communism.* Canberra: Australian National University Press.

Sissons, R. & Stoddart, B. (1984). *Cricket and empire: The 1932-33 bodyline tour of Australia.* London: Allen and Unwin.

Strenk, A. (1979). What price victory? The world of international sport and politics. *Annals of the American Academy of Political and Social Science,* 445.

Stoddart, B. (1981). Sport and society, 1890-1940: A foray. In C.T. Stannage (Ed.), *A New History of Western Australia.* Perth: University of Western Australia Press.

Stoddart, B. (1982a, September 3). How sport became a political weapon. *Age.*

Stoddart, B. (1982b, October 14). Why the empire's gold has a hallow ring. *Age.*

Tatz, C. (1983). Sport in South Africa. *Australian Quarterly,* **55**, 4.

The story of the British Empire Games (1950). Auckland: BEGMC.

Tomlinson, A. & Whannel, G. (1984). *Five ring circus.* London: Pluto.

Trainor, L. (1978). The primacy of internal policy: National, sport and external relations, 1975-78. *Political Science,* **30**, 2.

Whannel, G. (1983). *Blowing the whistle: The politics of sport.* London: Pluto.

PART III

III

Politics and the Olympic Games

SECTION A
Political Aspects of Individual Olympic Games: 1932, 1976, 1980, and 1984

17

The Olympic Games of Los Angeles 1932, as Seen by the Nationalist and Racial Ideology

Hajo Bernett
SPORTWISSENSCHAFTLICHES INSTITUT DER UNIVERSITAT BONN
FEDERAL REPUBLIC OF GERMANY

The Political Meaning of Sport of the German Expedition

The return of the Germans into the Olympic arena after World War I resulted in an unexpected triumph: They emerged as the second best team from the fights of Amsterdam. The 1928 success of the German sport leadership was the basis of winning the International Olympic Committee (IOC) over to awarding the Games of 1936 to Berlin and Garmisch. From this point of view, the participation in the Olympic Games of 1932 was propagated as a test and national question of prestige.

But the world economic crisis set sharp boundaries to the proof of the achievements. Facing 5 million unemployed people, Olympic sport appeared a luxury. Nevertheless, it was possible to win the goodwill of the German president and the political support of the chancellor. After Hindenburg had shown his sympathy, Chancellor Bruning addressed a letter to Theodor Lewald, the President of the German Olympic Committee, which acknowledged the sport as a "support of relations of friendship between the nations."[1] The German Chancellor welcomed the participation of the German sport youth and expressed the hope that they would form "new ties of feelings of friendship in a competition with the American youth." With the publication of this let-

---

[1] "Zeitspiegel der Leibesübungen." In *Die Leibesübungen* 1932, Nr. 4, 177.

ter, Lewald underlined the political type of mandate. In the name of the Olympic Committee, he explained that Los Angeles was not supposed to be simply a sportive event. Rather, people will have to "recognize the effect on foreign affairs" and to "behave themselves according to the rules of foreign politics." Irritated, the editorial staff of the German journal of sport teachers reported about the sports leadership's new way of seeing itself: "Taking part in the Olympic Games is a political affair."[2]

Carl Diem, the secretary-general of both the Deutscher Reichsausschuß für Leibesübungen (DRA) and the organization committee of 1936, was the sovereign organizer of the Olympic expedition. In his "war diary" from 1932, he explained what he meant by sport politics. To him, "The trip to Los Angeles did not only go with sport politics, but also with German politics." Therefore, the meeting with people of German origin belonged to the program of the Olympic expedition. Diem hoped to "heighten the belief of the world in our message"[3] by Olympic triumphs.

The Confrontation With the Black Race

The meeting of sportsmen with the black race became a problem which, for the Germans, implied political as well as ideological coherence. The prejudice of racial predominance was the legacy of colonial times. According to this stereotype, the black man was regarded as inferior and stupid but good-natured. That is why indignation was high when the French lowered themselves to use black troops in World War II. This contempt changed into hatred when the Africans were put up as an occupying power after the Allied victory. Joseph Goebbels, who used a Renish party paper as mouthpiece of the National Socialist racism,[4] was the spokesman of this burst of hatred. Not even Carl Diem was immune to racial prejudices. When the Olympic Games at Paris in 1924 were near, he declared the participation of Germany to be preposterous. "Where is the German who wants to go to a cosmopolitan celebration to Paris while Negroes with French uniforms are standing along the German Rhine?"[5]

This "international Judaism" meant the Semites were the Nationalist Socialists' real concept of an enemy. According to their racial doctrine, though, the Semites were related to the Hamites, or North African tribes; thus the association emerged that Jews and Negroes were the embodiment of human inferiority. Bruno Malitz, an athlete and SA man, formulated the following with the intention of making internationalism in sport contemptible: "French people, Belgians, 'Pollacken' and Jewish Negroes all started on German cinder tracks, played on German football grounds and swam in German swimming

---

[2] "Beteiligung an den Olympischen Spielen ist eine politische Angelegenheit!" In *Die Leibesübungen* 1932, Nr. 6, 274.

[3] "Ergebnis von Los Angeles." In Diem C.: *Olympische Flamme. Das Buch vom Sport.* Vol. I. Berlin 1942, 386.

[4] Lochner, L.P. (Ed.): *Goebbels Tagebücher.* Zürich 1948, 15.

[5] Diem, C.: *Sport ist Kampf.* Berlin 1923, 35.

stadiums.''[6] After the Games in Los Angeles, an anti-Olympic reflection was published in the ''Nationalsozialistische Monatshefte'' and reprinted in the ''Angriff'' which was edited by Goebbels. The author attacked the ''democratic neglection of all differences in worth between nations and races.'' He accused Americans of having sent the ''still innocent black people'' to fight against the white athletes. The crowd ''was enthusiastically celebrating their black natives of the country as the winners over the white races, without thinking that perhaps a time is not too far away when the nations of the white races pay dearly for this inconsistency.''[7]

In this, the terrifying vision was spread that the ''black auxiliary troops'' of the United States, as they were contemptuously called, will stand up one day for a last ''worldwide fight between the nations of the white race and the primitive people.''[8]

A German Rescues the ''Honor of the Whites''

The public expected new Olympic medals, especially from the track and field athletes, after the success at Amsterdam. In Los Angeles, the Americans dominated because their black athletes achieved phenomenal results. In contrast to this, the German athletes were behind in expectations. While the bourgeoisie sports press got over the disappointment, the National Socialist *Westdeutscher Beobachter* expressed its dissatisfaction as follows:

> Black day for Germany's athletes (August 4, 1932).
> Germans expectations are falling (August 5, 1932).
> Again and again no success for Germany (August 6, 1932).
> Another expectation destroyed (August 8, 1932).

But then followed an event which amply compensated the inwardly injured. The German sprint champion, Arthur Jonath, won the bronze medal in the 100-meter race. The Renish Nazi paper described this sporting success as a racially great feat: ''Jonath rescued the honor of the white race.''[9] This was not only just a way of speaking, but conviction, because ''honor'' was one central conception of the National Socialists' philosophy of life. From this point of view, the German sprint champion had not only demonstrated the reputation of German sports but also the prestige of the white race which had been pressured by the Negroes. The winners of the Olympic final, however, were the black Americans, Eddie Tolan and Ralph Metcalfe. The popular Eddie was awarded the victory only after the photofinish. Both Tolan and Metcalfe made their sporting careers as college students.[10] Their record performances

---

[6] Malitz, B.: *Die Leibesübungen in der nationalsozialistischen Idee*. München 1934, 21.

[7] Haller, G: ''Der olympische Gedanke.'' In *Nationalsozialistische Monatshefte* 1932, Nr. 30, 392. Shortened Reprint in *Der Angriff* 8.9. 1932.

[8] Ibid. 393.

[9] *Westdeutscher Beobachter* (Köln), 3. - 8.8. 1932.

[10] Pierro, A.A.: ''A history of professional preparation in physical education in selected negroe colleges and universities to 1958.'' In Zeigler, E.F. (Ed.), *A history of physical education and sports in the United States and Canada*. Champaign, IL. 1975, Ch. 19.

symbolized the entrance of black sportsmen into the establishment; therefore, this victory was celebrated as a milestone within the process of racial emancipation. "The performances of Eddie Tolan and Ralph Metcalfe were inspiring to Negro leaders who praised athletics to their people as one of the few "open" activities in which submerged people could manifest superiority."[11]

While on one hand, American society became more and more open to the process of social integration of racial minorities, the acceptance of Negroes, on the other hand, was denounced as a step into the fall of culture by the National Socialist propaganda. Thus the National Socialist philosophy of life showed its reactionary, anachronistic character even in sport politics.

Olympic Games at Berlin Without Black Athletes?

The "national" thinking people could not stop thinking about successful black athletes. According to their ideas, such a triumph as 1932 should not be repeated at Berlin. The Turnerführer, Edmund Neuendorff, who had been a member of the NSDAP since 1932, explained in the name of the younger generation, that the honor of the race prevented German sportsmen from "running a race with Negroes and colored people of every shade."[12] The protest of the "national" Turner outside the Reich was even stronger. The Austrian Deutscher Turnerbund, which had separated from the liberal Deutsche Turnerschaft in 1889 for racial reasons, welcomed the National Socialist revolution. They expected the principle of "racial purity" to gain acceptance in sports as well. At Vienna, the ideological fanatics urged the German government not to permit Olympic Games on German ground in 1936 because they still had not overcome the defeat of World War II and felt that Olympism, as a "French invention," should not gain a foothold in Germany. Another irrational impression was even more deeply rooted than this chauvinistic argument, and that the "shameful" moment in 1932 "when a Negro with wooly hair and thick lips defeated the German sprinter champion."[13] The National Socialists who shared this primitive racism were not willing to give up their Olympic strategy on foreign affairs for an ideological principle, and thus the Austrian Turnerführer were shamefully disappointed.

Also, the leadership of the Sudeten-German Turner was unable to realize that the constellation of Los Angeles could be repeated in Berlin, the Capital of Reich. Nevertheless, the Deutsche Turnverband that in 1919 was forced by Czechoslovakia to separate from the Austrian alliance, held to the principle of "racial purity." The idea that a German sportsman could be willing to do the same as in Los Angeles seemed unbearable because that would mean "to fight for the same award with colored people of every shade from European Semites and Asian Mongoles to African and American Negroes."[14]

The Sudeten-German Turnerführer, who were totally prejudiced in the

[11]Mandell, R.: *The Nazi Olympics*. New York 1971, 223.

[12]Neuendorff, E.: "Wettkampf gegen Neger." In *Die Schar* 1933, Nr. 2, 30.

[13]"Kein Olympia in Berlin." In *Bundesturnzeitung* 1933, Nr. 13, 169.

[14]"Die Olympischen Spiele 1936 wirklich in Berlin?" In *Turnzeitung des Deutschen Turnverbandes* 1932, Nr. 21, 335.

ideology of Friedrich Ludwig Jahns "Volkserziehung," warned of a repetition of the "Rassenschande" at Los Angeles.

> The racial blame is the same as in Los Angeles no matter whether it's a Negro, an Oriental or a German Jew who is the first recordbreaker to be celebrated on German ground as the best of his perhaps even German country.[15]

In the beginning, the precept of "racial purity" was directed towards Judaism, but now the first Olympic Games on German ground were near; and this "ground" was believed to be sacred ground which should not be desecrated by the triumph of foreign races. Here each defeat of "Aryan" sportsmen should be regarded as "Rassenschande." The bigoted decision of the foreign Germans met at this point with the criminalization of all "non-Aryan" by the National Socialists. This nonhuman thinking can be explained by the political situation of the Sudeten Germans who had to struggle under pressure for their "Volkstum."

The editorial staff of the *Völkischer Beobachter*, the "Kampfblatt" of the National Socialist movement, was dominated by the same views. The sports editors of the *VB* had close relations with the Deutscher Turnerbund at Vienna and supported the same sports political principles; therefore the same consequences were drawn out of the experiences of Los Angeles and the same demands arose. "Negroes have no business being at the Olympics." The *VB* implied that the American had used those "second class people" only to win points. Second-class people, however, have no business getting mixed up in a "competition between free men." "The next Olympic Games take place in 1936 at Berlin. Let's hope the responsible men know about their duties. The black people must be excluded, that's what we demand."[16] Although the editors were not national Socialists, this demand was even quoted in the specialist journal of the German sport teachers. The effect from Los Angeles was felt as an emotional pressure. "It weighs not only upon the mind of the Americans that some important competition had been won by representatives of the black race."[17]

But the "responsible men" who had been appealed to by the *Völkischer Beobachter* knew perfectly about their duties. They had to obey the rules of the IOC, and they even had to affirm that no Jewish athlete would be excluded. The Negro problem fell to the background in view of the serious collisions with the National Socialist principles. At any rate, it did not influence the reflections of the German Olympic officials.

In this context, the question of whether the appearance of black athletes at Berlin went off without conflicts is of certain interest, and it can clearly be answered positively. The results of the black athletes were not diminished by anyone, not even by the party press which had been chained up by Goebbels. Not even Hitler can be accused of having ignored the successes of the black people.[18] Jesse Owens even became the favorite of the crowd at Berlin.

---

[15]Ibid.

[16]"Neger haben auf der Olympiade nichts zu suchen." In *Völkischer Beobachter* (Berlin), 19.8. 1932.

[17]"Auswirkungen der Olympischen Spiele in Deutschland." In *Die Leibesübungen* 1932, Nr. 9, 418.

[18]See Mandell, R.: *The Nazi Olympics*. New York 1971, 227.

The National Socialist propaganda for the Olympics worked trouble-free.[19] Outside Berlin and Garmisch, the racial patterns of thought rested in force. When in 1936, Max Schmeling defeated the "brown bomber," Joe Louis was lowered to the level of a stupid and crafty "nigger"[20] with bulging muscles by the radio announcer.

The Political Right Demands More Fighting Spirit

After the surprising comeback of the German athletes at Amsterdam, public expectations rose too high, and the failure of Los Angeles injured the national ambition. The example of the fencer Helene Mayer shows how the reproaches against the German team hurt some athletes to the quick. Although the Olympic champion of 1928 reached the final and took fifth place, this was called an "unexpected defeat" and the "greatest disappointment."[21] Helene Mayer reacted with bitter words on the unfair criticism.

> If you are defeated only once immediately all hell's been let loose and people come out of their holes like rats and attack their victims. . .And after all that you are still to believe in the noble mission of sport.[22]

The reproaches of the political Right were directed, not against individuals, but against the leaders of German sport. This event may seem a little unusual, but the year 1932 took place against the background of National Socialist ideology of sports. At first the *Völkischer Beobachter* had shelved the political judgement and had reported objectively about Los Angeles. The triumph of the "Reichstagswahl" on July 31, though, made the National Socialists aware of a new power what was also reflected by sport politics. The NSDAP got 13.7 million votes, which doubled their seats in the Reichstag, and with this had switched the points to their takeover. A campaign against those responsible for Olympic sport was aroused by the feeling of growing political superiority, and the disappointment of Los Angeles brought about sport political signals that would herald a new era of fighting spirit. The *Völkischer Beobachter* published an article on principles under the significant headline "Fighting spirit brings the decision not only skills do" the day before the final Olympic act. This simplifying formula was exactly in accordance with the principle of the National Socialist philosophy of life. It was obviously regarded as being sufficient for a description of the situation of German sport. "The German sportman is unable to fight that means he is extremely seldom able. . .to give his best. That's the fact German sport suffers from." The active participants are in no way responsible.

---

[19]See Teichler, H.J.: "Berlin 1936—ein Sieg der NS-Propaganda?" In *Stadion* 1976, Nr. 2, 265-306.

[20]"Schmelings Sieg ein deutscher Sieg." Screen Record 1936. Bundesarchiv Koblenz.

[21]Reemtsma Cigarettenfabriken (Ed.), *Die Olympischen Spiele in Los Angeles* 1932. Altona-Bahrenfeld 1932, 95.

[22]Mayer, H.: Diary 1932, in Possession of Ludwig Ernst Mayer, Frankfurt.

Entirely our sport leaders are to blame for this because they think it is their task to see the only luck of modern competition in intellect, skill and tactics. In contrast to this the American athletes are educated 'to fight in sport.' Gemany can successfully compete with each nation, if we put more emphasis on the 'aspect of fighting.' The nation of 'only poets and philosophers' belongs to the past. The maxim of the 20th century is fighting especially even in sport.[23]

This motto of fighting is bound by tradition in both theory and practice of German sport. It is rooted in imperialistic tendencies but also in the wish of national revival after the defeat of World War I. The idea of fighting got a new political dimension by the social Darwinism of the National Socialists. The discrimination of intellectuality in sport is bound by tradition: The typical antiintellectuality of the National Socialists, though, gave new decisiveness to the principle of fighting.

The campaign was picked up by the party press and was brought into the provinces. Thus the *Westdeutscher Beobachter* published the article from the *VB* under the headline, "lack of fighting spirit" and added the subtitle, "The reasons for the German defeat at Los Angeles."[24] The paper, which had been founded and edited by Robert Ley, the NSDAP Gauleiter, commented on the Olympic disappointment with a demand for "a training of young people for fighting-sport-discipline." "Bourgeoise principles of sports" were declared unsuitable because "only the fighter inside the German man can last."[25] By the "bourgeoise sporting spirit," the propagandists of the Nationalist Socialist revolution obviously meant the increase of intellectuality and rationality in German competitive sport. This progressive shaping of the international sport did not fulfill the National Socialist ideal of a "political soldier"; therefore the heavy criticism of the National Socialists finally turned towards the (putative!) "unpolitical" understanding of sport by the bourgeoise associations.[26] Furthermore, the ignoring of women in this argument is characteristic of the masculine-voluntary character of the National Socialist doctrine.

An article in the paper of the Völkische association, *Der Werwolf*, attacked Los Angeles and "unpolitical" sport. Herbert Blank (whose pseudonym is Weigand von Miltenberg)[27] and who belonged to the circle around the reform National Socialist, Otto Strasser, inveighed against the "caboodle of the Olympic Games" and insinuated that the "liberalist-capitalist-sport" had been politically indifferent. "Especially this perverted idea of being unpolitical is the reason for our Olympic defeats." To put an end to the "internationally poisoned" Olympic sport, it should be replaced in Germany by national "Wehrsport."[28]

The party press prepared again to retaliate after the attacked sport leaders had defended themselves with the aid of the bourgeoise sport press. The

---

[23]"Kampfgeist, nicht Technik allein entscheidet." In *Völkischer Beobachter* (Berlin), 13.8. 1932.

[24]"Mangelnder Kampfgeist." In *Westdeutscher Beobachter* (Köln), 16.8. 1932.

[25]"Jugendliche Kampf-Schulung." In *Westdeutscher Beobachter* (Köln), 9.8. 1932.

[26]See the Sources and Comments in Bernett, H. (Ed.), *Der Sport im Kreuzfeuer der Kritik. Kritische Texte aus loo Jahren deutscher Sportgeschichte.* Schorndorf 1982, 211-230.

[27]Fest, J.C.: *Hitler. Eine Biographie.* Frankfurt/Berlin/Wien 1974[6.], 456, Note 120.

[28]Quoted in: *Sportpolitische Rundschau* 1932, Nr. 10, 156.

National Socialist Berlin newspaper, *Der Angriff*, spoke about "impudence" and "contortions" to the veiled "fiasco" of Los Angeles. They demanded the resignation of the sport leaders and threatened, "If it is not the sporting association, which discharges its 'great lords' then the people will do it."[29]

Half a year later, the National Socialist press referred to this threat. Meanwhile the "national uprising" had created a new power structure in the (abused!) name of the nation. Both *Der Angriff* and the *VB* demanded on April 1, 1933, "New men to the front." This attempt, however, was only a partial success because the National Socialist leadership of the nation had made the decision for a new Olympic strategy, and that is the reason why the "great lords" could still not be spared.

The Appreciation of the Olympic Games at Los Angeles

This should not give the impression that the public, in general, reacted in a disappointed, bitter way to the poor performances of the German athletes at Los Angeles. Rather it must be confirmed that the politically neutral daily press did justice to the special significance of the Olympic Games of 1932. An excerpt from press commentaries may clarify these facts. Looking back, the *Dusseldorfer Nachrichten* confirms that Germany had "left much to be desired" at Los Angeles, but they emphasized, respectfully, that the German athletes "accepted the rules of a fair play and that their sportsmanship and their attitude towards victory and defeat had been given an honorable mention."[30] The *Deutsche Allgemeine Zeitung* also admitted that the expected successes failed to materialize, but the paper compensated this impression for the appreciation "that the sporting manner of all our people had been satisfying in every respect" and that they had done justice to the Olympic idea.[31] The *Deutsche Reichszeitung* totally abstained from criticizing the German team. It drew this conclusion under the impression of a "splendid final ceremony . . .It will not be easy to surpass"[32] this Olympic celebration. A surprising positive report must be given of the Deutsche Turnerschaft, which according to Carl Diem, "held eternal resistance against the Olympic work."[33] After the end of the X Olympic Games, there were no signs of "national" resentment by the gymnasts left. Obviously, they have had the opportunity to correct their negative judgement of "Americanism." Two summarizing reports in the *Deutsche Turnzeitung* were full of recognition toward the organizational and cultural performance of the Americans.[34] The official *Jahrbuch der*

---

[29]"Die schuldigen Sportführer verteidigen sich." In *Der Angriff* (Berlin), 7.9. 1932.

[30]"Abschied von Los Angeles." In *Düsseldorfer Nachrichten*, 15.8. 1932.

[31]"Rückblick auf Los Angeles." In *Deutsche Allgemeine Zeitung* (Berlin), 18.8. 1932.

[32]"Der Schlußakt in Los Angeles." In *Deutsche Reichszeitung* (Bonn), 16.8. 1932.

[33]Diem, C.: *Ein Leben für den Sport.* Erinnerungen aus dem Nachlaß. Ratingen/Kastellaun/Düsseldorf 1974, 117.

[34]"Rückschau auf Los Angeles." In *Deutsche Turnzeitung*, 27.9. 1932, 902-905; "Deutschland auf den Olympischen Spielen 1932." In *Deutsche Turnzeitung*, 11.10. 1932, 945-948.

Turnkunst also drew an unimpeachable general picture.[35] The conservative *Amerikanische Turnzeitung*, though, expressed certain reservations toward the attitude that "a record run of 100 meters at Los Angeles can be considered as a great gain to civilization." Nevertheless, it applauded the great sportive triumph of the American athletes. They "rolled up a margin over the rest of the world" and "stowed away the biggest share of triumphs and points."[36]

By the gymnasts's movement of millions giving up the aversion, nothing was more standing in the way of a positive judgement of the X Olympic Games. Thus, standard works about the history of the Olympic movement say today that Los Angeles was a sportive piece of luck. Though the attempt of the radical Right to challenge the atmosphere of harmony and to fan the flames of conflict were wrong, it signalled a change in the Olympic movement that could only be stopped by the destruction of the Hitler regime.

---

[35]Naumann, R.: "Die X. Olympischen Spiele." In *Jahrbuch* der Turnkunst 1933, 30-37.

[36]"Reviewing the Olympics." In *Amerikanische Turnzeitung*, 18.9. 1932.

18

The Montreal Games: A Social and Political Comment

John D. Dewar
UNIVERSITY OF SASKATCHEWAN
SASKATOON, SASKATCHEWAN, CANADA

The XXI Olympic Games were a key contributor in fulfilling Mayor Jean Drapeau's 1965 vision of his beloved Montreal.

> We see rising before us the city that Malraux hailed a year ago as 'a city standing proud.' Now this great French city in North America will demonstrate with brilliance and dynamism that the French fact does not belong to the order of memory and museums but to the order of creation, invention, youth, and the future. Coinciding with the awakening of Quebec, the expansion and affirmation of 'Metropolis-Montreal' and 'Montreal, crossroads of the world' indicate in the most eloquent way the virtue of imagination, efficiency and vigour in a French culture which has inspired a modern type of civilization, and of a French language which can fully express the realities of this modern world and the aspirations, needs, dreams and hopes of the citizen of the twentieth century.

> What remains for us to do—and it is no small task—is to make this city, besides being progressive, powerful and dynamic, the high point of a new humanism and a certain pleasantness of life. It is perhaps here that we francophones of America have the greatest role to play in defining ourselves and setting an example. The challenge is enormous, but I like to think that the qualities of our people and the thrust of the quiet revolution are equal to it.

> (Le Devoir, May 19, 1965, from
> Stratford and Thomas, p. 202, 1977)

The Montreal Games

The Games placement of Montreal among the "who's who" of world cities created political, sport, and social contradictions for this complex Canadian city and its dervish-like mayor.

147

Jean Drapeau is so certain he will be recalled by a future generation that he has drawn up a political will. It stipulates that the Olympic Stadium is not to be named for him if he should suddenly die. At least, not right away. But if in twenty years, once the dust has settled about his reputation, they feel the stadium should bear his name, then by all means let them call it after Jean Drapeau. (McKenna, Purcell, p. 359).

On Tuesday afternoon I didn't know anything about gymnastics. By Thursday night, Olga Korbet had let me down. (Greenfield, *Time*, August 2, 1976, pp. 44-50)

Thank you so much for giving us a week of relief. I'd seen Jimmy Carter on your cover so many times, I was beginning to wonder if he weren't already President." Barbara Pavlovic, Stoughton, Wisconsin. (*Newsweek*, August 16, 1976, p. 4)

The organizers, spectators, competitors, and media blended to focus the eyes of the world on Montreal and the Games of the XXI Olympiad. The organizers, "the ship of fools," had problems before and continuing difficulties following the Games, but the 16 days of the competitions were their well-administered and orchestrated time of glory. The athletic accomplishments of the competitors were, at times, perfection themselves. The media, as never before, became the message, and many of the people of the world received the word for as much as 7 hours a day. The Montreal Games were a success, or were they?

His Worship, Jean Drapeau, mayor of Montreal and father of the XXI Olympic Games, has found, like the people and the Malouf Commission, that the Games were a mixed blessing. The Commission of Inquiry into the Montreal Olympics, headed by Superior Court Justice Albert Malouf, cited chapter and verse as to the wrong-doings associated with the Games and which of the Olympic cast of characters were involved. The report was officially released in four volumes to the public on June 5, 1980. The *Montreal Gazette* editorialized the following major blunders according to the Commission:

- Failing to set a cost limit either in the organization of the Games or the building of Olympic installations.
- Mayor Jean Drapeau's assuming the role of project manager even though "he was entirely lacking in the required aptitudes and knowledge."
- Selecting an architect, Roger Tallibert, who directed the realization of his unnecessarily grandiose and complex design from 3,000 miles away and was not subject to constraints of cost or feasibility.
- Building a 25 million dollar Olympic rowing basin which now is seldom used and has become a "real white elephant."
- Constructing a 75 million dollar Veledrome without any relation to Olympic requirements or the city's needs after the Games.
- Including expensive fountains and raised walkways as well as superfluous space in the planned mast in the Olympic Stadium.
- Plunging ahead with a plan for the Olympic Village before private financing was secured; leaving COJO, the Olympic Organizing Committee, to pick up the cost overruns.
- Choosing an Olympic Village without a call for tenders or competition.
- Misleading provincial government authorities about costs of Olympic construction work.
- Unions "shamelessly" taking advantage by the confused construction situation.

- Allowing Regis Trudeau and Associates to get out of their Olympic contracts with a no-damage-action agreement even though they had not completed work on a parking lot, and 3 million dollars had to be spent to repair what they had done (*Montreal Gazette*, June 6, 1980, p. 7).

Drapeau's cost-be-damned approach, labor manipulation, cost escalation, and secrecy in high places, almost destroyed the Games from within the City Hall of Montreal. As the Games approached, preplanned political problems raced to the front so as to be in the limelight when the games began. *Sports Illustrated* placed one of the major opening crises in perspective with this "ironic footnote."

> Sports buffs who seek the ultimate in Olympic memorabelia should pick up a pair of the athletic shoes that the Hanover chain now sells under the brand name 'Pony.' On the underside of the tongue of many of Hanover's Ponies is a label that reads, 'Official Shoe of the Canadian Olympic Team.' The inside of the heel is stamped, 'Made in Taiwan' (*Sports Illustrated*, August 16, 1976, p. 7).

The Taiwan team did not compete, and, as the later 1978 ruling of the IOC indicated, the political position of Canada's not allowing them to take part as China was upheld; only the athletes suffered. The same was true for the African athletes who were governments' pawns in a game unrelated to their emerging athletic prowess. The action of a New Zealand group with respect to South Africa resulted in African nations leaving Canada: Such are the ways of war and politics.

Opening of the Games

The political problems, government commission, and the criminal costs of facility construction continued to plague beautiful Montreal. The city and her people did, however, rise to the occasion and, "once more with charm," conducted, in the summer of 1976, an international spectacle that gave media direction to future competitions and may well have saved the Olympic Games.

The flame was lit by two young Canadians dressed in black and white, and the XXI Olympic Games were officially underway. More than the normal economic, sight, media, and political problems had preceded and would follow this beautiful summer day of July 17, 1976. Many experts had predicted that Drapeau's Olympic dream would never be realized. The Games went on, and they have continued to go because they have become more important than the people of the press and than the politicians of sport and government who hover around and dull the illumination of the Olympic flame. The people of Quebec, Canada, and the world wanted the Games, and Montreal, again as the perfect hostess, put on her charm and the competitions began.

The caliber of the competition and the breadth of their geographical base served notice that the young athletes of the world were ready to challenge the sport super powers of the United Socialist Soviet Republic and the United States of America. Jack Wszola (Poland), Lasse Viren (Finland), Alberto Juanteorena (Cuba), Guy Drut (France), Don Quarrie (Jamaica), John Walker (New Zealand), and Hasely Crawford (Trinidad), were examples of men in track and field who would serve as inspirations to a new generation of athletes in less-populated countries. Female swimmers and performers from the German Democratic Republic continued to dominate, and gymnastics was dominated by Nadia Comaneci. The outstanding performances of these and other athletes centered the focus of the Games on the competitions and away from the oppressing political problems of the opening days.

The power and weakness of the modern Olympic concept was provided in microcosm in Montreal. Where did the truth of sport lie following the 1976 Games? The articulate English pessimism of Brian Glanville reminisced of the past when English gentlemen, scholars, and sportsmen better fitted his idealistic male, Anglo-Saxon model of the Games athlete and concluded, "The heart of the Olympiad still seems to me to be athletics, but that heart is sick, and surely cannot beat much longer" (Innsbruck, Montreal, 1976, p. 85).

These pessimistic prognosticators had a familiar ring to them and may lead future students of the Games to question the knowledge and depth of such sports writers.

Selling the Games

The heart of the Games, however, may have been transported in boxes to the people. The media was selling the Games and many other products in Montreal.

> Madison Avenue is running hard in this year's Summer Olympics. No fewer than six corporations have launched TV advertising campaigns linking hamburgers, hair care products, and beer to the Olympic spirit of competition. . . . .
>
> The Joseph Schlitz Brewing Co. invested more than four million dollars for 122 spots showing divers, gymnasts, relay runners, and high jumpers in action. At the end of each spot an announcer simply says, 'Perfection. . .that's what you expect every time you open a Schlitz. (*Newsweek*, August 2, 1976, p. 79).

The soft-sell ads were strategically coordinated with ABC to appear on the night of that event's competition. Joe Namath and Faberge Brut was not quite so soft a sell or smell.

Newsweek pointed out that the biggest winner in the first week of competition could well have been the American Broadcasting Corporation.

> But the biggest winner in this year's competition was ABC, which once again outlapped the other networks in the ratings race and consistently captured nearly 50 percent of the TV viewing audience in the first week. (*Newsweek*, August 9, 1976, p. 51)

As half of the viewers in the United States and millions more around the world can attest, the televised countenance of the Olympics looked just fine. This was indicative of things to come: The cry of the Olympics now seems to be, it is not if you win or lose, but who gets the television contract.

The handsome high-hurdle champion, Guy Drut of France, exhibited the *joie de vivre* of the French and favored wine as his drink, while the great Finnish champion Lasse Viren trained on reindeer milk.

Quality Performance

More serious training questions and concerns with blood-doping, drugs, steroids, and restrictive diets emerged in Montreal. The new morality seemed to indicate a live-and-let-live attitude, reflected sometimes in macabre humor— "He looks just like any other runner, except for two tiny puncture marks in the jugular."

Possibly, people were beginning to place the rumination of the press and media in perspective and perceiving the competition in terms of the quality of the performance before them. One such performance was that of Bruce Jenner.

The Jenner saga was made for the media, who zoomed in on Bruce and his wife Chrystie, who had met at little Graceland College, a reformed Morman school in Iowa. They left the Midwest: She became a stewardess, he an athlete and part-time insurance salesman. Their American dream unfolded before the eyes of the viewing public. However, beyond the journalistic jargon was a true human-interest story and decathlon total of 8,618 points that improved on the world record by 94 points. The Jenner tale and performance was the type of tale that strengthened the Olympic image in the eyes of the beholders.

Conclusion

The divergence of winners, the media successes, and the minimum number of incidents during the Games resulted in the projecting of positive vibrations from Montreal to future Olympians and Olympics. The deficits linger on, and the legal fights and accusations continue, but Montreal held the Games and provided an expensive stepping stone into the new morality of the Olympic Games and Canadian Sport.

It was no longer the English medical student running for Queen and Country; this earlier model of noble bearing and true sportsmanship was not applicable to the XXI Olympiad. The new paradigms of the athleticism met neither the Brundage nor the de Coubertin criteria, but they were representative and reflected the expectations of the citizens of their respective nations. Many will decry the change; others will say it has brought the Olympics closer to those who are the most involved and to reality.

The athletes, the people, and the press profited from the Montreal Games. The administrators, le grand Jean Drapeau, Monsieur Roger Tallibert, and the IOC learned the wisdom of the Gospel according to St. Luke, Chapter 14, verse 28: "For which of you wishing to build a tower does not sit down first to calculate the outlays that are necessary and whether he has the means to complete it."

Gerald Clark, the last editor of the *Montreal Star*, commented on his city.

> Montreal is not a decaying city. It is a reshaped city: a reflection of the Province of Quebec, dominated by a fresh wave of French rather than English Canadians. This is a substantial development that should be regarded in an affirmative sense. Regardless of the doubts of many English-speaking residents, the quality of Montreal is positive and on the ascendancy. (Clark, Preface, 1982)

The cultural growth and quality of self-perception of Montreal's people give credance to Jacque Leveillee's analysis of the Olympic affair and Drapeau. "If there is any criticism of extravagance or overspending they say he is guilty only of a 'crime passionel." (Clark, p. 196, 1982)

They, the people, have kept him in office since 1954. Will history judge him as kindly as the citizenry?

19

The Canadian Boycott of the 1980 Moscow Olympic Games

Sandra L. Kereliuk
UNIVERSITY OF ALBERTA
EDMONTON, ALBERTA, CANADA

Origin of the Term

During the later months of 1880, tenant farmers in the area of Mayo, Ireland, became disenchanted with their governmental land agreement; specifically, with the methods their landlord used to extract rents. The farmers held meetings and discussed the types of levers which Irish tenants could apply to elicit an improved land bill. The Mayo group resolved to somehow demonstrate its group discontent against the landlord. Rather than malevolently shooting the landlord, it was suggested that a ''more Christian and charitable way, which would give the sinner time to repent'' should be employed (Marlow, 1973, p. 135). A detailed form of social and moral excommunication was developed by the tenants, and it was effectively utilized against the landlord. The name of the landlord was Captain Charles Cunningham Boycott. This incident caused Boycott not only to become the first victim of organized ostracism, but also for his name to become a standard term in the English vocabulary (Marlow, 1973, p. 135). This was the initial use of the boycott method of disapproval, and over the next 100 years it would be used on numerous occasions to put pressure on individuals, organizations, social units, and governments. Included in this process were the modern Olympic Games.

Olympic Evolution

The Olympics were revived during the late 1800s, and the first Modern Games were held in 1896 in Athens. During their 88-year history, the Modern Games have evolved from a transnationalistic festival to a nationalistic encounter. The structure of the Games invited political interference from the start. Flags, anthems, and national teams were advocated, and not only did these help politicize the Games, but it allowed the movement to serve as an exploitable political forum (*The Annals of the American Academy*, 1979, *445*, p. 139). As nations acquired a greater interest in the Games, principally due to the glory and prestige they offered, the Olympics grew in size and stature and developed into an event of global importance. Along the way, the Olympics fell under the influence and control of international trends, conflicts, and events (Espy, 1981, p. 176). The Games began to mirror the problems in the world.

In theory, the Games had been touted as a challenge for youth worldwide, but they evolved into a battle for athletic superiority and political recognition. Disruptions almost became the rule rather than the exception. Between the time an Olympic boycott was first applied in 1908 by several Americans in a track event, to the time there was a complete withdrawal of 62 nations in 1980, no less than 18 actual or threatened boycotts occurred during the 14 Summer Games alone (Kereliuk, 1982).

Statement of the Problem

With the possible exceptions of the 1936 and 1972 Summer Games, the Olympics never really captured the center spotlight of international politics until the boycott crisis of 1980. When Afghanistan was invaded by the United Socialist Soviet Republic in December, 1979, it unintentionally became the catalyst for the most blatant sport-politics clash in Modern Olympic history. The invasion caused a Moscow-Washington conflict, and American president Jimmy Carter called for a massive Western boycott of the 1980 Moscow Games (*Toronto Globe and Mail*, 05-01-80, pp. 1-2).

The nation of Canada, because of its geopolitical location with respect to the United States, and because of its historical background as her strong ally, immediately became involved in the boycott issue. The Canadian Olympic Association (COA), the national committee whose key function is to represent Canadian athletes, and the Canadian federal government were at odds with each other over the boycott issue from the beginning. Eventually, both parties voted to withdraw Canadian athletes from the 1980 Moscow Summer Games.

This paper attempts to show that the COA supported the United States-led boycott because of pressure exerted by a number of critical power groups. These "groups" were the American federal government, the Canadian federal government, certain private American corporations, and the Olympic Trust (OT), a committee composed of influential Canadian businessmen which acts as the COA's primary fundraiser.

However, before the development of the COA decision is discussed, it is important to first understand the background of the boycott's catalyst, the invasion of Afghanistan by the USSR, and the development of the boycott decision by the leaders of the withdrawal, the United States of America.

Afghan Invasion

The Moslem country of Afghanistan is a snow-swept, mountainous land with few natural resources. It is placed between the USSR to the north, the oil rich fields of the Persian Gulf (through Iran) to the west, and the nations of Pakistan and India, which, in turn, hold the key to the warm-water ports of the Arabian sea to the east. It is precisely this geographical location which has made Afghanistan strategically important to both the USSR and the West.

In a lightening-quick invasion between December 24-31, 1979, Soviet aircraft and troops took control of Afghanistan. A coup of the 3-month-old government of Mafizullah Amin was engineered, and the USSR installed its own man, Babrak Karmal, at the top. For the first time since World War II, the USSR had not only deployed ground troops outside of its sphere, but it had taken control of a country that had not been a member of the Warsaw Pact bloc. In doing so, the USSR had violated a fundamental ground rule of East-West relations (*Time*, 14-01-80, p. 11).

USA Boycott

It was not surprising that the Carter administration called for a boycott as punishment against the USSR. Not only have the Olympics evolved into a highly visible political event, but Carter's acceptance of the boycott as a political tool was already known; in the spring of 1978, he had first raised the possibility of boycotting the Moscow Olympics. He had intended to use the boycott threat, at that time, to show American disapproval of human rights' violations in the USSR. Reports issued during this time had suggested that dissidents were being brought to trial and sentenced to lengthy terms in prison and labor camps. When the prominent, Western-backed dissidents were cleared of charges through court proceedings, the boycott talk subsided (*Journal of Sport and Social Issues*, Fall-Winter, 1982, p. 15). Therefore, although it was not surprising that a boycott was threatened in response to the Afghan invasion, it was surprising that it was turned into virtually the only response.

By January 20, Carter made the boycott threat official. The President, speaking on a television interview show, declared that he would use the Olympics to punish the Soviet Union if they did not withdraw their troops from Afghanistan within one month (*New York Times*, 21-01-80, p. A1).

On February 20, Administration officials announced that there were 70,000 Soviet troops in Afghanistan. This left Carter with no alternative other than to announce a certain boycott. In what was termed a "final and irrevocable decision," Carter announced that the United States should not send a team to Moscow, and that he expected the USOC to abide by his decision (*New York Times*, 21-02-80, pp. 1-2).

The boycott vote of the USOC was scheduled for April 12 and by this date, the Administration made it very clear that the USOC had no choice but to vote for a boycott. The final vote was not even close. The tally was 1,604 in favor of the boycott, 797 opposed, and 2 abstentions (*Sports Illustrated*, 21-04-80, p. 32).

After Carter had formal acceptance of the boycott in his own country, he turned to the task of seeking assistance from American supporters. Without the backing of respected sporting countries and important allies, the American boycott would fail.

The Canadian Boycott

An important ally on which the United States counted for support was its neighbor Canada. For Canadian decision makers, there were unique factors which confronted their country in the boycott issue, due to Canada's geopolitical location with respect to the United States. Geographically, Canada is situated alongside the United States. No other nation comes in direct contact with Canada's borders. This exclusive proximity to the United States contributes to a much greater feeling of "closeness" to this nation. Politically, Canada and the United States share the same basic ideologies; that is, they share similar assertions, theories, and aims which constitute their political, social, and economic programs. These two major factors have historically combined to make the countries close allies who share many advantages such as mutually-beneficial economic agreements. This close association was the single most important factor in the Canadian boycott decision.

This association compelled Canada to base its decision on whether or not it was its unofficial duty to demonstrate its political alliance to the United States. Carter forced this issue when he turned the invasion of Afghanistan into a Moscow-Washington confrontation and asked Canada to take sides by presenting it as an East-West dispute. The decision for Canada was not whether or not the boycott was a viable sanction to employ against the USSR. Rather, the decision was whether or not to support the United States boycott endorsement.

Initially, prominent Canadians did not perceive this. The first reaction of the Canadian Prime Minister, Joe Clark, to the boycott suggestion was negative. At a January 4, 1980, news conference, Clark said that Canada was unlikely to withdraw from the Games because such action would have "no practical effects" on the Soviet position in Afghanistan (*Toronto Globe and Mail*, 08-01-80, p. 33). The COA position, announced 3 days later, was also non-supportive. COA President Richard (Dick) Pound, in a Montreal interview, stated that the Association would defy a government decree to boycott the Games unless the athletes' safety was in doubt. He warned that Clark could not make a boycott decision because "the Association acts independently from the government" (*Toronto Globe and Mail*, 08-01-80, p. 9).

But on January, 27, one week after President Carter had issued his nonparticipation ultimatum to Moscow, Clark completely reversed his position. His change of heart seemed to be a direct result of the first trace of pressure the United States applied on Canada which came in the form of a personal message from Carter to Clark asking the Canadian Prime Minister to support the boycott.

Four days after receiving the message, Clark stated, for the first time, that he was prepared to seriously consider a boycott (*Toronto Globe and Mail*, 26-01-80, pp. 1;3), and, 2 days later, Clark completed his reversal when he announced that Canada, following the example of the United States, would boycott the Games if the USSR did not remove its troops from Afghanistan by February 20 (*Toronto Globe and Mail*, 28-01-80, p. 9).

However, the entire issue of support was complicated by a major political event which occurred during the height of the Afghan and Olympic debates. Prime Minister Clark and his Conservatives were ousted from office when the Liberals, under the leadership of Pierre Elliott Trudeau, were returned to power in the national election of February 18. This occurred only 2 days before Clark's ultimatum deadline. The boycott stance was an election issue which left the athletes and general public uncertain of the final decision.

The new prime minster was in no hurry to make a final decision, and, the first major political announcement came on March 19 during the Liberals' transitional period into office. At this time, External Affairs Minister Mark MacGuigan said an official decision would be reached by the latter part of April after consultations with other countries had been completed (*Edmonton Journal*, 20-03-80, p. A2).

However, an announcement by the OT inadvertently sped up the decision-making process. On March 27 Willy Halder, an OT Director, stated that the group had raised enough money to send Canadian athletes to Moscow without receiving federal assistance (*Edmonton Journal*, 28-03-80, p. A8). This announcement, which caused the COA to erroneously assume that the OT would sign over the fund, combined with the Association's unhappiness over the lingering uncertainty of the decision, probably caused the COA to take action on its own. Barely 4 days after the OT announcement, the COA's Board of Directors met and passed a resolution of intent to participate. The resolution, which was couched in diplomatic language, was not an ultimatum. However, this action not only placed tremendous pressure on the COA, but it also publicly displayed the magnitude of its financial and political vulnerability.

The OT applied the first pressure in the form of a financial threat. One day after the COA announced its resolution, the OT threatened to withhold all donations if Canadian athletes were allowed to compete (*Toronto Globe and Mail*, 01-04-80, p. 49). The OT, comprised of influential Canadian businessmen, many of whom worked for American-based corporations, reported that most

corporate donors, such as the American-owned Simpson-Sears Ltd. and Eatons, requested that their substantial pledges be withheld if the team were sent to Moscow (*Toronto Globe and Mail*, 03-04-80, p. 51). A form of political pressure was applied next. Three days after the COA resolution, representatives of the federal government (MacGuigan and Sport Minister Gerald Regan) met with representatives of the COA (Pound and Canada's International Olympic Committee member, James Worrall) to discuss the boycott. When the meeting concluded, Pound announced that an agreement had been reached between the two parties. The COA had asked the two cabinet ministers to make a decision on whether the athletes should compete. After the government made public its stance, Pound said, "The COA would then reconsider its position and do whatever the government told it to do with regard to the boycott" (*Toronto Globe and Mail*, 03-04-80, p. 51).

Nothing could be formally approved until the new Liberal government opened its parlimentary session on April 14. Four days later, Trudeau announced that the government would make its decision before the COA met for its annual meeting on April 26. This deadline may have been announced, not only to allow the COA to hold its meeting, but because of the scheduled April 23 visit by American Secretary of State Cyrus Vance. This final application of pressure by the American government seemed to have occurred because of Trudeau's repeated delays in making a decision. In fact, a spokesman for the prime minister stated that Vance was "pressuring" Canada to join the boycott (*Edmonton Journal*, 19-04-80, pp. A1; A3).

Canada's decision was formally announced on April 22, the day before Vance's visit. Speaking in the House of Commons, MacGuigan announced that the USSR action of Afghanistan made it completely inappropriate to hold the Games in Moscow, and that the government would boycott the Games in retaliation for the invasion. Taking a strikingly different stance from the USA, MacGuigan added that the government would not use coercion, such as seizing passports or interfering with foreign travel to keep individuals from competing but noted, "If Canadian athletes participate in Moscow, they will do so without the moral and financial support of the government of Canada" (*Toronto Globe and Mail*, 23-04-80, pp. 1-2).

It was now up to the COA to make the boycott decision official. In an unprecedented move, the athletes were invited to give a presentation at the COA meeting. Twenty-four athletes from 19 sports met for 2 days to formulate the presentation. After voting 13-7 to attend the Games, the athletes prepared a brief and presented their position to the COA just before its scheduled vote. If the presentation had an effect on the association's members, it was not reflected in the final tally. On April 27 the COA voted to boycott the Moscow Olympic Games by a count of 137 to 35. In a noble and respectful gesture, the athletes issued a statement accepting the decision.

Summary

The decision by the Canadian government to boycott the Moscow Olympics was greatly influenced by the position taken by the government of the United States. For Canada, the boycott seemed to reemphasize Canada's position as a supporter of the United States. The mixing of sport and politics was not a major issue; the perceived loss of glory and prestige through nonparticipation was not a significant item of concern; the needs and concerns of the athletes were not major factors. Rather, the issue which had the greatest effect on Canada's decision was whether or not it was even possible to make a decision independent of the United States. It seems the verdict reached, for this specific incident, was that it was not.

References

COA has money for Moscow Games. (1980, March 28). *Edmonton Journal*, p. A8.
Canada almost certain to boycott Olympics. (1980, April 19). *Edmonton Journal*, A1; A3.

Canadian Olympians balk at boycott. (1980, January 8). *Toronto Globe and Mail*, 3.

Clark asks athletes to boycott Games. (1980, January 28). *Toronto Globe and Mail*, 9.

April decision of Games boycott. (1980, March 20). *Edmonton Journal*, A2.

Espy, R. (1981). *The politics of the Olympic Games*. Los Angeles: University of California Press.

Fraser, J. (1980, April 23). Canada joins in boycott of Moscow Olympics. *Toronto Globe and Mail*, 1-2.

Gross, J. (1980, January 21). Leader welcomes time for decision through 'proper channels.' *New York Times*. A1-A4.

Kereliuk, S. (1982). The Canadian boycott of the 1980 Summer Olympic Games. (M.A. Thesis, University of Alberta).

Marlow, J. (1973). *Captain Boycott and the Irish*. London: Andre Deutsch Limited.

Martin, L. (1980, January 5). Carter slashes grain to Soviet Union. *Toronto Globe and Mail*, 1-2.

McCabe, N. (1980, April 1). Head of Canadian team vows to skip Moscow trip. *Toronto Globe and Mail*, 49.

McCabe, N. (1980, April 13). COA retreats from Moscow stance. *Toronto Globe and Mail*, 51.

Moore, K. (1980, April 21). The decision: No go on Moscow. *Sports Illustrated*, 30-33.

My opinion of the Russians has changed most drastically. . .(1980, January 14). *Time*, 6-13.

Sheppard, R. (1980, January 26). Could send troops to Gulf, P.M. says. *Toronto Globe and Mail*, 1; 3.

Shinnik, P. (1982). Progressive resistance to nationalism and the 1980 boycott of the Moscow Olympics. *Journal of Sport and Social Issues*, 13-21.

Smith, T. (1980, January 21). Carter proposes taking Olympics away from Moscow. *New York Times*, A1-A4.

Strenk, A. (1979). What price victory? The world of international sports and politics. *The Annals of the American Academy*, **445**, 128-140.

Weisman, S. (1980, February 21). As deadline passes White House says its Olympic decision is final. *New York Times* A1, A4.

20

The Politics of the 1984 Los Angeles Olympics

Dale P. Toohey
CALIFORNIA STATE UNIVERSITY, LONG BEACH
LONG BEACH, CALIFORNIA, USA

> Politics is the process in a social system, not necessarily confined to the level of the national state, by which the goals of that system are selected, ordered in terms of priority, and resources are allocated and implemented. It, thus, involves both cooperation and the resolution of conflict, by means of political authority and if necessary coercion.[1]

Sport constitutes an exceptionally strong element of social interaction and, as such, becomes the perfect vehicle for implementing political objectives. Thus, nations have used international sporting events to further their own political causes. The more important the sporting event, the greater the accompanying publicity, and the greater the exposure to draw attention to political causes.

The Olympic Games are the pinnacle of amateur athletic achievement. The Summer Games and the Winter Games are the focus of world attention once every 4 years and, as such, are the perfect settings to demonstrate issues to millions throughout the world. For this reason, since their inception, especially since their rise to prominence, the Games have been subject to a variety of political intrusions. These forces do not merely extend during the period of the Games although they are most conspicuous during this time but are a continuing phenomena reflecting the current political trends in the world at large.[2]

---

[1]Ritter, P. The Olympic movement in the service of peace and brotherhood. *Olympic Review*, No. 130-131, 503-505.

[2]Toohey, D., & Warning, K. (1980, February). *Nationalism: Inevitable and incurable.* Presented at the Pre-Olympic Symposium. Skidmore College, New York.

Los Angeles Wins the Bid

Los Angeles' bid for the 1984 Summer Olympic Games began on October 25, 1967, when the United States Olympic Committee urged Los Angeles representatives to bid for the 1984 Summer Olympics. By late July, 1977, New York and Los Angeles were in competition to be the United States representatives.

September 26, 1977, was the date that the United States Olympic Committee would nominate its representative city to bid for the 1984 Games before the International Olympic Committee had its meeting in Athens in May 1978. Los Angeles defeated New York for the right to host the Games after Mayor Tom Bradley of Los Angeles, and the then-Governor of California, Gerry Brown, stressed that Los Angeles wanted to turn the Olympics away from the spiral of increasing deficits seen in recent years. New York Governor, Hugh Cary, had, by contrast, promised New York would put on the greatest Olympiad in the history of the world with New York state guaranteeing to pay any deficit.

It was revealed that it had actually been Los Angeles' hard line against high costs that had been a crucial factor in its victory. While New York had a strong commitment for money, Los Angeles had a commitment to save money and to run the Olympics at no cost to the city, state, and, in particular, local taxpayers. Mayor Bradley favored a tough, competent, and rather small organizing committee that would carry out this pledge of a "spartan financially sound Olympics."

Even the Los Angeles delegation to the United States Olympic Committee Headquarters in Colorado Springs were cost-restricted. New York spent $400,000 to make its presentation to the Olympic Committee; Los Angeles spent only $30,000 of a budget allocation of $40,000, all from private donors. Governor Brown, in keeping faith with his pledge to avoid use of state funds, along with three others who traveled by charter jet to Colorado Springs to help solicit the 1984 Games, paid for the charter himself. Brown said, "That is our contribution because we want to encourage contributions from the private sector and encourage other citizens to participate in the same vein."

At the Athens meeting where the 1984 Games were to be awarded, the Los Angeles delegation ran into a major stumbling block when the International Olympic Committee insisted that the city and the United States Olympic Committee assume complete financial responsibility for the organization of the Games. Los Angeles' representatives were given an ultimatum to negotiate on terms of the International Olympic Committee draft contract or lose the Games. The extensive, involved negotiations that followed resulted in some give and take from both sides and represented contrasting political philosophies. The International Olympic Committee held an idealistic stance in attempting to maintain the Olympic ideal while the Los Angeles committee had a very pragmatic approach, especially where cost factors were concerned.

On October 20, 1978, at approximately 1:30 p.m., Mayor Bradley and Lord Killanin signed the Olympic contract at a White House ceremony in Washington, D.C., formally designating Los Angeles as the 1984 Summer

Olympic city.[3] After being awarded the 1984 Olympics, the Los Angeles Olympic organizers had to continually deal with world political events. The threat of Eastern bloc government officials, if not Olympic officials, being tempted to organize a boycott of the 1984 Games in reprisal for the American boycott of the 1980 Moscow Olympics was always present.

World Political Events

In many areas of government in the United States, and with athletes in particular, the virtues of the 1980 boycott were regarded as dubious at best. In an interview with Pete Axthelm of *Newsweek* magazine, former President Jimmy Carter revealed his feelings on the 1980 Olympic boycott. Carter feels the boycott did work stating,

> The fact that the troops are still in Afghanistan indicates that we generated enough international reaction to make their takeover more difficult. The boycott damaged their international standing. It could be argued that without it, they would have also sent troops to Poland.[4]

As a result of the shooting down of a Korean Air Lines 747 on September 1, 1983, by a Soviet jet fighter, some politicians and private citizens in the United States sought to bar the Soviets from competing in the 1984 Games. On September 14, 1983, the California State Legislature, by a unanimous vote, called upon President Reagan and Congress to ban Soviet athletes from participating in the 1984 Los Angeles Games. This resolution, by Senator John Doolittle (Republican-Citrus Heights), was approved 74 to 0 in the Assembly and 36 to 0 in the Senate.

Reaction from Olympic and other government officials was immediate. United States Olympic Committee President, F. Don Miller, was highly critical of the Legislature's action stating, "Everyone has been invited to Los Angeles and to renege on this at this time would be very, very dangerous to the survival of the Olympics and the Olympic Movement."

Government officials in Washington said, in light of letters written to the International Olympic Committee by both President Reagan and former President Jimmy Carter pledging the United States Government would admit any athletes or sports officials accredited to participate in the Los Angeles Games, the United States believes that it has entered into commitments and will not go back on them.

Peter Ueberroth, the president of the Los Angeles Olympic Organizing Committee, stated that he "remains opposed to any efforts to punish athletes for political purposes. History has proven that the use and abuse of athletes for political purposes, only hurts young individuals rather than achieving any political gain."[5]

---

[3]Toohey, D. (1980, May). *The 1984 Summer Olympic Games—The Los Angeles story*. Presented at the National Olympic Academic, Indiana University.

[4]Axthelm, P. (1983, October 10). The Olympics: Boycotts can work. *Newsweek*, p. 68.

[5]*The Independent Press Telegram*. September 17, 1983. Section B, p. 2.

The International Olympic Committee's Athletic Commission also opposed any boycott of the 1984 Games. World champion hurdler, Edwin Moses, proposed that no action be taken to prevent any qualified athletes from attending the Games, and that the Olympics be held without political influence. With this resolution approved, Moses and others viewed it as an "auspicious sign for universal participation in Los Angeles."[6]

Soviet Withdrawal

Following these events, Soviet sports officials notified the Los Angeles Olympic leadership that they were cancelling plans to send 17 Soviet athletes to compete in a pre-Olympic rowing and canoeing regatta. Soviet teams later withdrew from the pre-Olympic competitions in archery, basketball, and volleyball. The Soviets also stated they would not send an ice hockey team to the United States to compete against the American Olympic team.[7] This decision was later revised and in December 1983 the Soviet team completed a series of contests against the American team.

During this period, American athletes competed in the Soviet Union in wrestling and judo. On returning to the United States, Judo officials made allegations stating that they were harassed while in Moscow. Prior to the attack on the Korean airliner, Olympic President Peter Ueberroth was informed in a telephone call that Soviet entertainers would not participate in the Olympic Cultural Festival to be held prior to the Olympics.

Soviet-United States relations were strained even further by the American invasion of Grenada and the Soviet walkout from the Geneva arms limitations talks following the United States delivery of nuclear missiles to Western Europe. These events caused further speculation that the Soviet Union would not compete in the Los Angeles Games.

The Soviets did, however, appear to take a step closer to participating in the Games following a week-long inspection of facilities and arrangements by officials of the USSR National Olympic Committee. Following this early December visit, Mort Grasnov, USSR sports commissioner stated,

> I do not see any reasons at this time that won't make us participate. Somewhere around May 28, we shall hold a meeting of the General Assembly of the U.S.S.R. Olympic Committee. That is when and where we will make the decision.[8]

Another positive step toward Soviet participation was taken by the Soviet National Olympic Committee when they placed a ticket order for the 1984 Games. No details were released on the number of tickets ordered.[9] Also, in August 1983, the Soviets agreed to pay $3 million for domestic television rights to the Games.

[6]*Los Angeles Times.* November 21, 1983. Part I, p. 3.

[7]*Los Angeles Times.* September 8, 1983. Part 2, p. 12.

[8]*U.S.A. To Day.* December 8, 1983. Section C, p. 1.

[9]*The Los Angeles Olympic Organizing Committee.* News Release. June 3, 1984.

On other fronts, in Eastern Europe, the East German sports authorities made a sharply written complaint to the Los Angeles Olympic Organizers about the wording of the United States' visa application questionnaires that their team auxiliaries, but not their athletes, needed to fill to go to the 1984 Summer Games.

The State Department questionnaire put membership in the Communist Party in the same category as that of heinous crime, drug addiction, or a contagious disease. Olympic President Ueberroth then made inquiries in Washington regarding the wording of the questionnaire, and the appropriate sections were dropped.

Then, on May 8, 1984, just 2½ hours after the transcontinental Olympic torch relay began its journey to Los Angeles, the Soviet Union announced it would not attend the Los Angeles Olympics. Within a few days, Bulgaria, East Germany, Vietnam, Mongolia, Czechoslovakia, Laos, and Afghanistan followed suit. These countries were later joined by Cuba, Ethiopia, Hungary, North Korea, Poland, and South Yemen.

The Soviets withdrew on the grounds that their athletes would be endangered by "anti-Soviet hysteria." A statement from the Soviet National Olympic Committee was released that said, "The cavalier attitude of the U.S. authorities to the Olympic movement, are aimed directly at undermining it. In these conditions, participation of Soviet sportsmen in the Games of the XXIII Olympiad in Los Angeles is impossible."[10] The Soviet allies gave similar reasons for withdrawing from the Los Angeles Games.

Reaction from around the globe to the Eastern Bloc withdrawal was immediate. International Olympic Committee leaders openly stated they deplored the boycott. The Los Angeles Organizing Committee defended their security arrangements and again declared that *all* athletes would be welcome in Los Angeles. Los Angeles organizers visited the IOC; IOC President Samaranch visited Moscow; and Ueberroth visited Cuba in unsuccessful attempts to persuade these countries to attend the 1984 Olympics.

Romania alone broke with the Soviet Union in accepting the invitation to attend the Games. The Romanians would be the only Warsaw Pact nation represented in Los Angeles, and about two-thirds of the cost of transporting the Romanian Olympics team was borne by the Los Angeles Olympic Organizing Committee and the International Olympic Committee. Marxist South Yemen, a radical Middle-Eastern nation, became the first Arab country to drop out of the Games when it withdrew on May 26, 1984.

June 2 was the deadline for countries to accept the International Olympic Committee's invitation to take part in the Games. On June 3, the Los Angeles Olympic Organizing Committee announced a record number of 142 contries would participate. This total exceeded by 20 the previous high of 122 countries at the 1972 Munich Games. Indications were that 7,800 athletes would be participating which would also be a new record. An estimated 2,200 athletes were lost to the Games as a result of the Soviet-led withdrawal.[11]

---

[10]*Newsweek Magazine* "Special report—are the Olympics dead," May 21, 1984, p. 18.

[11]*The Los Angeles Olympic Organizing Committee*. News Release. June 3, 1984.

Subsequently, Angola, Bolivia, and Upper Volta also withdrew. The Bolivian government withdrew in protest to an article written by a *Washington Post* reporter that suggested that Bolivian athletes could finance their way to the Games by selling beer for Budweiser, the "official beer" of the 1984 Olympics. The reporter later apologized, and the Bolivian team attended. The West African nation of Upper Volta withdrew in protest to a recently completed tour of South Africa by the English rugby team. On July 26, the United States Government denied entry visas to three Libyan journalists on the ground that they represented a threat to United States' security. The team from Libya, of one athlete and two officials who were already in Los Angeles, withdrew.

Nations which withdrew from the Games were the Soviet Union, Afghanistan, Bulgaria, Czechoslovakia, Cuba, East Germany, Ethiopia, Hungary, Laos, Mongolia, North Korea, Poland, South Yemen, and Vietnam, as well as Iran, Albania, Upper Volta, and Libya for reasons unrelated to the Soviet withdrawal.

Reasons for the Soviet-Led Boycott

The Soviet-led boycott of the 1984 Games was probably due to a number of reasons rather than any single event; namely reaction to President Carter's boycott of the 1980 Moscow Olympics; fear of demonstrations against and defection by Soviet and other Eastern Bloc athletes; the current tensions in American-Soviet relations; concern for the overall-athletic ability of the current Soviet team, especially in men's track and field, the showcase event of the Olympics; and the new leadership of the Soviet Union's view of the boycott as a political tool to be used as a springboard for further political confrontations with the American Government. Violations of the Olympic Charger, while given as a major reason for the withdrawal, probably were minor considerations as any deviation from Olympic rules had the approval of the International Olympic Committee and were known well in advance by the Soviet membership on the International Olympic Committee. The fear that a successful Olympics could be viewed as an extension of the capitalist system, as these are indeed the "Capitalist Games," concerned the Soviets and their allies, and they probably did not want the risk of being part of a successful program representing the American political ideology since success in Soviet sport is viewed by the Soviet authorities as an extension of its political system. Representatives of the 41 African National Olympic Committees visited Los Angeles in January 1983. President Peter Ueberroth of the Organizing Committee said that as a result of this visit, communications and cooperation with African National Olympic Committees have taken a major step forward. Ueberroth cited a message received from the president of the Association of National Olympic Committees of Africa (ACNOA) on his return:

> I would like to sincerely thank the LAOOC in the name of the African National Olympic Committees and in my own name for the warm welcome that was shown to us and the facilities that were offered to us.

If all the delegates are unanimous in recognizing that the meetings in Los Angeles were a success, it is without doubt thanks to your good organization, we are already convinced, due to the dynamism of the Organizing Committee, that the Games of the XXIII Olympiad will meet with success without precedent.[12]

Remembering the African Nationals' withdrawal from the Montreal Olympics following the New Zealand rugby tour of South Africa Olympic leaders feared a similar reaction from the African continent following the England rugby team's South African tour. The inclusion of Zola Budd, the South African-born runner, on the British Olympic team also worried officials, as Budd had received preferential treatment from the British Government in order to gain citizenship to be eligible for the British team. The Organization of African Unity and the Supreme Council of Sport in Africa left the decision up to each country. South African journalists were refused press credentials to cover the Games.

Two weeks from the Opening Ceremony, racist hate leaflets were mailed to the National Olympic Committees of Zimbawe, Sri Lanka, South Korea, Malaysia, China, and Singapore. The letters had no signatures except for a cartoon insignia of a white-robed horseman over the caption "Ku-Klux Klan." The United States State Department stated the letters were probably "not written by a native English speaker" and suggested that the Soviet Union was behind the campaign.[13]

China sent an Olympic team to Los Angeles. Relations between the United States and China became tense, when on July 20, 1983, Chinese tennis star Hu Na defected while taking part in a tennis tournament in California. She formally applied for asylum July 26 and on March 10 lobbied Congress for support. The United States Government granted asylum April 4, 1983. The Chinese government, in turn, cancelled all cultural and sporting exchanges between the two countries. As a result, Chinese athletes did not compete in the pre-Olympic events in cycling and swimming during the 1983 summer as they had planned. The Los Angeles Organizing Committee questioned the United States Government's decision and did everything it could to ensure China's presence in Los Angeles in 1984.

Shortly after the teams from China and Taiwan arrived in Los Angeles, a friendship gesture by the California Chinese community to build international solidarity during the Olympics failed when Taiwan's Olympic team did not attend an all-China luncheon in Pasadena, California. The Taiwan delegation objected to the fact that 100 athletes and coaches from the People's Republic of China attended.

Security for the Olympics

Since the advent of the Modern Olympics by Piere de Coubertin at Athens in 1896, the most tragic political interference to the Olympic movement came

---

[12]*The Los Angeles Olympic Organizing Committee*. Press Release. March 18, 1983.

[13]*Los Angeles Times*. July 12, 1984. Part 1, p. 13.

in Munich at the 1972 Olympics. The murder of Israeli athletes by Palestinian terrorists in Munich has caused security arrangements to safeguard against terrorism and other forms of crime to be of utmost importance for Olympic organizers.

Security arrangements for Los Angeles were directed by Edward Best, who worked for the Federal Bureau of Investigation (FBI) for 22 years. the FBI, Los Angeles Police Department, and other area low enforcement agencies combined their efforts to make Los Angeles safe during the Olympics. The FBI established its own 42 member antiterrorist squad which trained in Washington to learn to deal with well-armed, trained terrorists. In addition, Los Angeles-based paramedics trained to do rescue missions by rappelling from a helicopter, if required, during the 1984 Olympics. The Reagan Administration asked for $50 million in military aid during the Olympics.

Antiterrorist specialists acknowledge that the threat of terrorism at these Olympics was probably greater from groups within the United States than from countries outside, the belief being that ethnic-oriented extremist groups in the United States may have grudges left from their old countries which still linger. It is difficult for authorities to cover these groups as they come from large ethnic areas and not many officers can slide into the group undetected as few members speak any English. In the past, local terrorism in Los Angeles has been mainly Armenian-related, and, as a result, Turkish cyclists did not ride in the open-road races during the Olympics as the security forces felt they could not provide adequate protection during these events.

In September 1983, Monsignor William Barry, the president of the Inter-religious Council of Southern California, at the request of Los Angeles Olympic President, Peter Ueberroth, cancelled a proposed interdenominational Hollywood Bowl celebration to be held just prior to the Olympics. Barry believed Ueberroth was convinced the service would have pro-peace overtones, and, as a result, the religious rally would attract politically oriented peace groups.[14] The American Civil Liberties Union of Southern California filed suit in Los Angeles Superior Court on August 11, 1983, on behalf of over 50 world-class women athletes from 19 countries who charged that the International Olympic Committee (IOC) is discriminating against them for failing to provide 5,000 and 10,000 meter track and field events for women at the 1984 Olympics. Also, named as defendants in the suit were the United States Olympic Committee and the Los Angeles Organizing Committee. Peter Ueberroth denounced the suits' inclusion of local officials as defendants as "unfortunate" and "exploitive." He stressed that the IOC and not the local committee makes decisions on events for the Olympics. He stated, "They have sued the wrong party at the wrong time for the wrong reasons. We are offended by the suit, especially since we have singularly fought for the women's marathon and other important women's events."[15] The Courts eventually turned down the suit as filed.

Even the lighting of the Olympic flame took on major political overtones when the authorities in Olympia threatened to cancel the traditional lighting

---

[14]*Los Angeles Times.* September 18, 1983. Part 2, p. 1.

[15]The Los Angeles Olympic Organizing Committee. Press Conference. August 12, 1983.

ceremony at Olympia and the transfer of the flame to Athens where it was to be laser-beamed to the United States. The Greeks objected to the commercialization of the flame during its journey across the United States. The system of each torch bearer paying for the privilege of carrying the torch on American soil did have the approval of the International Olympic Committee and the money raised was donated to youth groups and charity organizations. The International Olympic Committee responded by saying the Olympic flame and the lighting ceremony belong to the Olympic movement and not Greece, and, if necessary, the lighting ceremony could be held at the International Olympic Committee headquarters. The dispute was resolved 2 days prior to the lighting ceremony following a visit to Greece and political negotiations by Tom Bradley, the mayor of Los Angeles.

The Organizing Committee, in the wake of team withdrawals, made appropriate adjustments and emphasized the positive aspects of the Games. Their hope was that all nations who attended would enjoy the Games, and that the 1984 Los Angeles Olympics would exemplify "human brotherhood."

SECTION B
Analysis of Olympic Politics: Four Examples

21

Historical Relations Between Modern Olympic Games and Japanese Political Situations

Hideaki Kinoshita
NIHON UNIVERSITY
TOKYO, JAPAN

Historical Background

The Tokugawa feudal government (1603-1868) had not maintained diplomatic and commercial relations with Western nations except Holland since 1633. Accordingly, the Japanese had no experience of competition in either domestic or foreign affairs during this period. By the middle of the 19th century, Japan had opened its doors. This was brought about in 1853 by Commodore Perry's fleet threatening to use force, and only after much pressure were the conditions agreed upon. In 1868, the Meiji government overtook the Tokugawa government, and this period signaled Japan's status as a modern state. The Meiji government's modernization slogan was "Fukoku Kyohei," which meant "a rich nation; strong military." Militarism and industrialization marked this period, means by which Japan intended to defend itself against the gunboat diplomacy taken by Western nations during the 19th century.

This kind of international situation nurtured "competition," a term, not found in traditional Japanese vocabularies. Yukichi Fukuzawa, the founder of Keio University, found it difficult to translate that term into Japanese. Even today the term *kyogi* is generally employed to mean competition. Kyogi actually means sport; therefore, *sport* in Japanese implies ones performance by comparing his technique and skill with others in sport. In the beginning of modern Japan, the Japanese concocted new words for competition. For example, *kyoriki* which means comparing strength, and *kyoshin* which means comparing what one has perfected culturally. Eventually, the term *kyoso* also came into being;

it is the term that comes closest to competition, but, in competitive sport, only the term *kyogi* is used. It means comparing one's technique and skill. Kyoso, in its true meaning, was more pronounced in the field of foreign affairs, including trade and war, and also in realizing one's upward mobility in society.

In modern Japan, international games progressed as rapidly as interschool games. In the Tokugawa period, martial art matches were not permitted between different schools, but, in the modern periods, they have been permitted as in the case of Kendo. In the minds of most modern-thinking Japanese, the feudal principle of anticompetition ceased to exist.

Purpose

The aim of this paper is to demonstrate the parallel patterns of thought involved in the Japanese concept of Olympic Games and the Japanese manner of perceiving international and domestic political situations. To discuss this matter, the relationship between Japanese participation in Olympic Games and international political situations will be described.

The First Period (1896-1905)

Japan did not participate in foreign affairs with the Great Powers of the world or in the Olympic Games. The Japanese government had been subjected to "unequal treaties," which the Tokugawas concluded with the 1984 United States of America in 1857. One was the treaty of consular jurisdiction, and the other was the treaty of disadvantageous tariff.

The Japanese attempted to do away with these treaties. First, the Japanese government succeeded in abolishing the United Kingdom consular jurisdiction in 1894. The Sino-Japanese War took place that same year, but the Japanese were forced by the European powers to resign certain rights of the peace treaty with China. This demonstrated the government's inability to deal with international powers.

Of course, at this time, the level of athletics in Japan was still very primitive. For example, in 1896, the top baseball club of The First High School had just begun to engage in this kind of sport with foreign residents in Japan. From that time, other games of this sort were held frequently.

The Second Period (1905-1920)

Japan was recognized by the Great Powers and participated in Olympic Games without governmental subsidy. Japan engaged in the Russo-Japanese War of 1904. As a result, the Great Powers recognized the international position of Japan; hence, Japan gained the right to impose tariffs in 1911.

Japanese participation in international sport was recognized. *First*, Dr. Masatsugu Yamane, the inspector of the Japanese Physical Education Society, received an invitation on November 24, 1905, from the Chairman of the Organizing Committee for the 1906 Olympic Games in Athens. These are known as the Memorial Games and were to commemorate the first modern Olympic Games held a decade before. In this letter, the Chairman asked the Japanese to organize a Japanese Olympic Committee and to participate in the Games; this was the first opportunity for the Japanese to participate in the Olympic Games. Japan could not capitalize on this chance because of the lack of leadership and organization.

Second, the records in the pole vault (3 m 90 cm) and the 100 m dash (10.24s) by Minoru Fujii in 1906 were found in the *Almanac of 1907* issued by Spalding Company. These were listed as the most valuable records in the world that year.

Third, Jigoro Kano, famous as the founder of judo, was nominated as a member of the International Olympic Committee in 1909. Accordingly, he took the initiative in organizing the Japanese Amateur Athletic Association. The Japanese then participated in the V Olympic Games in Stockholm in 1912. It was extremely difficult for this Association to gather funds. Before these games, it had collected only 5,992 yen (about $3,000), and the team consisted of only two members because the round-trip cost was 4,465 yen (about $2,240), almost all the Association's money. Over the following 4 years, they collected only 5,348 yen (about $2,680). The government at this time declined comment on whether or not they financially supported Japanese participation in Olympic Games. The majority of money would, therefore, come from wealthy sponsors and officials of the Association. In 1920, the Association could collect only 20,000 yen (about $10,000), only enough for one-way tickets for the 15 participants. To force sponsorship for their return, the participants left Japan for the Games. The giant family trusts of Mitsui and Mitsubishi then had to donate 30,000 yen (about $15,000) needed for their return trip. The companies paid on the condition that they would in the future withdraw all sponsorship.

The Third Period (1921-1930)

Government subsidy supported the Japan Olympic Committee, and Japan began to win prizes in the Olympic Games. In 1921-1922, Japan joined in the Naval Limitation Treaty in Washington as it was by then recognized as one of the five great powers of the world. The government, on one hand, attempted to limit its armaments, but, on the other hand, strengthened war preparations, in particular, by developing physical fitness among its youth. In 1924, the government established the National Institute for Research in Physical Education, sponsored the Meiji Shrine Games, and proclaimed the 3rd of November, "National Physical Fitness Day." The government also provided financial support for the Association to enable the Japanese to participate in Olympic Games by supporting the Japanese Amateur Athletic Association with 1,000 yen (about $500) in 1921, when the Fifth Far East Championship Games were held in

Shanghai. It was the first subsidy to enable Japanese athletes to compete in international games held abroad.

Subsidies were increased to 30,000 yen (about $14,500) in each year of 1922 and 1923, but the Association was to save half of each grant to use for participants in the next Olympic Games. When the VIII Olympic Games were held in Paris in 1924, the governmental subsidy for the Association was raised to 60,000 yen (about $25,200). The Japanese team consisted of 18 men, and the total cost was 68,350 yen (about $28,700). All the expenses were paid for by the government. In addition to this financial assistance, Prince Chichibu, a brother of the Emperor, gave a national flag to the team. This meant that the Japanese Olympic team was authorized as a representative of the empire of Japan, as well as the emperor's army. After that, the government continued to increase its subsidy.

On the commencement of government subsidies, Japanese participants produced good results. In the 1924 Paris Olympics, some participants were ranked sixth. In the 1928 Amsterdam Olympics, two men won gold medals, Oda in the hop, step, and jump; and Tsuruta in the breast stroke. One woman, Hitomi, won a silver medal in the 800 m run. They were the first Japanese medalists in the Olympics.[1] Japanese teams did well in the subsequent Los Angeles and Berlin Olympics, too.

Government subsidies automatically increased from 100,000 yen (about $28,000) for the 1932 Los Angeles Olympics to 300,000 yen (about $87,000) for the 1936 Berlin Olympics. As a result of the large increase in subsidies, the team achieved excellent results, far better than when compared with the results of previous Japanese Olympic teams.

The Fourth Period (1931-1937)

Japan attempted to hold the XII Olympic Games in Tokyo in 1940. Around 1930, because Japan faced difficulties in domestic and foreign affairs, the government arrogantly entertained the idea that Japan was the most powerful nation in the world. The government began to formulate policies to make people believe that Japan, ruled by the emperor, was the most superior power in the world, and the government sought to demonstrate this power in international politics. To host the Olympic Games in Tokyo was one such means.

In 1931, the Tokyo Municipal Council passed a resolution to hold the XII Olympic Games in Tokyo in 1940. Furthermore, in 1935, the mayor of Tokyo would make available to foreign teams 1,000,000 yen (about $290,000) in subsidies if the Games were held in Tokyo in 1940. In this same year, the National Diet passed a resolution to hold the Olympics in Tokyo in 1940. As a result of these efforts, the general meeting of the International Olympic Committee in 1936, decided that the XII Olympics would be held in Tokyo in 1940.

---

[1]Katsutoshi Naito was the first medalist in the Olympics, but he joined the 1924 Olympics in Paris, after staying and training at The Pennsylvania State University in the United States without any relation to the Japanese Amateur Athletic Association. Therefore, he has to be omitted in the trend of Japanese participation in Olympics.

Japan also gained the rights to hold the V Olympic Winter Games in Sapporo and the International Exposition in Tokyo in 1940.

The Fifth Period (1938-1945)

Because of World War II, the XII Olympic Games in Tokyo were cancelled, and the Japanese Olympic Committee was dissolved. The Sino-Japanese hostilities, triggered by Japan, began in 1937. Though realizing local victories, Japan failed to bring about total victory; war expenses mounted, and Japan was forced to cancel the XII Olympic Games planned to be held in Tokyo in 1940.

After Pearl Harbor, the Japanese government mobilized the country for total war. Following this, in the field of sport, the Japanese Amateur Athletic Association was reestablished as the controlling body of all sports in 1942 and was utilized for military purposes. The Olympic Committee was dissolved; thus, Japanese athletes were isolated from contact with athletes of other countries.

The Sixth Period (1945-1951)

World War II ended in 1945, and Japan was occupied by the Allied Nations. It was prohibited from participating in the Olympics. Naturally, as distaste for war still existed throughout the world, Japan would not be allowed to participate in the 1948 Olympics in London. Even if the Japanese had organized a National Olympic Committee of their own accord, they would not have been asked to participate in the 1948 London Olympics.

The Japanese were, of course, eager to compete in London. To demonstrate this, Furuhashi surpassed the records in the 400 m and 1500 m freestyle swimming events that were set on the same day of the London Olympics. Eventually, in spite of the occupied status of Japan, the International Olympic Committee agreed, in principle, that the Japanese should again join the international sporting community in 1949.

The Seventh Period (1952-Present)

Japan participated in Olympic competition again and sponsored the XVIII Olympic Games in Tokyo in 1964. As a result of the Japanese peace treaty in San Francisco in 1951, Japan recovered its independence and returned to international society. Consequently, in the XV Olympics in Helsinki in 1952, the Japanese team consisted of 69 members, and almost 50% of the expenses for this team were subsidized by the government. Since then, the government has assisted Japanese participation in Olympic Games as a matter of its national policy. The XVIII Olympic Games in Tokyo in 1964 were successful because they had almost the full support of the government. In this respect, the political value of the 1964 Tokyo Olympics was equal to that of the 1940 Olympics. By supporting the Olympics from 1940 through 1964, the government was declaring, from the viewpoint of domestic and foreign policy, Japan's superior position in international society.

Conclusion

There are two major periods in the history of Japanese participation in Olympic Games. The first period consists of the first to the fifth phase and the latter period from the sixth to the seventh phase. The former represents the prewar period; the latter the postwar period. Japan attempted to consolidate her position internationally by participating in the Olympics before the war. In conclusion, the history of Olympic participation in the prewar period closely parallels that the postwar period when related to the internationally competitive and political situations surrounding Japan.

References

Note: The following reference books are available in Japanese only.

The Editorial Committee of the Encyclopedia of History in Modern Japan. (1978). *An encyclopedia of history in modern Japan*. Tokyo: Toyo-Keizai Shinpo.

The Japanese Amateur Athletic Association. (1936). *The history of the Japanese Amateur Athletic Association Book 1*. Tokyo: JAAA.

The Japanese Amateur Athletic Association. (1953). *A report on the XV Olympic Games in Helsinki in 1952*. Tokyo: JAAA.

The Japanese Amateur Athletic Association. (1958). *The 80-years history of sports in modern Japan*. Tokyo: JAAA.

The Japan Amateur Sports Association. (1963). *The 50-years history of the Japan Amateur Sports Association*. Tokyo: JASA.

The Japanese Amateur Athletic Association. (1982). *The encyclopedia of sports*. Tokyo: JASA.

The Japanese Physical Education Society and Nihon College of Physical Education (Eds.). (1973). *The 80-years history of the Japanese Physical Education Society and Nihon College of Physical Education*. Tokyo: The Same Society and College.

Kinoshita, H. (1970). *History of sport in modern Japan*. Tokyo: Kyorin-Syoin.

Kinoshita, H. (1971). *Basic study on the history of physical education in Japan*. Tokyo: Fumaido.

22

A Comparison of the United States Olympic Athletes Concerning Political Involvement in the Olympic Games

Debbie J. Denbeck
COLLEGE OF SAINT MARY
OMAHA, NEBRASKA, USA

> Keep to your old customs: protect your country, avoid war, and give the world
> a sign of brotherly friendship whenever the joyful time of the four-year games
> approaches.[1]

This statement, from an oracle of the God Apollo, states an ideal of what
the Olympic games once stood for, but raging wars and unharmonious relationships between countries have brought political disturbance into greater
awareness.

Now an area which was founded on both unity and peace has been stricken—
the Olympic Games. Research has shown that political involvement in the
Olympic Games has become more prevalent in recent years. The blatant
occurrences at the 1972 Olympics could have initiated a more intensive era
of political manipulation in conjunction with the events as evident by continued
politically related activities. For the first time in the history of the modern
Olympics, 11 athletes died, and competition was halted for 24 hours.

The purpose of this study was to compare the opinions concerning political
involvement in the Olympic Games of the United States Olympic athletes com-

---

[1]Mckay, J. *My Wide World*. (New York: MacMillan, 1976). p. 2.

peting in the 1960-1976 Olympiads with the United States athletes competing in the 1972 Summer Olympic Games. In addition to the original statement of the problem, this study includes two other concerns to the researcher.

1. An additional purpose of the study was to research the effect of the political controversies that occurred at the 1972 Summer Olympic Games on the United States Olympic athletes.
2. A further interest of the researcher was to determine if the athletes felt that the controversies that occurred at the 1972 Summer Olympic Games had an effect upon their own performances.

Methodology

The subjects for this study were randomly selected from the United States athletes who participated in the 1972 Summer Olympics in Munich, West Germany. Those athletes who competed in the 1960-76 Olympiads were randomly selected and tested by Dr. Udodiri Okafor in a doctoral dissertation, "The Interaction of Sports and Politics as a Dilemma of the modern Games," completed at The Ohio State University in 1979.

This researcher received permission to conduct the study and to obtain addresses of the athletes who participated in the 1972 Summer Games through the United States Olympic Committee. Copyright permission was also obtained to use the measuring instrument, a questionnaire—The Interaction of Sports and Politics (ISP)—from Dr. Okafor.

The 4 supplemental questions were attached to the questionnaire concerning specific events which occurred at the 1972 Summer Olympics and involved United States athletes. These questions were devised to measure four separate occurrences which dealt with political controversies as well as to determine if the controversies affected the athletes' performances.

The purpose of the ISP instrument was to measure opinions concerning the interaction of sports and politics in the Olympic Games through the use of a 5-point Likert scale. The four supplemental questions were measured by a four-response scale, with a space left for additional comments.

The initial mailing was sent to 120 athletes. As 23 were returned, it decreased the sample size to 97. In order to protect each subject's anonymity, each athlete was assigned a code number, and two follow-up letters and questionnaires were sent to those athletes who had not responded. A total of 60 questionnaires were completed for a return percentage of 63.8%.

An independent t-test was used in the interpretation of the data compiled from the ISP instrument. The mean scores of the 1960-1976 United States Olympic athletes were calculated by Dr. Okafor and used for computation in this study. The statistical analysis used to interpret the data compiled from the four supplemental questions were in percentages.

Analysis of the Data and Discussion

The analysis of data revealed that the calculated t-score was .155984, and that the standard error of the mean of the 2 groups was .174275. With 74 being the degrees of freedom, the critical value for significance at the .05 level was: t. 05 (74df) − 1.994. Therefore, there was no statistically significant difference between the 2 groups.

Discussion of the Findings

Section A: Purpose of the Olympic Games

The results suggested that the athletes still believe in the original purpose of the Olympic Games. Despite the numerous accounts of international happenings which have occurred during the time of the Games, the athletes are still there to compete and to develop friendships among the athletes of different countries. Question 8 states, Do Olympic athletes want to use the Games to make friends from other nations? This idea was supported by 46 out of 60 athletes who answered, "strongly agree" or "agree."

Section B: Olympic Athletes, Sports, and Politics

The answers to questions strongly suggest that athletes do not welcome politics into the Games. The question which received the highest response on the questionnaire was Question 1: Do Olympic athletes wish to keep sports free from politics? All the athletes who responded to this question either circled "strongly agree" or "agree." The question which received the lowest total was Question 3, Do Olympic athletes welcome the politics in sports because it enables their country to assert themselves?

Section C: Economy of Sports and International Relations

Question 3—Are the Olympics becoming too expensive for many nations and require cost curtailment?—is supported by the athletes and research as 41 of the athletes either strongly agreed or agreed with the above question. Since 1960, the costs of hosting the Olympics have increased significantly.

A staggering 59 out of 60 answered Question 8 with "strongly agree" or "agree." The question was, Is the interaction between sports and politics a thorny problem for the Olympic Games? The additional comments from the athletes supplied increased support for this concern. They responded that it is impossible to eliminate politics from the Games, but there should be more emphasis on the athletes' performance instead of the nation's policies.

Section D: Nationalism and Government Involvement

The results of the questions in this section revealed that nationalism could possibly play a very important role in the Olympic Games. For Question 1—Are the Olympics now used as a strong avenue to project the image of one's country?—54 athletes answered with a "strongly agree" or "agree." In Sugden and Yeannakis' four levels of politicization in sport, the first level supported these findings as, "The quest for national prestige in which nations seek to make their mark in the world community by achieving success at the Games."[2]

Government involvement in the Olympic Games was also an issue of great concern. The athletes were split when answering Question 2—Is government involvement necessary for the success of their Olympic national teams? Twenty-four athletes answered either "strongly agree" or "agree"; 29 athletes responded with a "disagree" or "strongly disagree." According to Loy, McPherson, and Kenyon, "Sport and politics are prevalent at the international level because national governments are involved in the Olympic organizations; also, athletes are used as symbols to show the strength of the nation."[3]

Section E: Measures for Separating Politics and Sports

According to completed research in this area, three solutions have been suggested: (a) eliminate the national anthems, (b) eliminate the national flags and team dress, and (c) eliminate the medal tables. All three of these ideas appeared as questions in this final section. Twenty-four answered Question 4—Should national anthems of a winning athlete's country no longer be played if there is to be a low-key national identity?—with a "strongly agree" or "agree." The results from Question 5—Should national flags and team dresses be the only allowable conspicuous identities for countries?—indicated that 28 athletes circled "strongly agree" or "agree." Twenty-two of the athletes answered "strongly agree" or "agree" to Question 6 which was, should there be no medal tables published during the Olympic Games? The overall results of these questions indicate that a majority of the athletes did not feel these were likely solutions to decrease or separate politics from the Olympic Games.

Table 1. Percentage results of the four supplemental questions

Subject	No Number Answered/%	Yes Number Answered/%	No Opinion Number Answered/%	Occurred After Performance Number Answered/%
Question #1	29 = 48.3%	9 = 15%	0 = 0%	22 = 36.7%
Question #2	11 = 18.3%	40 = 66.7%	9 = 15%	0 = 0%
Question #3	47 = 78.3%	3 = 5%	10 = 16.7%	0 = 0%
Question #4	23 = 38.3%	26 = 43.3%	11 = 18.3%	0 = 0%

[2]Coakley, J.J. *Sport in Society: Issues and Controversies*. 2nd ed. (St. Louis: C.V. Mosby, 1982), p. 32.

[3]Kenyon, G.S., Loy, J.W., Jr. and McPherson, B.D. *Sport and Social Systems*. (Reading, PA: Addison-Wesley, 1978), p. 287.

Question 8—Should we eliminate problems of amateurism in the Olympic Games by making them open to all athletes?—received a great deal of criticism. Thirty-one of 60 athletes felt that the Olympic Games should be open to all athletes regardless of their athletic standing; and 21 indicated only amateur athletes should be allowed to participate.

It is evident, when comparing the mean score of each question used in the ISP instrument, that little difference existed between the groups. It can be speculated that no statistical difference is prevalent between the groups for two reasons: (a) the United States athletes will have a strong commitment to the original idea of the Olympic Games, and (b) the athletes do not welcome political intervention in the Games.

Supplemental Questions

This study also revealed that the Arab takeover of the Israeli athletes did not affect 48.3% of the United States athletes who participated in the 1972 Summer Olympic Games and were subjects in this study. The additional comments indicated that the athletes said they were so intense about competing that they did not allow their emotions to get involved. Also, 36.7% of the athletes had already finished their competition. Many of them did indicate that this incident would have had some impact upon their own performances if they had been competing at that time. One athlete who responded was competing at that time. This athlete noted a personal loss of competitiveness due to the questionable continuation of the Games and recurring rumors of other violent acts.

Over half of the athletes, 66.7%, felt the Rhodesian incident set a political overtone on the Olympic Games, while only 18.3% felt it did not. Finally, on a vote of 36-31 by the International Olympic Committee, the invitation to Rhodesia was withdrawn.

A majority of the athletes, 78.3%, felt the final basketball games between the United States and the Soviet Union were not handled without political overtones. From the additional, comments it appeared that some of the athletes felt the refereed sports were blatant occurrences of political involvement because decisions were continually changed.

In the final question concerning the decision by the International Olympic Committee to remove the two American black runners from further Olympic competition, the athletes were divided: Twenty-three (43.3%) felt it was a justifiable decision; 26 athletes (38.3%) disagreed with the decision. Of the athletes who opposed the decision, many indicated that they felt the decision was made on poor evidence. It was also pointed out by one athlete that track and field was a televised major sport, and they wondered what the outcome would have been if this had occurred in a nontelevised, minor sport. Many of the athletes who agreed with the decision believed that athletes should not express their political opinions at the Games.

The results of this study may bring about a better understanding of the opinions of the athletes concerning politics in relationship to the Olympic Games and be useful for future competition.

References

Brundage, A. *Personal Olympic Collection, 1908-1975.* (Collection, University of Illinois.)

Coakley, J.J. (1982). *Sport in society: Issues and controversies.* (2nd ed.). St. Louis: C.V. Mosby.

Daley, A., Jordan, P., & Kiernam, J. (1977). *The story of the Olympic Games.* (2nd ed.). New York: J.B. Lippincott.

Espy, R. (1979). *The politics of the Olympic Games.* Berkeley: University of California Press.

Kannin, D.B. (1981). *A political history of the Olympic Games.* Boulder, CO: Westview Press.

Kenyon, G.S., Loy, J.W., Jr. & McPherson, B.D. (1978). *Sport and social systems.* Reading, PA: Addison-Wesley.

McKay, J. (1976). *My wide world.* New York: MacMillan.

Okafor, U. (1979). *The interaction of sports and politics and a dilemma of the modern Olympic Games.* Doctoral dissertation, The Ohio State University.

Warning, K.M. (1980). *A political history of the modern summer olympic games.* Master's thesis, California State University—Long Beach.

23

Theoretical and Practical Confusion About the Olympic Games

David A. Rose
THE VIEW FROM LEFT FIELD
LOS ANGELES, CALIFORNIA, USA

Events leading up to the 1984 Olympic Games again brought to the fore two questions which have long plagued both sports scholars and enthusiasts. (a) Are Olympic athletes amateur or professional? (b) Are the Olympic Games sport or politics? Answers to these questions are not merely theoretical; they bear directly upon the potential of the Olympic movement to attain its stated objectives: bringing the athletes of the world together, encouraging international good will, and constructing a better, more prosperous, and more peaceful world ("Rules of the International Olympic Committee," 1976). The purpose of this paper is to critically examine the debate over these questions, to identify and evaluate the two leading positions on the issues, and to expand the debate by offering a third postion which attempts to clarify problems unresolved by the other two.

The Debate

 The conservative position, as it may be called, holds that Olympic athletes are amateur, that the Olympic Games are sport, and that sport should *not* be political. This position is an outgrowth of 19th century British notions about sport (Dunning & Sheard, 1976), carried into the Games by their founder, Pierre de Coubertin (Spears & Swanson, 1978).

To the conservative, there are only two kinds of participants, amateurs and professionals (Rose, 1980). An amateur plays for the love of the experience; a professional plays for money. Conversely, not participating is seen as a matter of individual choice: A person's "right" vis a vis sport is a "right to choose" to participate (Rose, 1982). In this view, sports programs emerge and are sustained by their ability to satisfy individual motives. However, the governance of such programs tends not to be coordinated in any way (Zornow, 1976). What compels interaction between programs is the skill of the athletes. Improvements in skill bring about either a shift to a different program or a concession by governors of one program to let an athlete play in another one for a given period or event. To the conservative though, there is a gulf between amateur sport and professional sport, which, if crossed, cannot be recrossed. This notion gives rise to the perception of sport as two disconnected line segments.

Given this separation, the Olympics are seen as the pinnacle of amateur sport competition. The essence of this pinnacle is the display of *arete*, individual excellence of mind, body, and spirit (Spears & Swanson, 1978). The organizers of the Games envisioned them as a festival celebrating arete, with control resting in the hands of private committees charged with promoting the movement internationally.

Before proceeding, two points should be emphasized. First, while this conception of Olympic sport is often held up as "pure sport," as if free from other motives, they are not sport for sport's sake. They are rather sport for honor's sake. The second point is related to the first: Amateurism is a socially-based, not sport-based, idea. People who are amateurs are the "right sort," in the British sense of the phrase.

The second position, which may be called *centrist*, asserts that Olympic athletes are elite, that the Olympics are political, and that athletes should be supported financially in order to eliminate unfair advantages. To this way of thinking, an "athlete's right" is the "right to compete to the best of one's ability" (Rose, 1982). The dominance of this position began in 1936 and has escalated steadily since 1952, when athletes from the USSR first participated in the Games.

Soviet participation changed the content of Olympic competition in two significant ways. First, the Soviets proposed to the capitalist countries that one could stay within the bounds of their definition of amateur but operationally decide who is amateur differently—by applying different standards for measuring who is the "right sort." What Soviet participation emphasized was that the concept of amateur in practice meant someone who was not participating in programs called professional sport. It emphasized the subtle but accepted distinction between those who received money (or other forms of support) while they improved their skills, and those whose motive for playing was money (Rose, 1985).

Given the mood of the times since the war, the presence of athletes from communist countries also emphasized that the honor won in sport was not confined in its effects to the sports world; that is, that the Olympics were political. While this premise existed before Soviet involvement, their participation raised considerably the sociopolitical stakes of winning and losing. The reason is well known. By predicting the inevitable decline of capitalism and the rise of socialism and then communism, Karl Marx transformed the social meaning which could be attached to Olympic outcomes: They became nothing less than a barometer of the relative health of the two contending systems.

Given these stakes and conditions, leaders in capitalist countries have gradually loosened the definition of amateurism and gradually increased their coordination of programs feeding Olympic teams—all in the name of competitive fairness (Zornow, 1977). The resultant blurring of old distinctions (Reed, 1984) has led slowly but steadily to the rise of new terminology and concepts: *mass sport* and *elite sport*. The distinction here is strictly sport-based: The mass athlete has little skill or desire to win; the elite athlete has both great skill and great desire. These concepts, in turn, yield a notion of sport as a continuum.

Calls for reform of the present situation consistently fall along lines predicted by the positions. On the one hand are those who want to push the system further in the direction it appears headed, by opening the Games to the best athletes—whatever you call them (Simon, 1984). The danger here is that "faster, higher, stronger" will be transformed from the display of arete to a titillating spectacle where winning is its own morality and, thus, no morality at all. On the other hand, there are those who call for a return to the simpler past (Moore, 1984), urging that "pure" amateurism be restored and that the Games be held on a permanent site. The problem with these latter recommendations is that they fail to explain how to move back from the present and how to avoid destructive escalation in the future.

An Alternative

Given this predicament, it may be postulated that neither the conservative nor the centrist position offers an adequate understanding of the past and, thus, that neither can provide adequate guidance for the future. In the space remaining, therefore, the task of exploring a new position will be developed.

This new position is based on Rose's (1980) research into similar conceptual problems in the United States sports world, especially in college athletics. His research revealed the existence of four distinct categories of sport (see Table 1).

Several points are worth noting about these categories. First, each is defined sociologically; or structurally, according to the setting in which participa-

Table 1. Sport categories

Sport category	Contextual definition	Structural dialectic
Amateur	Recreation	Arousal/anomie
Quasi-amateur	Education	Synergy/anarchy
Semi-professional	Deferential	Community/rivalry
Professional	Ritual	Authenticity/illusion

tion takes place, not according to the motive of the participant. Second, the nature of each category is dialectical with each category containing within itself the potential for its own transformation. Third, the four categories are interconnected: No category is devoid of elements of the other three, but each is distinguished by its own dialectic. Fourth, because categories are both transformable and interconnected, the structure of sport, as a whole, is a tetrahedron.

One of these categories, semiprofessional sport is especially relevant to the present discussion. Semiprofessional sport is defined as programs in which participation is undertaken to represent the quality of the sponsoring organization. In view of the points made earlier, it may be seen that the Olympic Games are, at the least, semiprofessional sport (Rose, 1980). In this case, teams represent sociopolitical entities called nations; thus, in this framework, the Olympics are both sport and politics. The answer to the second question falls with the answer to the first: Olympic athletes may be said to be at the least semiprofessional.

Note, however, the use of the phrase, "at the least." This phrase alludes to what has been called the "professionalization of amateur sport," but which, in the tetrahedronal conception of sport, is more properly called the "professionalization of semi-pro sport." Furthermore, the definition of semiprofessional sport exposes two points about this process heretofore overlooked (Rose, 1982). First, it exposes as the mechanism of increasing professionalization the interaction between the representative relationship and the social reality encircling the semiprofessional program. Second, the definition also exposes the significant stages of the process: semiprofessional sport, acceptably professional sport, and unacceptably professional sport.

In the intermediate stage, the representative relationship is genuine, but the relative priorities between being an athlete and being a member of the organization are reversed by the actions of the organization. In the latter stage, the representative relationship is broken, as the organization gives membership and support to individuals whose only claim to such treatment is their athletic skill. If this description seems abstract, it is intended to be, because the specifics depend on the kinds of organizations involved.

In applying these ideas to the Olympic Games, it is appropriate to borrow terminology from United States' college sport. In the stage of semiprofessional sport, Olympic teams are composed of citizen-athletes, individuals who are citizens first and athletes second; individuals who are contributing members of their nation, whose life chances are consistent with their contribution, and who have an interest and ability in sport. In the stage of acceptably professional sport, Olympic teams are composed of individuals who are athletes first and citizens second; people whose life chances are contingent on sport, and who contribute to society through work opportunities sport brings them. In the stage of unacceptably professional sport, teams are composed of people who are athletes first and citizens not at all; people who are not contributing members to their society, but whose life chances are consistent with, or better than, other members, solely because of their athletic ability.

Two points are worth noting about these stages relative to Olympic history. First, they refute the claim that certain nations, by virtue of their political economic system, cannot have professional athletes. Instead, these concepts open the possibility of having professional sport programs other than those owned by capitalists, including ones in noncapitalist countries and in the Olympic Games. Second, the concepts reveal that the debate previously understood to be a debate over amateurism, professionalism, and broken-time payments, is really a debate over the forms which support for athletes can take without serving the representative relationship between team and nation. In this regard, the answer given earlier must be amended: Rules under which the Games are presently conducted mean the Games are professional sport. The question is, Are they acceptably professional or unacceptably professional sport?

It should be readily apparent that questions of acceptability depend on three matters: Who makes the rules, what are the rules, and, as a result, who gets a chance to play and who does not? The nature of these questions is such that they are both empirical and normative; that is, political and ultimately moral. As moral questions, they demand answers which are consistent with, not the political realities of today's world, but with the aspirations of individuals and nations who want peace and prosperity. Thus, one can answer the question of acceptable professionalism in the Olympics by posing a normative answer against which present practices may be judged. The following three principles stand out:

1. A sport can be an Olympic sport only if it represents sporting interests of the people.
2. A nation's team may be invited to the Games only if the nation promotes other societies' right to develop.
3. An individual is eligible to participate in the Games only if he or she promotes other individuals' right to develop.

Principle 1:

National representatives would meet to establish the minimum level of international interest a sport must attain to be recognized as an Olympic sport. This level would be a minimum number of nations participating at a minimum level of national interest. This minimum national level would be a ratio of the number of individuals in amateur sport programs relative to the relevant gender-population in the country. Only those countries meeting this minimum level would be eligible to have a team representing it. Thereafter, national committees would pay dues and have voting representation in regional and international Olympic committees proportional to the number of recognized sports in which they field teams. An individual residing in a country not represented by a team may be eligible to compete under the aegis of the appropriate regional committee.

Principle 2:

Invitations would be voted on a sport-by-sport basis by the national committees whose teams participate in the sport. A nation's team would be presumed invited unless a predetermined number of committees vote to reconsider. The case for and against inviting the challenged team would be presented to the full Olympic community, who would vote, one-vote-per-country, for or against an invitation. In each sport, the nation voted by the others to have done the most to promote the right to develop would be designated the official site of Olympic competition for that sport. Events in each sport would be televised, with rights' fees for a country paid on a per capita TV basis at a minimum rate relative to the Gross National Product per capita. Rights would be sold for the entire package of sports, with income distributed between the host nations, the International Olympic Committee, the Regional Olympic Committees, and the National Olympic Committees whose teams were invited to participate. International Olympic Committee and Regional Olympic Committee's monies would be used to cover administrative costs, costs of eligibility enforcement, and two special funds, an international exchange program used to assist the development of programs at the local level and a research development fund used to support the study of sport in society.

Principle 3:

An individual would not be eligible to participate if he or she participates during any pre-Olympic year in an unacceptably professional sport program. Each national committee would be responsible for certifying eligibility, with regional and international committees performing periodic verification checks. National Olympic Committees would, in turn, certify programs conducted by each national federation. A challenge to a federation's practices could be brought through petition signed by a predetermined number of athlete-members. A federation losing such a challenge would lose its Olympic accreditation in the sport.

When one compares these regulations to the way the Olympic movement and Games are presently conducted, answering the last question is straightforward: In their present form, the Olympic Games are unacceptably professional sport.

References

Dunning, E., & Sheard, K. (1976). The bifurcation of Rugby Union and Rugby League: A case study of organization conflict and change. *International Review of Sport Sociology*, **11**(2), 31-72.

Moore. K. (1984). Oh, for the days of a county fair. *Sports Illustrated*, **60**(20), 26, 31-32.

Reed, J. (1984). Chariots of litigation. *Time*, **123**(80), 80-81.

Rose, D. (1980). *Physical culture. A critique of the American sociological study of sport*. Unpublished doctoral dissertation, University of Massachusetts, Amherst.

Rose, D. (1982). Olympic athletes: Amateur or professional? In J. Partington, T. Orlick, & J. Samela (Eds.), *Sport in Perspective* (p. 81). Ottawa: Coaching Association of Canada.

Rose, D. (1985). The controversy over college sport: Will it ever end? In D. Chu & J. Segrave (Eds.), *Sport in Higher Education*. Champaign: Human Kinetics.

Rules of the International Olympic Committee (1976). In M. Killanin & J. Rodda (Eds.), *The Olympic Games*. New York: Macmillan.

Simon, W. (1984). If disruptions continue, we'll destroy the Olympics. *US News and World Report,* **96**(20), 28.

Spears, B. & Swanson, R. (1978). *History of sport and physical activity in the United States.* Dubuque: Wm. C. Brown.

Zornow, G. (1976). *President's Commission on Olympic Sports. First Report to the President.* Washington, D.C.

Zornow, G. (1977). *Report of the President's Commission on Olympic Sports, 1975-1977.* Washington, D.C.: US Government Printing Office.

24

De Coubertin and the Olympic Games as Symbols of Peace

Arnd Krüger
GEORG-AUGUST-UNIVERSITÄT
FEDERAL REPUBLIC OF GERMANY

The Olympic Games have been considered a symbol of peace ever since the ancient games when an Olympic truce was kept which applied to athletes, coaches, judges, and spectators (Lämmer, 1976). The unity of the Greek world and a common code of ethics required that this truce be kept. Violators were punished. A longing for peace is now part of the rules of the modern Olympic Games. Rule 3 states that the purpose of the Olympic Games is,

> De contribuer au respect et au maintien de la paix entre les peuples. [To contribute to respect and maintain peace between people.]

On the other hand, physical education and sport in ancient Greece also served to prepare able soldiers. The English victories over Napoleon were supposed to have been "won" on the playing fields of Eton, the military strength and the imperial expansion of Britain at de Coubertin's time, resulting partly from participating in sports together (Mangan, 1981). For de Coubertin (1894), the root of German Turnen was simply warfare. The dichotomy of war and peace has thus constantly been present in ancient and in modern Olympic history.

Not only in the instance of Afghanistan have organizers of Olympic Games been actively involved in warfare. In 1896, the athletes went to compete in a country ready for a war which started right afterward (Crete at war with Turkey); in 1900, the organizers of the Olympic Games were in the process of occupying major parts of China; and just prior to the 1904 Olympic Games, the United States staged a civil war in Columbia to have the northern provinces separate as Panama, which the United States immediately recognized and received the Canal Zone in exchange. During the 1904 Olympic Games, the United States still had troops stationed in Panama. Wars of participating countries were so frequent that one cannot name them all: In 1900 the British fought the Boer-War, and French troops occupied the Niger; in 1904, German troops were in the Cameroun. The Balkan war of 1912 was fought between participants of the Olympic Games (Krüger, 1980). The list, even under de Coubertin's presidency, is too long to include. There is no Olympic truce for the modern Olympic Games, and the International Olympic Committee (IOC) has never expected it.

Olympic Games and Warfare

As the IOC bases itself on the philosophy of de Coubertin, the relationship to peace and war becomes most obvious in key decisions such as those at the occasion of the 1940 Olympic Games. Although this occurred after de Coubertin's death, Count Baillet-Latour, who followed him in office, had been picked and prepared by him and took basically the same stand on all major issues (Krüger, 1980). The Summer Games were given to Helsinki in 1938, after Tokyo had given them back (Bernett, 1980), and the Winter Games to Germany on June 9, 1939. This was after the annexation of Czechoslovakia by Germany. Having to decide to cancel the Olympic Games or to give them to the organizer of the last Olympic Games, who was the only one who would be able to organize them on such short notice, the IOC decided to give them to the obvious aggressor. Olympic Rule 1—that Olympic Games are to be celebrated every 4 years—was valued higher than the knowledge that Germany was preparing for war, had invaded its neighboring countries, and was threatening others. In the first vote, it was 2 to 27 against cancellation; in a second vote, the Olympic Games could only be given to Germany.

Two weeks after the beginning of World War II, the president of the IOC, Count Baillet-Latour, asked the members of the Executive Committee (EC) how one should behave now that there was war. Could the Olympic Games be held in a country at war? "Yes," they voted, 4 to 3. Should countries at war be excluded? "No," they voted, 7 to 0. Are the Olympic Games technically organizable? This question was handed over to the international federations, and they agreed by a large majority. Is it conceivable that athletes of countries at war could compete against each other in sports? "Yes," they said, 7 to 0. Is the EC alone competent to decide these questions? "No," they said; the whole IOC should be asked, they voted 4 to 3. This decision is the precedent by which the IOC later handled decisions all the way to the Afghanistan situation. The Winter Olympic Games of 1940 were given back by Germany on November 25, 1939, when, after the invasion of Poland, the Western Allies remained at war with Germany. The Summer Olympic Games of 1940 were given back by Finland on May 6, 1940. The hope that one could celebrate the Olympic games lasted that long (Krüger, 1982).

De Coubertin and the Education for Peace

For de Coubertin as educator and historian, the question of war and peace was always present in his work. Ever since one of his first papers on education for peace, published in 1889 when he was only 27, until his late work in the Union Pédagogique Universelle (1927) and the Bureaux international de pédagogie sportive (1933a), he was concerned with peace education. For the historian de Coubertin (1933, p. 175f.), warfare was not the most important part of historiography. He attempted, rather, to write a social history which would orient itself to the leaders of the contries (1925). The catalog of his library (Meylan, 1944) proves that this was also his main interest.

His attitude toward war and peace remains surprisingly constant during the 44 years it can be followed. Peace for de Coubertin is armed (1904). Pacifism he resents, as "wars come over a country like a tempest" (1903b), and one should be prepared. As an educator, de Coubertin was aware that education for peace started with the individual. It meant for him that the individual should be strong and have courage. To maintain peace, one had to be sure that one was not afraid of the other: Mutual respect should be achieved on the basis of a balance of power (1933a, p. 161). As Volume Three of his *L'Education des Adolescents au XXe Siècle*, he published a timely *Education Morale* on mutual respect (1915). While war was raging in Europe, he was concerned with respect for beliefs, for conditions, for conventions, and for individuality, and felt that all should be guided by a culture of the conscience. How is this realized in practice? While in 1889 de Coubertin thought about peace in small terms and advocated boxing as in the British public schools; later he started to develop a theory of peace which was applicable to nations. Here again, he felt that peace should be strengthened through sports.

A country of beautiful, strong athletes conscious of their power would be ready to fight for family and community: This, for de Coubertin (1923), was more effective than any treaty or the equality of fear. One of the fundamental errors of European education was rooted in not knowing enough about the other countries (1932). The best service to one's own country should, therefore, be to know more about other countries: This would lead to an internationalism which had been de Coubertin's guiding principle throughout his life. This manifested itself for de Coubertin in volunteering for military service at the beginning of World War I and also showed in his writing, particularly in French history (1899). He resented cosmopolitanism of society if it were not based on firm patriotism (1898).

De Coubertin and the Nazis

One of the possible touchstones of de Coubertin's attitudes toward war and peace can be seen in his later work. In a detailed archival study, Teichler (1982) linked de Coubertin with the German Nazis, as he was not sufficiently critical of them and also corresponded with high Nazi officials on friendly terms. This, de Coubertin's flaw, proved that he was not the humanist he was supposed to be on whom the Olympic Movement is based (Seillière, 1917). While de Coubertin's integrity seems to be perfect in the view of his biographers (Boulogne, 1975; Eyquem, 1966; Krüger, 1980; Lucas, 1962; MacAloon, 1981; Mandell, 1976; Senay & Hervet, 1956; and Ullrich, 1982), Teichler pictures him as an old man who is a weak and ready vehicle of Nazi politics at a time when he should have known better. He is said to have helped the Nazi regime by providing them with the reputation of the Olympic Movement, a symbol of peace, thus helping camouflage preparations of war. As the figurehead of the Olympic Peace Movement, de Coubertin should have disassociated himself from the Nazis. Of course, one can question whether by 1933-1937, the Nazi cruelties had already become known so that de Coubertin felt discredited by dealing with them. After all, the IOC had given the Olympic Games to Berlin and Garmisch-Partenkirchen, so why should the honorary president of the organization speak up?

After 1925, he had resigned from the presidency, retreated into educational matters, and did not keep up-to-date with elite sports; yet he was a keen observer of political matters. The IOC was 100% in favor of the Berlin Olympic Games. After the expulsion, Ernest L. Jahncke, the only American in the IOC who had spoken up against the Nazis (Krüger, 1972), impressed everyone. It may be asked if, in such a situation, de Coubertin's relative reluctance to propagate the Nazi Olympics was not, indeed, a minor form of critique. It should not be overlooked that de Coubertin was financially ruined and that he turned down a favorable offer by the Nazis to do public relations for them. Can this not be interpreted as being consistent in his thought?

In 1904, the IOC staged the Olympic Games in St. Louis, in the American South where strict racial segregation was kept between athletes and between spectators until the 1950s. Lynching, suppression, and lack of opportunity for black Americans was not unknown. de Coubertin had voted for the Olympic Games to be held in Chicago where he wanted to travel. When the United States Olympic Committee went to St. Louis instead, he did not go and called the IOC to a meeting in London instead. He was not only antagonized by the president of the organizing committee (Lucas, 1977), but also accepted the inequality of races and the rules on which segregation was based; however, he could never accept the personal consequences for the individual (de Coubertin, 1903a).

His relationship to Jews was different; Jews were among his oldest friends and collaborators in his educational initiatives. In his political interpretation of the Dreyfus Affair, he showed that racism was no issue for him, and he explained the whole matter in social terms (1899, p. 984ff.). There is no indication that de Coubertin resented German racism. What he publicly condemned was the burning of books as this ran counter to his notion of mutual respect by knowing each other (1933b).

De Coubertin could not understand the peculiar relationship of Germany to the League of Nations as this organization did what he favored: It helped people to know more about each other, by talking about problems, by informing, and by assuring the self-determination of people. In the final analysis, it can be said, however, that, until his death, he was never certain how to evaluate the Nazis. In one respect, he admired a country such as Germany which did so much for the physical education of its citizens, but on the other hand, he was against any form of intolerance. This is most obvious in the last newspaper interviews which he granted (Krüger, 1972, p. 177f.; Saint-Vallier, 1936). It can therefore be argued that for de Coubertin as a historian, the Nazi rule until 1937 was not such a touchstone after all. For de Coubertin, as a political scientist who has been compared to Tocqueville (MacAloon, 1981, p. 273), he realized that the Nazi propaganda would only help the Olympic Games as it was making it the media event of its time. This counted for him; he did not care whether it was done to advertise the climate of southern California or a racist regime (Saint-Vallier, 1936). His life and sport philosophy of *mens fervida in corpore lacertoso* (a fermenting spirit in a muscular body) was not too far away from some of the body cults of the Nazis (Krüger, 1979) prior to the Second World War. De Coubertin died in 1937, and so he never witnessed the war-mongering of the Nazis.

In the middle of World War I, de Coubertin (1915) wrote a book on mutual respect and advocated contacts between the victorious and the defeated. These basic positions on the basis of knowledge and respect for national identity he did not forsake the rest of his life. Politicians without conscience he termed "monsters" (1915, p. 104).

The Symbolism of the Olympic Games

Avery Brundage's "The Games must go on" (Guttmann, 1984) has been criticized as a perversion of the Olympic idea into mere actionism. De Coubertin also advocated this last resort of Olympism, as competing with each other and talking together is the basis of knowledge and respect. The Olympic Games of modern times cannot be taken as a symbol of peace nor of love of peace; they are no symbol for pacifism but a symbol of the longing for peace which is apparent in mutual respect and acceptance of the rules of the game.

The Olympic slogan, *citius-altius-fortius*, expressed the hope for progress and expansion of an industrial society. *Mens fervida in corpore lacertoso* stands for the ideals of dynamism, optimism, and strength. The always-changing Olympic site, the Olympic rings, and its flag are symbols of the unity of the world coupled with the respect for the individuality and the nationality of every participant. In this respect, the desire that the games must go on is the continuation of this longing for peace, as it helps maintain the unity of the world (1925, vol. 4, p. 32ff.).

In his last major newspaper interview, de Coubertin assured the press (Saint-Vallier, 1936) that he wanted the Olympic Games the way they became: a major media event for the sake of propaganda. He also pointed out that the basis for mutual respect is not in the competition of elite athletes, but is rooted in the education for athleticism which starts with children. De Coubertin's notion of peace can therefore be said to be one of peace education for mutual respect on the basis of strength for which the Olympic Games and elite sports are but a small portion.

References

Bernett, H. (1980). Das Scheitern der Olympischen Spiele von 1940. *Stadion*, **6**, 251-290.

Boulogne, Y.P. (1975). *La vie et l'oeuvre pédagogique de Pierre de Coubertin*. Ottawa: Leméac.

Coubertin, P., de. (1889). L'éducation de la paix. *La Réforme Sociale, 7*, 361-363.

Coubertin, P., de. (1894). Le rétablissement des Jeux Olympiques. *Revue de Paris,* 1, 170-184.

Coubertin, P., de. (1898). Does cosmopolitan life lead to international friendliness? *Review of Reviews,* New York, 17, 429-434.

Coubertin, P., de. (1899). France since 1814. *Fortnightly Review,* 65 (N.S.), 186-211, 572-585, 817-834, 1025-1037, 66, 240-255, 843-855, 977-990.

Coubertin, P., de. (1903, Sept. 26). La question nègre. *Figaro,* p. 1.

Coubertin, P., de. (1903, Dec. 23). L'oeuvre de paix. *Figaro,* p. 1.

Coubertin, P., de. (1904, Jan. 26). Les bases de la pédagogie prochaine. (2) la paix armée. *Figaro,* p. 1.

Coubertin, P., de. (1915). *Le respect mutuel.* Paris: Félix Alcan.

Coubertin, P., de. (1923a). *Discours prononcé par le président du comité.* 21st IOC session Rome. Lausanne: IOC.

Coubertin, P., de. (1923b). Où va l'Europe? Paris: Editions G. Crès.

Coubertin, P., de. (1925). *Histoire universelle.* (vols. 1-4). Aix-en-Provence: Société de l'histoire universelle.

Coubertin, P., de. (1927). Histoire pourvoyeuse de guerre ou de paix. *Union Pédagogique Universelle, 2,* 5-10.

Coubertin, P., de. (1932). *Les assises de la cité prochaine.* Conférence donnée à Berne le 19 avril. Geneva: Burgi.

Coubertin, P., de. (1933a). *Anthologie.* Lausanne: B.I.P.S.

Coubertin, P. de. (1933b). *Lettre à S.E. le président du Conseil de la Société des Nations.* Lausanne: IOC.

Coubertin, P., de. (1935). *Les assises philosophiques de l'olympisme moderne.* Geneva. Le Sport Suisse.

Eyquem, M.-T. (1966). *Pierre de Coubertin. L'épopée olympique.* Paris: Calmann-Lévy.

Guttmann, A. (1984). *The games must go on. Avery Brundage and the Olympic movement.* New York: Columbia University Press.

Krüger, A. (1972). *Die Olympischen Spiele 1936 und die Weltmeinung.* Berlin: Bartels & Wernitz.

Krüger, A. (1979). Mens fervida in corpore lacertoso oder Coubertins Ablehnung der schwedischen Gymnastik. *Proceedings of the 8th HISPA Congress,* Uppsala, 145-153.

Krüger, A. (1980). Neo-Olympismus zwischen Nationalismus und Internationalismus. In H. Ueberhorst (Ed.), *Geschichte der Leibesübungen* (vol. 31, pp. 522-568). Berlin: Bartels & Wernitz.

Krüger, A. (1982). Deutschland und die Olympische Bewegung. In *ibidem* (vol. 32, pp. 1026-1047).

Lämmer, M. (1976). The nature and function of the Olympic truce in ancient Greece. *History of Physical Education and Sport, 3,* 37-52.

Lucas, J.A. (1962). *Baron Pierre de Coubertin and the formative years of the modern international Olympic movement. 1883-1896.* Unpublished doctoral dissertation. University of Maryland.

Lucas, J.A. (1977). Early olympic antagonists. Pierre de Coubertin vs. James E. Sullivan. *Stadion, 3,* 258-272.

MacAloon, J.J. (1981). *This great symbol Pierre de Coubertin and the origins of the modern Olympic Games.* Chicago: University of Chicago Press.

Mandell, R.D. (1976). *Die ersten Olympischen Spiele der Neuzeit.* Kastellaun: Henn.

Mangan, J.A. (1981). *Athleticism in the Victorian and Edwardian Public School: The emergence and consolidation of an educational Ideology.* Cambridge. Cambridge University Press.

Meylan, L. (Ed.), (1944). *Catalogue de la bibliothèque du baron Pierre de Coubertin*. Lausanne: La Guilde du Livre.

Saint-Vallier. (1936, Aug. 28). Tout va très bien monsieur le baron. *L'Auto*, p. 1.

Seillière, E. (1917). *Un artisan d'énergie française. Pierre de Coubertin*. Paris: Henri Didier.

Senay, A., & Hervet, R. (1956). *Monsieur de Coubertin*. Paris: S.E.S.

Teichler, H.J. (1982). Coubertin und das 3. Reich. *Sportwissenschaft, 12*, 18-55.

Ullrich, K. (1982). *Coubertin. Leben, Denken und Schaffen eines Humanisten*. Berlin. Sportverlag.

PART IV

Sport and Politics:
A Positive View of the Future

25

In a Nuclear Age, Sport is Man's Best Hope

Donald W.J. Anthony
AVERY HILL COLLEGE
LONDON, ENGLAND

When I accepted to present a keynote paper on 'sport and politics,' I had no idea that this theme would be the most significant for the 1984 Games. I had no idea that a new cold wave of world political tension would invade the Olympic family. I had the feeling that Los Angeles—despite its warts—would bring together a great family of sporting nations and strike a major blow for peace in the world. I still cherish the hope that it *will* strike this blow—despite the several seats reserved for absent friends. Nevertheless I did not realize that, in 1984, the political future of the Games would be at stake.

Even those of us who love sport and who have spent our whole careers dedicated to its propagation must realize that we can only do so much. Pierre de Coubertin warned us many years ago, "Don't expect too much from sport." Unless political leaders contrive to build a positive environment for the Olympic movement, the Games cannot alone bring about international peace and understanding—hopes which are enshrined in the fundamental principles of the movement itself.

Even if the militarists and the chauvinists feel happy that 1984 is tarnished, we can always remember what G.K. Chesterton said about Christianity and apply it to Olympism. It is not, he said, that it has been tried and found wanting, but that it has been found difficult and not tried!

Militarism, chauvinism, and *christianity*—these words focus attention on the man whose life and work are the basis of this paper: Philip Noel-Baker, an outstanding human being whose 93 years were spent predominantly in the areas of sport and politics, crusading for peace, especially through disarmament, and being the binding force linking these two areas.

Who Was Philip Noel-Baker?

Philip Noel-Baker was the Nobel laureate for peace in 1959. He was a major creative force in the League of Nations and later, the United Nations; a minister four times in the British Labor Party governments; an elder of the Society of Friends (the Quakers), and a pacifist and founder of the Friends Ambulance Units. In 1915, he was awarded the Mons Star (France), in 1917 the Silver Medal for military valour (Italy), and the Croce de Guerra in 1918.

He competed in the 1912 Olympic Games and was captain of the British Olympic team in 1920 and a silver medalist at 1500 meters in those Games. In 1948, he was the minister who, with the Olympic Organizing committee, coordinated the London Olympic Games. In 1952, he was commandant of the British contingent in Helsinki. At the age of 70, he was asked to preside over UNESCO's International Council of Sport and Physical Education. For 16 years he did just that with extraordinary energy and foresight.

In his lifetime, he had personally known every president of the International Olympic Committee, and he had corresponded with de Coubertin. At every moment in Olympic history, he stood up to be counted for his loyalty to the Olympic movement. In a lifetime spent in international organizations, he saw his involvment in sport as "the most noble." He felt that sport was "life as it could be and should be"; that sport would help all people, especially those in developing countries, to "make the best use of all that education had to offer them."

A convinced socialist, he did not, however, let ideology intrude in an obstructive way. He liked people, especially of the female gender. I spoke to his friends in Japan recently, and one of them said, "When he was older and walked with the aid of a stick he managed quite well—until he saw an attractive young lady who might support him; he then became, almost immediately, a helpless invalid." He was persona grata as much in Washington as in Moscow, in Mexico and Havana, in Paris and Rome, and in Belgrade and Tokyo. Not only was he a fine orator, but he could converse well in French, German, Greek, and Italian. For 5 years, he was professor of international relations at London University. He was exactly the same in spirit and attention whether dealing with the Pope, his housekeeper, my students, or those with a mental handicap. If necessary, he could match the intelligent, concept by concept, or the witty, joke by joke.

One of seven children of a Canadian-born Quaker, Philip was educated in Quaker Schools: Bootham in Yorkshire, and Haverford College in Pennsylvania. He had study periods in Paris and Munich and took an honors degree in economics and history at Kings College, Cambridge. At Cambridge, he was president of the Union (the debating society) and also of the Athletics Club. After marriage to Irene Noel, a nurse he met in the First World War, he took her family name, an early sign of his commitment to the feminist movement.

He was born in 1889, the year in which the Japanese Meiji constitution was promulgated. The colonists had the world neatly parcelled into large estates, and education for all was making a start in the richest of the industrial states. There was only one international sports federation in existence, that for gymnastics, and de Coubertin was in the preliminary stages of organizing an international committee to revive the Olympic Games and was, actually, organizing an international symposium on physical education. In the United States, the Boston Conference on Physical Training was held; in his lifetime, he thus saw the unfolding of the whole world sports phenomenon.

During his early life, he would have known of the suicidal action of a suffragette who threw herself under the king's horse in the Derby to bring attention to the "votes for women" campaign—the first time, perhaps, that a major sports spectacle was seized upon to make a political point. He watched the 1908 Games as a spectator. Before the age of 30, he was writing letters to the *Times* about Olympism. He even proposed that the 1920 Olympic Games might be delayed in order that participant nations, after the first World War, could be better prepared for them.

> In his obituary to Philip in 1982, Ernst Jokl said, 'Together with de Coubertin, Philip Noel-Baker ranked, and will always rank, as the founder of the contemporary sports movement.' De Coubertin was the romantic who recreated the Olympic Games in the image of what he believed the great religious festival had been in Hellas. But to Philip Noel-Baker the modern Olympic Games were to be more than a festival. He conceived the Games as a vehicle for the attainment of his ultimate goal, that of the establishment of peaceful relations between the nations of the world.

If you believe in the great leader theory of history, Philip John Noel-Baker must be counted in the history of sport. It is for these reasons that his views need special attention. They are the views of a most significant human being. They are views which need restating to each succeeding generation, and that is why I take advantage of this Eugene Olympic Scientific Congress to present them to you.

There was also the fun side to Philip's life. He could bring us to tears or laughter with a turn of phrase. He said that throughout his life as a socialist minister, he was plagued by the fact that his brother-in-law was chairman of the London Stock Exchange. But, he said, "all *his* life *he* was plagued by the fact that *his* brother-in-law was a socialist minister." In his later years, the honors were bestowed upon him. He was made a papal Knight of Saint Sylvester ("I rather like the Romans," he said). He accepted a peerage in the House of Lords, badly needing a platform for his deeply felt sociopolitical views. At the family party to honor this event, he said, "My father, who fought two by-elections on the abolition of the House of Lords, would have vetoed my decision!"

He was a preacher who practiced. He was also an athlete—a tennis player, mountaineer, walker, swimmer, and teetotaller. Even in advanced old age he was a keen devotee of simple aerobics. I can hear him now, proclaiming that he owed his continued intellectual energy to his strict regime. I had the great advantage of knowing him as a friend and colleague for 20 years and more. I have said before, and I repeat, every moment was an education for me and a great joy. In the beginning, I knew him as a famous man; I asked how I should address him—"Sir, Mr. Noel-Baker, whatever?" "Why not call me as they do at Battersea Park athletics track," he said. "What's that?" I asked. Just "Philip." It was this humility—the conquering of the ego as the Buddhists say—which made him particularly happy with his Japanese friends in Hiroshima and Nagasaki. If it was the carnage of the First World War which crystallized his pacifism, it was the dreadful nuclear bombardment of the Second World

War, in those cities, which reinforced his belief in the rightness of his lifelong crusade.

I was with him a few hours before he died. He had worn himself out at the United Nation's Special Conference on Disarmament in New York. On return, he sat down and completed his ongoing manuscripts on Nansen and a history of the League of Nations. He found it difficult to speak but easy to listen. He had with him his nurse, his secretary, and his granddaughter. I listed these bedside sitters, and he said, "Nothing more stimulating than the company of beautiful women." He then whispered what we thought might be his last words, and we craned forward to hear the great man ask, "What was Alan Wells' time for the 100 meters in Brisbane?" A balanced view of life indeed!

There were three great ceremonies after his death: at the Royal Institute of International Affairs; at the Friends Meeting House; and at Saint Martins-in-the-Fields in Trafalgar Square. All were meetings packed with people who admired and loved him. The lesson read at the last ceremony by an Anglican vicar but with a catholic priest in support (not bad for a Quaker), was a passage from the Bible which he had known by heart: "And they shall beat their swords into ploughshares—war shall be no more."

Political Concerns

His life encapsulated most of the issues which appeared in the introductory brochure of this Congress as "concerns.' These issues included sports as political strategy, as propaganda, as terrorism, as foreign aid, and as diplomacy for developing countries.

Philip Noel-Baker spoke simply and directly on all these issues. A few years before his death, we discussed the possibility of a collection of all that he had written and spoken about sport. "I haven't really said very much," he mused. "I have said the same thing again and again for 70 years!" Here are a few gems from his collection:

The number one question for the world, he said, was disarmament. He let the facts speak for themselves.

> The money required to provide adequate food, water, housing, education and health, for everyone in the world has been estimated at 17 billion dollars. A huge sum of money. About as much as the world spends on arms every two weeks.
>
> *(New Internationalist, 1983)*

> Every minute of every day one million dollars is poured into the black hole of the arms race.
>
> (Sony Ramphal Secretary-General Commonwealth Secretariat)

> The cost of ten advanced fighter aircraft equals the cost of preventing, by immunization, the death of five million children a year and the crippling effect of malnutrition on many millions more.
>
> *(The Observer, March 1984)*

On Politics to Sport

Thus for Philip there was no long-term problem with the size and cost of the Olympic Games. No Games yet, he often said, cost as much as the petrol used by military aeroplanes in all countries in one day. No Games yet have involved a logistical problem greater than that faced by even the smallest countries regarding annual military maneuvers. On the relationships of *politics to sport*, he said, in addressing the General Assembly of the International Sports Federations in 1969,

> I would say of course that everyone desires to keep politics out of sport. Of course everyone here can think of follies and disasters that have happened because that was not done. But I would say that politics are part of life and so is sport. Politics, as a politician I dare to say it, politics are part of civilisation and so is sport. They overlap problems which inevitably arise in which the international federations, and perhaps their national committees, must make decisions. I venture a general assertion that these problems can only be solved by the frank and loyal application of the basic principles of our civilisation. In many matters that will mean, as we have all learned, the full and loyal recognition of universal and equal human rights. But I believe that sport can, itself, play its part, perhaps its greatest part, in shaping the thinking, the ethos, the moral framework of the international community of nations.

On Sport at the Community Level

As a practicing politican with a constituency in Derby to care for, he was careful not to forget the political role of *sport at community level*. In 1981, addressing the International Olympic Committee Congress in Baden-Baden, he reiterated a view expressed many times before.

> Violence is increasing in Great Britain. In 1973 the cost of crime to our nation was £5000 million. Only a small percentage of the enormous increase is inflation.
>
> Punishment is not the answer. Prison and death are ineffective; they are violences. There are 18 million unemployed in the industrial countries of the North. 18 million for whom society can find no useful work. In Britain there are three million. They lead empty lives, they have no purpose, no dignity, no achievement in their lives. There is no training and no facilities for their physical and intellectual energies.
>
> In unbearable frustration they seek revenge in senseless acts of force. Punishment is not the answer. But there is an answer. Suppose the British government spent £500 million a year in support of the policy they urge—Sport for All. £300 million on facilities—tracks and pools, gymnasia, tennis courts and playing fields. £200 million for a great service of leaders, administrators, coaches, and trainers to ensure that every individual finds his chosen sport. As people took seriously to sport there would be a big reduction in the cost of crime; there would be a big reduction in the unemployment benefit which is now given to people to live in idleness.

His case was not that all violence would cease or that all would turn to sport, but that a big percentage would, and gladly. He believed that over 5 years as much as £3000 million a year would be saved, and that the quality of life for people would be enriched.

Terrorism

On terrorism in the Games, he wrote to *The Times* after the events in Munich (September 8, 1972).

> How many political kidnappings and murders have been in various lands in recent years? The arms producing countries have flooded the world with new and obsolescent weapons. Since 1962 five million people have died in U.N. Charter breaking wars. Lawless violence has been allowed to menace civilised society, national and international, at every level. This is the true cause of the tragedies like that in the Olympic Village. Your sports editor says that the events of yesterday will tend to confirm the arguments that the Games have outlived their usefulness. With respect this seems to me as logical as to say that, if the murders had happened at Victoria Station, Britain Rail should be closed down.

Propaganda

Philip did not attend the 1936 Olympic Games in Berlin. The grounds of principle which led to this decision were his view that Hitler had violated the Olympic Charter. Jews, Catholics, and "workers" (members of the German Workers' Sports Association) were excluded from the German team. He wrote to Karl Halt, the chairman of the German national Olympic Committee to protest. They had been club mates in 1913. "My self sacrifice," said Philip, "did Hitler no harm, just as my presence would have done him no good—it was just a futile loss to me." Politicians and others have agreed, he continued, that the fact that Hitler sat in the "Royal Box" in the stadium, greatly increased his power over the German people, as well as his prestige with them and with the world.

> It is a totally unjustified illusion. Of course he did his best to advertise and exploit that view. But the Games did nothing to increase his power—it was already absolute. They did nothing to add to his prestige. Just the opposite. They brought him a crushing humiliation.

The International Olympic Committee demanded that he remove Swastikas and Nazi slogans from the stadium. The message of the Games was that all the nations were one great happy family inspired by the same ideals of sportsmanship. The message "made the Nazi doctrine look abhorrent to anyone with eyes to see."

Philip once confided in me, "I have always wished I had been in that stadium in 1936 to see the nonsense that that wonderful black man, Jesse Owens, made of the Aryan-racialist theories of Adolf Hitler."

Racism

Similarly with racism in South Africa, he did not flinch. Writing to the *Daily Telegraph* (September 3, 1982) on the cricketers who had played in South Africa against all advice and for what Philip called "the temptation of huge bribes," he said,

I have always striven to keep controversial politics out of sport. But the South Africans have brought their odious politics of apartheid into their whole social system. To participate in sport with them is to condone this uncivilised and hateful system.''

Nationalism

On nationalism and its manifestations, he was not one to disregard the Olympic ceremonies. He turned to Fridhof Nasen (leading Norwegian internationalist and explorer who played a major part in the League of Nations) for guidance. Quoting Nansen, he said that to be a true internationalist, you must be a true nationalist as well. You must understand your own nation's genius, take an ardent pride in its national achievements, and in its national contribution to the international civilization of mankind. "To me," he said, "The Victory Ceremonies in the Olympic Games are a supreme example of this marriage of national and international patriotism and pride. Like Lord Killanin, who once stated that whatever he did, "For half the world it was too quick and for the other half too slow," Philip Noel-Baker tried to think both historically and globally. Historically because the ceremonies tried to marry the traditions of the ancient Games with those of the new, and globally because there were enormous differences in the social systems of the competing teams. For some, it was easy to discard what appeared to be problematic symbols; for newly developing countries such symbols were important in efforts to build national identity and pride in indigenous cultures.

In 1980, he was to the fore in helping the British Olympic Association to counter governmental pressure, for sport was "too precious to be made the shuttlecock of politicians." The great sports championships and the Olympic Games were a marvellous and heartening contrast to the wars, the violence, and the terrorism that have disgraced our world since "science was made the prostitute of war." Sport was not to be so prostituted.

The Games in Moscow would not, in his opinion, make the world think that "Communism is the best and most successful political system." or that "the President of the USSR was the greatest man on earth." "What facile vapourings." Everybody at the opening ceremony will be thinking only

> of the greatness and the glory of the Games, of the pageant and the emotion
> of the athletes parade, of the Olympic flame kindled by the sun in the sacred
> olive-grove in Greece, of de Coubertin's magnificent oath, so magnificently
> honoured by a hundred thousand athletes since 1896.

Philip Noel-Baker hoped that the Moscow Games might be "the turning point of history from violence and conflict—to the harmony and welfare of all the nations of the world." Sadly, in 1984, they were not. We are faced with another series of withdrawals and another dangerous moment in history. I have tried to envisage how Philip Noel-Baker might have reacted when the Soviet Olympic Committee made its announcement about nonparticipation in May 1984. I think he would have written to them as follows: I first visited Moscow in the aftermath of the revolution. From that moment, I was struck by the imagination of Lenin who understood the crucial importance of physical culture in the building of nations. Indeed, throughout my life I have often said that the two men who did most for the sport in this century were Lenin and Pierre de Coubertin—a Russian communist and a French aristocrat. Throughout my political life, I struggled to ensure that your viewpoint was given a fair hearing—and not only in sport. In my major speeches, I have drawn attention to the magnificent performance and the gracious behavior of your athletes.

In 1980, I worked with my colleagues in the British Olympic Association to prevent attempts to destroy the Olympic movement at that time. It was not easy for us. The militarists, the chauvinists, those who stand against peace and coexistence were in full cry. But, under the strident leadership of Denis Follows, chairman of our national Olympic committee, we stood by Moscow. Others followed our lead. Your Games were a great success. You followed the Olympic principles to the letter. In years to come, historians will see clearly that the only reason there is a Los Angeles Games is because there was a Moscow Games.

It is when the Olympic Games are under attack that its real friends stand up to be counted. Sadly, there are many who fail in this duty. There are some ex-Olympians who owe their professional success to Olympic participation, and who would deny other young people their chance. There are some sports writers, living like parasites on the body of sport, who glorify in the sordid attempts to despoil the Olympic idea. I have said, again and again throughout my life, that of all the international causes I have served, sport is the most noble. I have even ventured the thought that in a nuclear age, sport is man's best hope. Many "Western" political leaders misunderstood the Olympic idea. This idea means that the period of the Olympic Games should stand out as a model of life as it could be and should be. If you followed the logic of these political leaders you would have announced your decision not to go to Los Angeles after the invasion of Grenada. But, rightly, this was not your view.

The Los Angeles Games

Your criticism of the Los Angeles structure and process has much truth. To sell the Olympic flame is as unworthy as the sale of Holy Communion. The intense commercialism angers me as much as you. But, if we look deeper, there is much of great worth in United States sport. California, indeed, illustrates municipal "sports socialism" at work. The community makes excellent use of university sports facilities; in many cases they have a major stake in them. Los Angeles was able to host a major Games because of its lavish provision for community/university sports and recreation. The populace use the facilities at little or no cost. By law, a percentage of oil revenues must be invested in recreational amenities along the California coast. Many of the best sports people in the United States teams are there because of scholarships provided at universities—and provided very often because of generous state funding. The cry that this is a "private enterprise" Games has a hollow ring. The generosity of the sponsors should be seen against the fact that the money they donate is money which under a different social system, would be money paid in tax.

Your complaint about security is understandable. It is incumbent on the host Olympic nation to try to create the best possible environment, to create a climate of opinion which emphasizes all that is positive in the human spirit and all that is positive in the cultures of the nations taking part. When the German flag goes up, we should think of Beethoven not Bismark; each flag and anthem should remind us of the cultural greatness which is to be found in all nations.

If your complaint is that some leading politicians in the United States have not been seen to be fulfilling this role with great enthusiasm, you are right. It is my dearest wish that you will be assured sincerely that you will be really welcome in Los Angeles, that your young people will be safe and well cared for. I pray for creative statesmanship of this kind. The modern world is much too short of it.

But, the whole is greater than the sum of the parts. Even if you are right on the different factors involved, I feel, with respect, that you are wrong in your conclusion. I ask you, from my heart, to reconsider your decision. I am sure that in the stadiums of Los Angeles, the public will welcome you warmly. Your presence will strike a blow for peace. If you do not go to Los Angeles, the world will be the poorer for your decision. The chauvinists and militarists will gloat. Those who proclaim their belief in "freedom" will rub their hands with pleasure at another success in their campaign against international understanding. History is, in Olympic terms, on your side. Can you not—even at this last minute—think again? Should you not ask yourself whether this time you are on the side of history?

For most of his involvement in world sports administration, he had joined with de Coubertin in trying to combat the propaganda of the anti-Olympians. "The chauvinists have always hated the Olympic Games," he wrote in 1980. "I still have the letter which de Coubertin wrote to me in 1928." He said that ever since he had proposed the first modern Games in 1896 he had been the subject of attacks in the press, in personal correspondence, and in other ways. His enemies did not hesitate "to facilitate false stories of quarrels and dissension in the Olympic movement"; they did not hesitate to misrepresent his motives, the nature of the Games, and the purpose which de Coubertin had in view. De Coubertin suffered long and hard from these attacks.

Those who attack the spirit, the content, and the procedures of the Games and the Olympic Movement, often call impatiently for an alternative. Quite often, these critics have done little or nothing for the Olympic movement, but there is no easy alternative. Philip would, I am sure, have accused many of the critics as having used their intelligence destructively, a very easy thing to do. Any alternative must be worked out by people of goodwill, wedded firmly to the basic principles of a relatively young historical movement, yet to see its contenary. Taking the Games to the continents has boosted the growth of the sports and physical education movement in those regions. Smaller scale, separate sport-championships such as the 1983 World Athletic Championships have, indeed, been successful, but not because they were world championships on merit alone. Merit championships would exclude most countries in the world; six Americans in the best ten at 100 meters; four Russians in the hammer, and so on.

No, the reason for their success is that they modeled themselves on the Olympics. The ceremonies, the splendor, the parades and the determination that all the member athletic associations in the IAAF should have representation. The best athletes from the North meet with those of the South. Iran and Iraq took part. There was a place for both Israel and Palestine. Helsinki, 1983, was an "Olympic" festival—it was not a technical and clinical event concerned only with how fast, how far, how high.

I mention the South. In 1981, Noel-Baker returned to this theme—one of many which were dear to his heart. He called on UNESCO and the IOC, together, to "make a reality of sport for all." They should change the thinking and the accepted values of our rulers, they should "make the rulers see the empty nothingness of power." They should make them understand that the only valid aim of government "is human happiness." The IOC and UNESCO should launch a great crusade: They should "plead the cause of the Third World and seek to end its poverty." When such a campaign of education has been launched, he—Noel-Baker—would "nominate the IOC for the Nobel Peace Prize."

Had he lived, he would have been heartened by the superb success of the Sarajevo Winter Olympics: a region of the world with a Moslem culture, emerging into the industrialized North; a state rapidly developing; a city proud to host the Games and determined to make a human and organizational success. He would have applauded the sentiments of J.P. de Cuellar, secretary general of the United Nations: "At a time of increased international tension it is gratifying that the eyes of the world may focus on an enterprise which is motivated by the spirit of peaceful cooperation and friendship between peoples. And that of the President of the IOC, Juan Samaranch;

> We are convinced that once again we will demonstrate to the whole world the true meaning of sport as an illustration of friendship and fraternity within the Olympic Flag as their symbol. This is the image of peace as we conceive and practice it.

It was the view evidenced by Tom Bradley, Mayor of Los Angeles, who joined with his counterpart in Sarajevo to issue, "a joint message of peace, friendship, and cooperation among peoples." They called for an international truce to affect all wars; they issued a joint friendship medal.

There are some who find this message of peace through sport unconvincing. Recently, I was researching opinion about the words to be inscribed on a bronze relief to be made of Philip and placed at the British National Sports Centre in London. "Peace through sport" said some. "Why? That is a communist slogan; the sort of thing you see in the stadiums of Eastern Europe." "What pernicious nonsense," would have been Philip's reaction. "I want to see that slogan outside every stadium, communist or capitalist, monarchist or republican, North and South—in the world." We must not abandon the word *peace* to the chauvinists, he would say. We must hang on to it—this idea of international understanding through sport. This fundamental principle of the IOC. We must hang on to it and transmit it to future generations. It is one of the essential ingredients of Olympism, a major factor in the Games which gives this remarkable multisport, multiculture festival, a charisma which no other sporting event possesses.

There will be many among you, philosophers and sociologists of sport, who will say that most of Noel-Baker's speeches and writings are purely *rhetorical*.

Even if that were so, and it is not so, but even if it were totally true, rhetoric, like peace, must not also be allowed to become a dirty word. The critics will scoff at rhetoric. They should bear in mind the advice of Aristotle who said, "Rhetoric must enunciate simple principles, be based on empathy with the audience addressed, and find forms of persuasion appropriate to them."

Quoting this advice in the *New Statesman*, writer Bernard Crick had this to say to Philip's old party—the labor party: "The Labor Party needs to come out of its hole and revive a long term public rhetoric. It must persuade the unpersuaded, the wavering and the volatile." This was always Philip's style.

Is this not just what the Olympic Movement needs now? We have had another shock to the system. Those of us who hoped that Los Angeles would thrill to the sport dialogue between the East and the West, and between the North and the South—a dialogue crowned with the transfer of the Olympic flag from Moscow to Los Angeles—we do not know, now, just what to expect. What would Noel-Baker have done if the worst comes to the worst and the "socialist world" does not arrive in Los Angeles?

Certainly the old fighter would not surrender to the enemies of Olympism. Without doubt, he would have stood by Juan Samaranch and Monique Berliox, president and director of the IOC, in their further hours of trial. He would have expressed his great personal loyalty to such friends. His word would have been his bond. He would have emphasized that the great idealistic movements of mankind cannot often reach total fulfillment as they exist as symbols of hope—targets to which one can aspire. Even if their theoretical basis can be faulted, their actual effect might still be to produce and inspire constructive works.

Like de Coubertin, Philip Noel-Baker was born of the privileged elite but spent his life working for the underprivileged. I hope this is what people mean when they proclaim their belief in Victorian values. If he stood here now, he would be urging us to stand fast on the Olympic ideals.

As a politician, he would have called upon his colleagues worldwide to try harder to create a world better fitted for such a brilliant idea as the Olympic Games. As a diplomat, he would have searched for new ways to protect the old ideas, perhaps not just one permanent Olympic site, but a circuit of cities tried and trusted as great Games organizers with the regional Games taking on the role of regional sports "boosters." Perhaps more thought for the Red Cross analogy. He would have spoken strongly in favor of "Olympic Solidarity"—that unique world bank of sports expertise which enables knowledge to percolate up and down, and sideways, between the National Olympic Committees and the federations of North and South. He would be against malicious revenge and against great power rivalry in the Olympic movement. He would focus on areas of collaboration. Speaking in Paris at the contenary of the birth of de Coubertin, he proclaimed his belief in the theory of Wilfred Legros-Clark, president of the British Association that year and a famous biologist. His theory was that the ascent of man could be attributed to two qualities in brain and heart which were much more developed than in any other form of living organism: a *sense of altruism* and a *power of cooperation with others*. He would, I am sure, try to ensure that this altruism and cooperation should be foremost in the minds of those who are the custodians of the Olympic idea today. He would end by repeating a section of his Honorary Doctrate acceptance speech at Loughborough University in 1979:

> Every man and every woman and every child in every nation stand today before a double danger—nuclear doom with unimaginable description which none who has not been in Hiroshima can begin to understand; and world poverty and hunger. Millions have died in recent years of the torturing death of slow starvation. Hundreds of millions live out their lives in squalor, in mud huts, in slums and shanty towns. Hundreds of millions are the victims every year of preventable diseases which our nation knows no more. It is a double danger, it is a double evil, and the twin evils could be cured together if mankind would transfer the resources given to preparing nuclear war to preparing welfare, economic development, public health. If nations would transform the world from war and armaments and conflict, to cooperation, understanding and peace, we could see a change for the better within a decade which none of us present could think possible.

Philip Noel-Baker would have wanted Los Angeles 1984 to conquer its disappointment, to refrain from further recrimination, and, immediately, to lay plans for continual international sports dialogue between all the peoples in the world.

An intense emotion, it is said, like love or death can transcend the gulf between people or nations. That of death is temporary; that of love can be permanent. Philip John Noel-Baker had such a love of sport and of the Olympic idea. He would have presented that love to us with intense emotion; he would have won us to his cause. We would have left this hall persuaded that the world-family of sport should not be divided. I hope that even this second-hand attempt to represent his life and work leaves you with the firm belief that, despite the serious problems we face, his most powerful aphorism still has great force: "In a nuclear age, sport *is* man's best hope."

PART V

Suggestions for Further Reading

Selected References

Ali, R. (1976). *Africa at the Olympics*. London: Africa Books.

Brickhill, J. (1976). *Race against race: South Africa's 'multinational' sport fraud*. London: International Defense and Aid Fund.

Cheffers, J. (1972). *A wilderness of spite*. (Rhodesia denied). New York: Vantage Press.

De Broglio, C. (1970). *South Africa: Racism in sport*. London: Christian Action Publications.

Dobrov, A. (1972). *Highlights of Soviet sport*. Moscow: Novosty Press Agency.

Draper, M. (1963). *Sport and race in South Africa*. Johannesburg: South African Institute of Race Relations.

Edwards, H. (1969). *The revolt of the black athlete*. New York: Free Press.

Espy, R. (1981). *The politics of the Olympic Games*. Berkeley: University of California Press.

Goodhart, P., & Chataway, C. (1968). *War without weapons: The rise of mass sport in the twentieth century, and its effect on men and nations*. London: W.H. Allen.

Green A. (1964). *Recreation, leisure and politics*. New York: McGraw Hill.

Hain, P. (1971). *Don't play with apartheid*. London: George Allen and Unwin.

Hanna, W.A. (1962). *The politics of sport*. Washington, DC: American Universities Field Staff.

Hoberman, J.M. (1984). *The Olympic Crisis: From its origins to the Moscow Games*. New Rochelle, NY: Caratzas.

Hoberman, J.M. (1984). *Sport and political ideology*. Austin: University of Texas Press.

Hoch, P. (1972). *Rip off the big game: The exploitation of sports by the power elite*. New York: Doubleday.

Homes, J. (1971). *Olympiad 1936: Blaze of glory for Hitler's reich*. New York: Ballantine.

Kanin, D.B. (1982). *A political history of the Olympic Games*. Boulder, CO: Westview.

Kolatch, J. (1972). *Sport, politics and ideology in China*. New York: Jonathan David.

Lapchick, R.E. (1975). *The politics of race and international sport: The case of South Africa*. London: Greenwood Press.

Lowe, B., et al. (1978). *Sport and international relations*. Champaign, IL: Stipes.

Mandell, R.D. (1971). *The Nazi Olympics*. New York: Macmillan.

McIntosh, P.C. (1979). *Fair play: Ethics in sport and education*. London: Heineman.

Noll, R.G. (Ed.). (1974). *Government and the sports business*. Washington, DC: The Brookings Institution.

Olsen, J. (1969). *The black athlete: A shameful story*. Boston: Little, Brown.

Orr, J. (1969). *The black athlete: His story in American history*. New York: Lion.

Ramsamy, S. (1980). *Racial discrimination in South African sport*. New York: United Nations.

Riordan, J. (1977). *Sport in Soviet society*. London: Cambridge University Press.

Riordan, J. (Ed.) (1978). *Sport under Communism: The USSR, Czechoslovakia, the GDR, China, Cuba*. London: C. Hurst.

Segrave, J., & Chu, D. (Eds.) (1981). *Olympism*. Champaign, IL: Human Kinetics.

Sport and politics: Proceedings of an international seminar (1983). Israel: Wingate Institute.

Stone, G.P. (1972). *Games, sport and power*. New York: E.P. Dutton.

Thompson, R. (1975). *Race and sport*. London: Oxford University Press.

Thompson, R. (1975). *Retreat from apartheid: New Zealand's sporting contacts with South Africa*. London: Oxford University Press.

Woods, D. (1981). *Black and white: Should we play South Africa?* Dublin: Ward River.

DATE DUE

JAN 0 8 1991			
MAR 0 1 1992			
MAR 2 3 1992			
APR 1 2 1992			
NOV 2 3 1992			
DEC 1 4 1992			
APR 0 8 1993			
MAR 0 6 1998			
APR 0 2 1998			
NOV 2 4 2005			